Bloom's Modern Critical Interpretations

Bloom's Modern Critical Interpretations

Miguel de Cervantes's
Don Quixote
New Edition

Edited and with an introduction by
Harold Bloom
Sterling Professor of the Humanities
Yale University

BLOOM'S
LITERARY CRITICISM
An imprint of Infobase Publishing

Bloom's Modern Critical Interpretations: Don Quixote—New Edition
Copyright © 2010 by Infobase Publishing
Introduction © 2010 by Harold Bloom

Bloom's Literary Criticism
An imprint of Infobase Publishing
132 West 31st Street
New York NY 10001

Library of Congress Cataloging-in-Publication Data
Miguel De Cervantes' Don Quixote / edited and with an introduction by Harold Bloom.
—New ed.
    p. cm. — (Bloom's modern critical interpretations)
   Spine title: Don Quixote
   Includes bibliographical references and index.
   ISBN 978-1-60413-821-4
1. Cervantes Saavedra, Miguel de, 1547–1616. Don Quixote. I. Bloom, Harold. II. Title: Don Quixote.
   PQ6352.M455 2010
   863'.3—dc22
                          2009053338

Contributing editor: Pamela Loos
Cover design by Takeshi Takahashi
Composition by IBT Global, Troy NY
Cover printed by IBT Global, Troy NY
Book printed and bound by IBT Global, Troy NY
Date printed: May 2010
Printed in the United States of America

10 9 8 7 6 5 4 3 2 1

Contents

Editor's Note

My introduction casts *Don Quixote* as the central narrative of the last half millennium, a masterwork to which all the great Western novelists owe a debt.

Carolyn A. Nadeau discusses invention and imitation in the work, as Cervantes challenges but does not altogether reject literary tradition. Howard Mancing then explores the interrelation of the novel's narrative voices.

The role of objects and, in particular, the objectified book in *Don Quixote* is traced by Edward H. Friedman, after which Mario Vargas Llosa posits fiction as the central theme of Cervantes's work.

Roberto González Echevarría suggests that love and law are the book's great themes, while Manuel Durán and Fay R. Rogg cast Cervantes as a pioneer in the creation of the self-referential novel.

Bryant Creel identifies the duke's household as the novel's domain of malicious satire, after which Myriam Yvonne Jehenson and Peter N. Dunn detect a cultural polyphony in the way Cervantes responds to his changing world.

In the volume's final essay, Barbara Fuchs contends that the novel's sustained reflection on history is as central as Cervantes's subversion of romantic tropes.

HAROLD BLOOM

Introduction

Don Quixote is to the Spanish language what Shakespeare is to English, Dante to Italian, and Goethe to German: the glory of that particular vernacular. There is no similar singular eminence in French: Rabelais, Montaigne, Molière, and Racine vie with Victor Hugo, Baudelaire, Stendhal, Balzac, Flaubert, and Proust. Perhaps Cervantes's masterwork is the central book of the last half millennium, since all the greater novelists are as much *Don Quixote*'s children as they are Shakespeare's. As I have remarked elsewhere, Shakespeare pragmatically teaches us how to talk to ourselves, while Cervantes instructs us how to talk to one another. Hamlet scarcely listens to what anyone else says (except it be the Ghost), while Falstaff so delights himself that Prince Hal can seem merely the best of resentful students and half-voluntary audiences. But Don Quixote and Sancho Panza change and mature by listening to each other, and their friendship is the most pervasive in all of literature.

Don Quixote or Hamlet? Sancho Panza or Falstaff? The choice would be difficult. But Hamlet has only Horatio, and Falstaff ends in solitude, dying while playing with flowers and evidently dreaming of the table promised in Psalm 23 to be prepared for one by God in the midst of one's enemies. Don Quixote dies in Sancho's loving company, with the wise squire proposing fresh quests to the heroic knight. Perhaps Shakespeare did invent the ever-growing inner self, compelled to be its own adventure, as Emily Dickinson (an authentic heir of Shakespeare) proclaimed. Cervantes, whose life was arduous and darkly solitary, was able to achieve a miracle that Shakespeare evaded. Where in Shakespeare can we find two great natures in full communion with

1

each other? Antony and Cleopatra are giant forms, but they never listen to what anyone else says, including each other. Lady Macbeth fades out, Lear is most himself addressing the heavens, while Prospero has no human peer. I fantasize sometimes that Shakespeare, in eternity, brings together his most vital characters on one stage: Falstaff, Hamlet, Rosalind, Iago, Lear, Macbeth, Cleopatra. But in this life, he chose otherwise.

The reader needs no better company than Sancho and the Don: To make a third with them is to be blessed with happiness, yet also to be favored with self-insight. The Don and Sancho, between them, know all that there is to know. They know at least exactly who they are, which is what, finally, they will teach the rest of us.

CAROLYN A. NADEAU

Reading the Prologue: Cervantes's Narrative Appropriation and Originality

In Cervantes's work, the discussion of imitation surfaces many times, both in the prologues and through characters in the texts. In the prologue to the *Novelas ejemplares* (1612) [Exemplary novels], published seven years after *Don Quixote I*, Cervantes proudly declares his contribution to Castilian literature by presenting himself as the first and original composer of the Spanish *novela*. He dismisses imitating any of the Italian writers: "y éstas son mías propias, no imitadas ni hurtadas; mi ingenio las engendró, y las parió mi pluma, y van creciendo en los brazos de la estampa"[1] [And these are my very own {words}, neither imitated nor stolen; they are conceived in my imagination, given birth by my pen, and are being nurtured in the arms of the printing press].[2] Cervantes's declaration makes two important points. First, that his lack of imitation (novelas "no imitadas") coincides with his own invention ("mi ingenio"), thereby putting in opposition these two concepts. In the Renaissance invention was many times perceived as synonymous with imitation. The link between *inventio* and *ingenio* is put forth by the sixteenth-century prose writer Juan de Valdés: "'invention' and 'disposition' (*disposición, ordenación*) are the two principal parts of rhetoric; the former corresponds to the *ingenio*, the latter to the *juicio*."[3] Robert Edwards explains, "The purpose of invention, as the etymology (*invenire*) suggests, is discovery, and one rhetorical issue that bears directly on poetry is whether

From *Women of the Prologue: Imitation, Myth, and Magic in* Don Quixote I, pp. 35–53, 144–49. © 2002 by Rosemont Publishing and Printing Corporation.

3

such discovery entails original creation or the employment of existing commonplaces."[4] By the seventeenth century, invention became less associated with imitation strategies of finding subject matter in admired sources and more associated with the poet's imaginative ability. The second point that Cervantes makes is that in his *Novelas ejemplares* he sets aside notions of imitation, the rewriting of texts, in favor of invention, original creation. By juxtaposing the two modes of writing, Cervantes rejects imitation and endorses invention, thus clearly stating in which direction his writing has developed. Two years later in *Adjunta al Parnaso*, he discusses the parameters on imitation, using theft as a comparison.

> Item, se advierte que no ha de ser tenido por ladrón el poeta que hurtare algún verso ajeno y le encajare entre los suyos, como no sea todo el conceptoy toda la copia entera; que en tal caso tan ladrón es como Caco.[5]

> [Likewise, be advised that the poet who lifts some distant verse and inserts it among his own should not be taken for a thief, as long as it is not an entire concept or image; in which case he would be as big a thief as Cacus.][6]

Cervantes distinguishes between "lifting" a verse, an acceptable form of imitation, and "robbing" an entire concept or work, an action that, although it may be considered imitation, goes beyond acceptability. Cervantes is most opposed to indiscriminate borrowing; the imitation, above all else, must serve the writer's purpose. This judgment is more accepting of a selective, fragmented type of imitation than his stance in the prologue to the *Novelas ejemplares* in which he emphasizes his own originality or lack of imitation.

In Part II of *Don Quixote* the hero politely questions the court musician's insertion of Garcílaso stanzas in his song of the dying Altisidora. In his comic reply, the musician notes the irresponsibility of contemporary poets: "entre los intonsos poetas de nuestra edad se usa que cada uno escriba como quisiere, y hurte de quien quisiere, venga o no venga a pelo de su intento" (*IH*, II, 70:568) [For the novice poets of our day, the practice is for every one to write as he pleases and pilfer where he chooses, whether it applies to the subject or not] (*DQ*, II, 70:812). There is an unrestrained borrowing from other texts and a lack of justification in drawing from other sources that bother the musician. Imitation is here rejected as indiscriminate borrowing without regard to the writer's own needs and capacities. While all three examples focus on different concerns regarding imitation, in each Cervantes raises the question of imitation's relationship to thievery—"hurtadas," "hurtare," "hurte"—and doubts the legitimacy of established precepts. These later works, then, are clearly moving away from imitation toward invention. However, the fact that Cervantes is still writing about imitation shows that it is a powerful literary device and not one to be readily cast aside.

Curiously, centuries later, Alicia Ostriker also uses theft imagery to describe the work of American women poets in revising myths.[7] Estella Lauter best summarizes Ostriker's work: "[Ostriker] sees revisionist myth making by women as a complex act of theft from virtually any mythological pasture, regardless of its place in history, followed by re-evaluation of the cultural values previously enshrined there, and re-presentation of the stolen elements in experimental forms to emphasize the poet's argument with tradition."[8] Describing revisionist mythmaking, Ostriker labels the first type "hit-and-run attacks"; it is essentially a "challenge to and correction of gender stereotypes embodied in myth."[9] This call to challenge and correct gender stereotypes is key to Cervantes's own project as he rewrites the mythological women of the prologue, particularly the "mujeres rameras" [loose women], Lamia, Laida, and Flora, and the cruel Medea. Ostriker also correlates revisionism with formal experiment, again echoing Cervantes's position that invention (the original creation or the experimentation) is key to any successful imitation (the revision).

The prologue to *Don Quixote I*, written approximately eight years before the *Novelas ejemplares* and *Viaje del Parnaso*, again revolves around the critique of writers who imitate and exploit established writing strategies. Here, as in his other works, Cervantes challenges the authority of tradition but does not, as one may hastily conclude, seek to discard it. Rather, he passionately tries to incorporate those elements of past cultural authority that are worthy of recognition with new standards of creativity, originality, and self-expression. Michael Gerli, in his study of Cervantes, states that "[a]s Cervantes composes he appropriates, combines, naturalizes, and effaces other texts by rewriting them and displacing them with his own themes, images, style, and ideology."[10] In *Don Quixote I* he gives greater consideration to imitation, the foremost literary convention of the Renaissance, as he attempts to incorporate new measures for the role of literary imitation. These measures include debunking authority, collapsing the difference between imitation and invention, granting a privileged status to the creative process, and investing in the reader a more assertive role in his literary project.

Debunking Authority

In the past, scholars have addressed issues of the prologue to understand better the rest of the text. Ruth El Saffar points out the relationship of authorial control and distance as essential to Cervantes's elaboration of his novel. For El Saffar, the prologue traces the process through which Cervantes translates his thoughts into fiction and the way in which he transforms himself into narrator and character.[11] In effect, El Saffar grants Cervantes ultimate authority even though she does point out those moments when he distances himself from that authority. Ralph Flores disagrees with this and several other readings that grant Cervantes so much authorial privilege.[12] He argues that Cervantes's "power" is only absolute when compared to the fictional authors of the text, and even then, only rhetorically. For Flores, authorship is questioned at all levels, including reading, and the text's intertextuality is not merely parodic or satirical but works to debunk control at all levels.

This notion intrigues me as I find the prologue to *Don Quixote I* a format for Cervantes's critical position on transmitting literary and, by extension, cultural authority in the early modern age. Part of Cervantes's contention with contemporary practices is the belief—albeit waning—in the authority of the written word. Extrapolating from Salvador Fajardo's insightful comments on the erosion of authority exemplified in the prologue, we can see how Cervantes undermines the idea of "sources" as authority. Fajardo explains that the anonymous friend's entire monologue of advice is "blatantly deceitful," because the book has already been written.[13] However, this advice is of little importance as his words are also "blatantly useless," because, in effect, no one will bother to check the sources.[14] In this way, Cervantes puts forth a double attack on the authority of sources: he is implying that neither the writer nor the reader cares about models for the text. However, in one of his many ironic twists, Cervantes stresses the erosion of this belief specifically by using imitative strategies to debunk the authority that writers attribute to their sources. For example, when the anonymous friend cites Virgil's Circe as a model for the sorceress, he is simultaneously pointing to Virgil's intentional dismissal of his model: Homer's Circe. Aeneas bypasses Circe's island. In fact, in terms of her role as lover, she is displaced by Dido and, as guide to the underworld, by Sibyl. . . . The most obvious debunking of the authority of models that is outlined in the prologue is, of course, that of the chivalric novels: "deshacer la autoridad y cabida que en el mundo y en el vulgo tienen los libros de caballerías" (*IH*, pró. 57) [to destroy the authority and influence which books of chivalry have in the world and with the public] (*DQ*, pro. 13). The authority that is scrutinized in the prologue extends not only to past authors, but also to contemporary ones, Cervantes included. As he pokes fun at his own "estéril y mal cultivado ingenio" (*IH* pró. 50) [sterile, uncultivated wit of mine] (*DQ*, pro. 9), as he suffers over the shortcomings of his project, and listens to his friend for advice on remedying the problems, he points to the limitations of writer as authoritative figure. Similarly, he imbues his reader with a sovereign power to judge his writing, "y estás en tu casa, donde eres señor della, como el rey de sus alcabalas" (*IH* pró. 51) [you are in your own house and master of it as much as the king of his taxes] (*DQ*, pro. 9), but then quickly cautions that to even a king harm can come—"que debajo de mi manto, al rey mato" (*IH*, pró. 51) [A man's home is his castle] (*DQ*, pro. 9).[15] Cervantes is alerting us to his skepticism on all levels. There are no specially sanctioned domains for sources, writers, or readers. Cervantes, then, is rethinking the notions of the authority of source, author, reader, and ultimately of the text itself.

Imitation and Invention

Along with this erosion of authority Cervantes blurs the differences between responding to past texts and focusing on his own innovations; between reiterating the classic works and obliterating them; between theories of imitation and those of invention. As is evidenced by the appearance of imitation years later in the *Novelas ejemplares*, Cervantes debated the value of imitation and invention throughout his literary career, always favoring the creative processes of both. E. C. Riley, a critic whose work has inspired scholars to reexamine Cervantes's stance on literary convention, states that "purposeful creation also lies behind the irony and the semi-serious apologetics of the prologue of *Don Quixote I*."[16] For Riley, Cervantes combines a traditional technique of incorporating critical material in the form of an animated dialogue with an innovative technique of visualizing himself thinking about critical approaches.[17] Riley's argument that Cervantes combines different writing techniques reveals a balance between new and old traditions that Alban Forcione also finds in Cervantes's understanding of language in *Don Quixote*. Forcione describes Cervantes's writing as a "'decentering' of language, the conscious turning away from any absolute authority that might be invested in a single and unitary language."[18] For Forcione, Cervantes's progressive view of language recognizes both the importance of imitation principles and the need for self-expression: "Cervantes enunciates a principle of imitation ('la imitación perfecta' [perfect imitation]) which, while recognizing the importance of the proper adjustment of the literary utterance to the nature of its subject and the propriety of simplicity and clarity of style for the limited, satirical aims of the *Quixote*, at the same time places a good deal of emphasis on authenticity and self-expression."[19]

I would like to take this line of reasoning further and suggest that Cervantes all but obliterates his sources: For example, in citing Guevara's "mujeres rameras" [loose women] and Ovid's Medea as sources for female identity, Cervantes gestures toward distant relationships that, while they in part unlock the meaning of who Cervantes's female characters are, are still only fragmented pieces of a complex whole. In citing Homer's Calypso and Virgil's Circe, Cervantes is also signaling a departure from, or more defiantly stating, an obliteration of the old writers and writing styles in an effort to focus on the new, modern possibilities of female identity. In spite of this radical stance, Cervantes's search for freedom for female characters is framed by very certain limitations. Like the modern possibilities that Cervantes proposes for writers that are still tied to a literary world defined, in part, by imitation, the possibilities for women in his text are very much defined by male textual and social activity. Sheila Fisher and Janet Halley explain that "for a male author to write women in these periods was to refer not to women, but to men—to desire not relationship with women, but relationship to the traditions of male textual activity, and, by extension, of male social and political privilege."[20] On the one hand, then, the "imitation" ceases to defer authority to its sources and takes on significance through the innovative, modern context in which Cervantes transforms it. No reader would mistake Don Quixote for his models Amadís, Roldán, Odysseus, or Aeneas, Likewise, the sources for females cited in the prologue share buried, distant ties with the women in the main part of the text who are undoubtedly seventeenth-century women defined by their self-proclaimed agendas of love and intimacy. But on the other hand, even within this radical rewriting of past myths, Cervantes's female characters, however free they may be, are still very much tied to their roles within a male-privileged society.

Cervantes's shift from traditional imitation, in which authority is deferred to the source but validated by its modern position, to a literary convention that endorses artistic originality is not a new idea. Anthony Cascardi, for example, discusses at length the transformation from a humanist perspective of literature, which relies on the past to assert itself, to a modernist one, which looks toward other contemporary institutions, and the role that secularization and self-assertion play in this transitional time period. Edward Friedman also discloses reasons for this confrontation with tradition but focuses more on the external factors—rise in literacy rate, changing technologies, increased skepticism in authorial figures—that contributed to the changes in writing and reading.[21] Finally, Charles Presberg argues (that the prologue, serving as a model for the rest of the text, blurs the distinctions between historical and poetic narratives and dramatizes the limits of discourse itself. This blurring of narratives echoes Cervantes's stance on imitation. There is no longer a privileging of the ancient texts. In fact, if anything at all, the writer aims to obliterate the past from the text in favor of the writer's creativity. In the prologue, behind the comic irony of the two friends' discussion, Cervantes endorses a limited imitation that will always yield to his own innovative writing style.

Yet Cervantes's prologue is more than just an ironic or parodic look at literary convention. Because the initial musings of the fictitious Cervantes—the writer who appears in the prologue—and the subsequent dialogue of two friends focus on the process of constructing the text, the prologue is simultaneously process and product. In fact, it is an example of the dynamic writer/reader/text relationship to which Cervantes aspires. Christine Gledhill refers to this type of relationship as "an ongoing process of give-and-take."[22] She explains that meaning is not imposed but "arises out of a struggle or negotiation between competing frames of reference, motivation and experience."[23]

The women cited in the prologue also exemplify how Cervantes plays out the humanist-modernist tension in the main part of the text. Cervantes introduces in the prologue and later fulfills in the latter part of his work a needed, moderate resolution to resolve the differences that are so apparent to him at this humanist-modernist literary juncture. This blurring of old and new, of authorizing old texts and legitimizing his own artistic creativity, is inevitable. While at the forefront of change and undoubtedly paving the way for new literary trends, Cervantes is no more capable of escaping Renaissance trends of imitation and launching into purely "original" creativity than postmodernists are today of escaping modernist claims of legitimizing authorial originality even as they seek to reappraise these "modernist" myths. The previous critical positions must, in one way or another, form part of the new critical position! Thus, while we may argue that Cervantes's novel is indeed revolutionary, we cannot discard the text's identifying relationship with past texts, that is, with Cervantes's need to imitate his models or at the very least respectfully bid farewell to them.[24] We must not discard Cervantes's reliance on imitative strategies to assert himself as a creative writer; the two, imitation and invention, go hand in hand.

A Privileged Status to the Creative Process

In *Don Quixote*, Cervantes privileges the creative processes of writing and reading. Because the creative process is the fundamental theme of the prologue, process and product, as mentioned above, collapse into one. In the main part of the text, the scrutiny of the library, the canon's attack on contemporary writing styles, and various discussions among the characters at the inn underscore the reader's input into what makes a successful text. The reader's creative interpretation of what makes a good narrative, in both the prologue and the main part of the text, holds a special position. In their analyses of the prologue, Américo Castro and Juan Bautista Avalle-Arce indirectly point to the creative process as they discuss the prologue's narrative functions.[25] For them, the prologue is best understood as an epilogue, and, as such, many of the connections between the sources cited in the prologue and the characters of *Don Quixote* are only understood after several readings of the text. Interpreting the prologue in this way grants the creativity of the prologue a unique position within the text. The reader needs the text to decipher the prologue. While this privileging is more relevant to Cervantes's questions concerning literary convention as a whole than to the specifics of imitation theory itself, it complements his concerns regarding imitation by once again highlighting the originality and creativity of those involved with the text. This prominent status to the process is what I define as Cervantes's third tenet of transmitting literary authority. All critics agree that the prologue is a critique of established writing strategies. While some highlight the ironic or parodic values, others stress the dialectic relationship between life and literature on which Cervantes elaborates in the main part of his text.[26] While these positions are informative, they address only part of Cervantes's project. I have already outlined three of the positions that the "author" and his "anonymous friend" take up: the privileged status to commentary on the creative process, the blurring of old and new writing strategies, and the erosion of the belief in the authority of the written word. The fourth tenet is a challenge to the reader to take the leap of self-assertion in the act of reading.

The Reader's Leap

Don Quixote begins with a call to the fictitious Cervantes's "Desocupado lector" (*IH*, pró. 50) [Idle reader] (*DQ*, pro. 9) to exercise freedom of thought when evaluating the merit of the text. His self-proclaimed relationship to his work as stepfather is an effort to distance himself personally, and to offer his reader greater interpretive freedom:[27]

> [S]oy padrastro de don Quijote, no quiero irme con la corriente del uso, ni suplicarte casi con las lágrimas en los ojos, como otros hacen, lector carísimo, que perdones o disimules las faltas que en este mi hijo vieres, y ni eres su pariente ni su amigo, y tienes tu alma en tu cuerpo y tu libre albedrío como el más pintado, y estás en tu casa, donde eres señor della, como el rey de sus alcabalas, y sabes lo que comúnmente se dice, que debajo de mi manto, al rey mato. Todo lo cual te esenta y hace libre de todo respecto y obligación, y así, puedes decir de la historia todo aquello que te pareciere, sin temor que te calunien por el mal ni te premien por el bien que dijeres della. (*IH*, pró. 50–51)

> [I am the stepfather of Don Quixote—[I] have no desire to go with the current of custom or to implore you, dearest reader, almost

with tears in my eyes, as others do, to pardon or excuse the defects
you may perceive in this child of mine. You are neither its relative
nor its friend, your soul is your own and your will is as free as
any man's, you are in your own house and master of it as much as
the king of his taxes, and you know the common saying, "A man's
home is his castle"—all of which exempts and frees you from every
consideration and obligation. And you can say what you will about
the story without fear of being abused for any ill or rewarded for
any good you may say of it.] (*DQ*, pro. 9)

In reading the text, the fictitious Cervantes argues, one should think freely
and disregard both the suppositions of established authority figures and any
supposed respect or sense of obligation to the text itself. In Kevin Dunn's
study on Renaissance prefaces, he points out that prefaces encapsulated
certain "discursive practices designed to discourage or to limit imitation by
readers, to keep readers as readers and not as writers" and that well into the
seventeenth century, such was the norm.[28] In his discussion of *Don Quixote*,
Edward Friedman persuasively argues that the reader displaces "the author
as the controlling instrument of message production" as he or she inserts the
necessary images and visuals into the reading process.[29] It would seem, then,
that once again, the fictitious Cervantes's insistence that the reader actively
participate in the story's development and critique is yet another attack on
literary conventions and is another attempt to alter culturally ingrained
norms of the entire textual process: both writing and reading.

However, I cannot help but wonder if Michel de Certeau's observations on the reader's inventiveness when he critiques bourgeois society might
also hold true in this seventeenth-century context: "Reading is ... situated
at the point where *social* stratification (class relationships) and poetic operations (the practitioner's constructions of a text) intersect: a social hierarchiza-
tion seeks to make the reader conform to the 'information' distributed by an
elite (or semi-elite); reading operations manipulate the reader by insinuating
their inventiveness into the cracks in a cultural orthodoxy."[30] Surely the previously mentioned proverb, "debajo de mi manto, al rey mato" (*IH*, pró. 51)
[A man's home is his castle] (*DQ*, pro. 9) or more literally, "Under my cloak, I
kill the king," which immediately follows the fictitious Cervantes's generous
gesture to his reader on whom he bestows complete freedom of mind and
body in evaluating the text and to whom he directly refers to as "rey" [king],
contains, at the very least, an ironic gesture regarding the expectations and
practices of the readers. Drawing from Edwin Williamson's investigations,
we can see that this proverb, which asserts an individual's—in this case, the
writer's—independence, names the reader as king, and cautiously warns him

of overconfident interpretations and judgments.[31] The reader, like the writer, cannot fully break from centuries-old cultural expectations. And although he begins the prologue with an invitation to the reader to judge his work unabashedly, the narrator restricts the invitation with this obscure proverb. Similarly, he finishes the prologue by specifically directing the reader how to interpret the text: "en el cual [el prólogo] verás, lector suave, la discreción de mi amigo ... y el alivio tuyo en hallar tan sincera y tan sin revueltas la historia" (*IH*, pró. 58) [this prologue, in which gentle reader, you will perceive my friend's good sense ... and why you find—to your relief—the story of Don Quixote of La Mancha so straightforward and free of extraneous matter] (*DQ*, pro. 13–14). Here the fictitious Cervantes directly tells the reader how to respond to his work, thus attenuating his open invitation.

The "unrestrained" liberty that the fictitious Cervantes offers his readers is further exemplified in the conversation with his anonymous friend, who is in fact a reader of the novel.[32] The narrator explains to him his concern over the novel's lack of adornment: sonnets, quotations in the margins, notes at the end, and philosophic adages.[33] His friend proceeds to offer solutions for each of the problems, which, in turn, the fictitious Cervantes warmly accepts. Here, then, we see the reader take the leap of self-assertion and how his critique affects the writing of the text. In this way, the experience of the reader tropes the experience of the writer as the reader follows or perhaps even transcends the writer's creative relationship with the text. As a result, the prologue itself serves as a model for the writer/reader dynamic for which Cervantes yearns. Yet as Fajardo has observed, the reader's argument is baseless because, as he well knows, the book has already been written.[34] Once again, the reader's "liberty" is held in check. While Cervantes seemingly attempts to augment the authority invested in both reader and writer, he complicates his assertions with clever twists in the text's development. It is precisely in the text—the mediator between writer and reader—that elements of intentionality exist that may, on the one hand, reflect what the author intended or may, on the other, reflect what the reader infers.[35] Therefore, we must turn to the text to dismantle how this dialogue of specifics—most importantly, how this pressing issue of imitation of models—is played out.

Dialogue of Specifics

The fictitious Cervantes begins the dialogue on how imitative strategies fit into his text by examining some problems, including the difficulty in remembering sources: "De todo esto ha de carecer mi libro, porque ni tengo qué acotar en el margen, ni qué anotar en el fin, ni *menos sé qué autores sigo en él*, para ponerlos al principio, como hacen todos" (*IH*, pró. 53, emphasis added) [Of all this there will be nothing in my book, for I have nothing to quote in the margin or to note at the end, and *still less do I know what authors I follow in it*, to place them at the beginning, as all do] (*DQ*, pro. 10, emphasis added). As critics have noted, Cervantes is attacking those writers who indiscriminately or fraudulently cite classical sources without understanding them, a point he drives home in his later works, *Novelas ejemplares, Viaje del Parnaso*, and *Don Quixote II*.[36] Because writers use imitation theory in a reckless way, the fictitious Cervantes, in an affected, modest tone, explains why imitation does not suit his writing style: "por mi insuficiencia y pocas letras, y porque naturalmente soy poltrón y perezoso de andarme buscando autores que digan lo que yo me sé decir sin ellos" (*IH*, pró. 53) [through my incapacity and want of learning . . . and because I am by nature indolent and lazy about hunting for authors to say what I myself can say without them] (*DQ*, pro. 10).[37] While ironically pointing out his lack of erudition and lazy nature to explain why he is incapable of imitation, he implicitly questions why authors have to repeat what others have already said. His conflict, then, is a struggle between incorporating accepted notions of imitation, manifested in the prologue as the adornment his novel lacks, and resisting those very same notions. This dilemma in turn reflects the general tension found in the shift from preexisting humanist modes of writing and reading to modernist claims of self-assertion and originality.

The narrator's friend easily remedies the problems presented. He suggests writing the sonnets, including some Latin, and citing classical authors: "En resolución, no hay más sino que vos procuréis nombrar estos nombres, *o tocar estas historias en la vuestra*, que aquí he dicho" (*IH*, pró. 57, emphasis added) [In short, all you have to do is to manage to quote these names *or refer to these stories* that I have mentioned] (*DQ*, pro. 12, emphasis added). The fictitious Cervantes only has to include the sources in the text; later, it will be the friend's job—that is, the erudite reader's job—to elaborate on the models at the end of the text: "y dejadme a mí el cargo de poner las anotaciones y acotaciones" (*IH*, pró. 57) [and leave it to me to insert the annotations and quotations] (*DQ*, pro. 12). The friend supports the interactive role between writer, text, and reader. After offering these solutions, the friend reverses his advice and explains that the novel needs none of these missing ingredients. Instead, the most important thing is imitation, as best as the fictitious Cervantes understands it: "Sólo tiene que aprovecharse de la imitación en lo que fuere escribiendo; que cuanto ella fuere más perfecta, tanto mejor será lo que se escribiere" (*IH*, pró. 57) [It (your book) has only to avail itself of imitation in its writing, and the more perfect the imitation the better the work will be] (*DQ*, pro. 13). While casting aside the preliminary and epilogic adornments, his friend does endorse the strategy of imitation in his writing style. The convention of adding introductory sonnets, eulogies, epigrams, and indexes only offers the writer a quick fix of authority, an assumed, inflated authority that may or may not actually sustain the adornment. The friend also insinuates that these adornments actually obfuscate the purpose and power of writing: "procurar que a la llana, con palabras significantes, honestas y bien colocadas, salga vuestra oración y período sonoro y festivo, pintando, en todo lo que alcanzáredes y fuere posible, vuestra intención; dando a entender vuestros conceptos sin intricarlos y escurecerlos" (*IH*, pró. 58) [take care that your sentences flow musically, pleasantly, and plainly, with clear, proper, and well-placed words, setting forth your purpose to the best of your power, and putting your ideas intelligibly, without confusion or obscurity] (*DQ*, pro. 13).

In the prologue there are arguments for and against traditional literary conventions that affect the role of the writer and the role of the reader, and that question accepted practices that flaunt inauthentic, fraudulent imitative practices. Reflecting the tension of how to transmit cultural authority, the fictitious Cervantes declares that he does not want to include these practices of citing well-known authors, annotating passages with classical references in the margins, or creating an inflated "authoritative" index; nonetheless, he states that his novel lacks them. The friend says to include them, then reassuringly adds he does not need them. The narrator ends the prologue by accepting the friend's advice: "sin ponerlas [sus razones] en disputa las aprobé por buenas" (*IH*, pró. 58) [without attempting to question them (my friend's observations), I admitted their soundness] (*DQ*, pro. 13). The arguments for and against traditional writing strategies are never fully resolved. At the end of their discussion, we, the readers, are persuaded to accept his friend's advice, but the friend suggests to follow two different directions. Thus, the reader is left to think freely, contemplating which direction is the better and which direction Cervantes will take.

The friend's final piece of advice serves as a reminder of the variety of readers to be accommodated: "Procurad también que, leyendo vuestra historia, el melancólico se mueva a risa, el risueño la acreciente, el simple no se enfade, el discreto se admire de la invención, el grave no la desprecie, ni el prudente deje de alabarla" (*IH*, pró. 58) [Strive, too, that in reading your story the melancholy may be moved to laughter, and the merry made merrier still; that the simple shall not be wearied, that the judicious shall admire the invention, that the grave shall not despise it, or the wise fail to praise it] (*DQ*, pro. 13). The friend ends the discussion with the same attention to the reader with which the fictitious Cervantes began the prologue. As the fictitious Cervantes, the writer, and his friend, the reader, discuss the novel, they keep in mind other readers, hoping the novel will affect them in many different, yet honest, ways. In spite of all the contradictions Cervantes establishes concerning the freedom of the reader, or perhaps because of them, he invites the reader to be more honest. The reader should not just accept the ideas the writer puts forth nor be deceived by an air of erudition as occurs with other writers who exploit imitative practices: "como veo que están otros libros, aunque sean fabulosos y profanos, tan llenos de sentencias de Aristóteles, de Platón y de toda la caterva de filósofos, que admiran a los leyentes y tienen a sus autores por hombres leídos, eruditos y elocuentes" (*IH*, pró. 52) [after the fashion of other books I see, which, though on fictitious and profane subjects, are so full of maxims from Aristotle and Plato and the whole herd of philosophers that they fill the readers with amazement and convince them that the authors are men of learning, erudition, and eloquence] (*DQ*, pro. 10). Rather, the reader should challenge the writer, honestly respond to the text, and in this way participate in the creative process. This notion is manifested in the text, for example, when the travelers at the inn explain the different reasons they enjoy reading chivalric novels (*IH*, I, 32).

Literary Freedoms

To understand Cervantes's imitation strategies, one must keep in mind that the reader is free to discover clues embedded in the narrative. The role of the reader and the multiple readings a text can generate were discussed by many Renaissance writers. Petrarch, in one of his letters to Boccaccio, explains that *quick* and *slow* readers interpret his work in very different ways: "Unquestionably if a polished, quick, and intelligent reader makes the material being read a delight, then a slow, hesitant and obtuse reader helps to uncover and detect errors."[38] Cervantes also accommodates different types of readers. However, the "quick" readers are those who content themselves with a light, superficial reading, simply following the story line, while the "slow" readers are the more erudite who also study allusions to classical sources and how literature and life intersect. Limiting readership to these two types is unthinkable in the prologue, where the fictitious Cervantes and his friend both allude to the numerous types of readers that span these two extremes. Thus, while the two characters present arguments for and against traditional writing strategies and present the complexities of literary creation, they propose greater freedom for both writer and reader. Thomas Greene points out that writers tried to open a "two-way current of mutual criticism," or at least expose "the poetic distance traversed" from the model to the writer's text.[39] Yet this explanation is inadequate for Cervantes, who does not structure his text in diachronic terms. While Greene's categorization of types of imitation—sacramental, eclectic, heuristic, and dialectical—are relevant to Cervantes's critique of contemporary writers who abuse imitative strategies, they are not useful for understanding where Cervantes strives to take his writing: beyond the diachronic debates. However, even for one such as Cervantes who rebels against the dialectical struggle, issues of imitation must be dealt with, if only to dismiss them.

As I have been suggesting, in some ways Cervantes moves away from traditional concepts of imitation. He does not seek a competitive edge nor flex his erudite muscles. He does not search for a sanctioned tradition or authority to validate his work nor does he need to justify links between Christian and non-Christian writers in order to substantiate the use of a given model. However, he certainly draws on some conventional aspects. His contribution to the development of imitation strategies is, then, more a question of the degree to which he maintains certain principles and discards others than a question of renouncing imitation strategies altogether.

For Cervantes there are two important reasons to imitate models. The first, to a certain extent, follows the innovative ideas of Erasmus, who emphasizes the demands of his own time. Forcione explains that "Cervantes' insight into the living nature of language and his emphatic rejection of his contemporaries' conventional view of imitation had been anticipated in the writings of his most influential humanist ancestor (Erasmus)."[40] Cervantes's imitation strategies pull away from the "likeness" between the models and his own text. This pulling away from the likeness and subsequent highlighting of differences becomes an important issue in examining the women of the prologue and their appearance in the text. At first glance, the women in the main part of the text share no resemblance with Guevara's "mujeres rameras" or the ancient mythological figures. The interested reader must dig deeper to uncover the traces of the past with which the women in *Don Quixote I* are endowed.

In Cervantes's imitation of Guevara's letter that deals with Lamia, Laida, and Flora, he recovers characteristics of these ancient women that are absent from or distorted in Guevara's letter. In doing so, he recuperates the classical women's intelligence, adeptness for public discourse, and independence in certain characters in the text. Cervantes cites Ovid's Medea because he is the classical writer that emphasizes her conflict between passion and loyalty instead of focusing on her infamous act of infanticide. Finally, in citing Homer's Calypso and especially Virgil's Circe, he signals a classical example of turning away from the likeness to the model in an effort to further the distance between the two texts. Cervantes points to Virgil's own liberation from his model, as he deliberately passes by Circe in the *Aeneid*. Later, in Cervantes's novel we glance at parodic snapshots of these powerful women in the characterization of Maritornes and Dulcinea. But it is only a glance before Cervantes, like Virgil, turns away from his models. With all the examples Cervantes chooses to cite in his prologue, there is a deliberate attempt to signal the differences from the model. It is not that the writer's relationship with past texts disappears, but rather that, in keeping with the progressive trends of the late sixteenth and early seventeenth century (such as those Cave has pointed to in his treatment of Montaigne), Cervantes's focus shifts from the relation with the past to the relation with the present. He emphasizes a stronger authorial invention, not dismissing imitation altogether but, rather, further loosening the ties with the classical past to allow for greater authorial creativity. In other words, Cervantes makes a change of emphasis from a diachronic perspective, measuring his works in terms of past texts, to a synchronic one, measuring his work in terms of his society. This point is directly tied to his concept of the role of the reader; his imitation is a function of his relationship with the reader.

But who is this reader, or, in a broader sense, the audience with whom the fictitious Cervantes is seeking a relationship? As Fisher and Halley and others have pointed out, male authors write about women to speak to other men. Although it is problematic to read literary images as representations of history, I would like to turn to the "readers" within *Don Quixote* to get a sense of the ideological function of literature and perhaps from this information chart who the historical "reader/audience" might be. Oftentimes (as in the prologue, or as in the case of Alonso Quijano, or when Don Quixote and Sancho are alone traveling) the audience is a single man; at other times (when Marcela defends herself, when Cardenio and Dorotea begin to tell their stories) a group of men; and at still other times (most notably at the inn when the priest reads "El curioso impertinente," when Dorotea defends her honor, and when the Captive relates the story of Zoraida) the audience is composed of both men and women. In these situations it is always a man who responds to the story at hand. At the end of "El curioso impertinente," only the priest gives his opinion of the tale. When Dorotea defends herself, Fernando responds, and when the Captive finishes his tale, Don Fernando is the only one who speaks up. The rarest of situations is that of a single woman "reader," as is the case with both Luscinda and Dorotea, who read chivalric novels, and with Clara when she later recounts her tale and confides only in Dorotea. Even here, in response to Clara's tale, Dorotea seeks Cardenio's assistance at the first possible moment, thus ensuring an appropriate male response to Clara's story.

I divide the reader/audience by gender to show the relative paucity of female "readers" and to exemplify the immasculation of the limited female readers.[41] In defining "gender," I turn to Joan Scott's work on gender as a category of historical analysis. She defines the term as having two interrelated parts: "[G]ender is a constitutive element of social relationships based on perceived differences between the sexes, and gender is a primary way of signifying relationships of power."[42] Furthermore in discussing women in this work, I only refer to specific characters or, as Lou Charnon-Deutsch explains, "to a category into which all women are placed, blindly and erroneously, by a specific phallocentric discourse; it will in no case mean women, in general."[43] Similarly, the terms *female* and *feminine* refer to a "mode of being that has come to be culturally identified with women but that is not biologically determined."[44] Although textual examples do not allow us access to historical women's selfhoods, we can see by the sheer quantity of examples and also by Dorotea's response to Clara's story how female readers may be induced to participate in the denigration of their own subject position.

While there are relatively few works that investigate women readers of the Golden Age, Sara Nalle's work on literacy and culture touches upon both gender and class as factors in determining literacy rates. Briefly, she documents the spread of literacy in early modern Spain and its effect on Castile's book market, and explores the relationship between people's book choices and their socioeconomic background. Her data includes gender as a variable and reveals that literacy for women ranged anywhere between 57 percent, as is the case with urban women of Cuenca, to 3 percent, as is the case with both rural and urban women of Santiago.[45] She also shows that of the eighty-eight book owners in Cuenca, the largest group, one-third, were farmers, while artisans, field hands, merchants, shopkeepers, professionals, hidalgos, and priests made up the rest.[46] Relevant to *Don Quixote* she notes that while chivalric novels were popular fiction for the aristocracy they were also incredibly popular with young people, including women. In Cuenca, for example, "the majority of readers were unmarried, often living at home" and not only social class and gender but also age, marital status, and, of course, individual taste were important variables in understanding who read what in early modern Spain.[47] Anne Cruz raises an important yet elusive issue in examining the role of women in early modern Spanish literature: "The clash between literary and didactic writings and 'real' life—the difference, that is, between the fictional representation of women's expected demeanor and their actual behavior, despite the notorious difficulties in documenting the latter—therefore invites us to reevaluate the complex connections and oppositions underlying historical and literary discourses in early modern Spain."[48] Nalle's findings suggest that Cervantes does faithfully represent the status of women readers at that time....

In the prologue, Cervantes initiates a kind of hide-and-seek with his readers as he focuses on a rule common to Renaissance treatises: that the imitator conceal his sources using innovative corrective strategies. Erasmus clearly argues that "if we want to be successful in our imitation of Cicero, the first thing must be to conceal our imitation of Cicero."[49] Moreover, this intricate act of concealing is accompanied by the act of revealing. Cervantes advertises his sources both in the prologue and at other points in the text, yet he does not deprive his reader of the pleasure of seeking out the dismantled, fragmented narrative pieces that are the result of a complex rewriting. As Michael Riffaterre argues in his discussion of Du Bellay, "[erudite poetry] veils [its idea], but it also points to where it is hidden and how it can be revealed."[50] In this way Cervantes exploits the dynamic between writer, reader, and text. The fictitious Cervantes identifies some of his sources in the prologue as he consults his friend on ways of improving his text. However, these sources, as they surface in the text, are thickly disguised through fragmentation, ambiguity, and contextual distortion. Cave, in discussing Montaigne's writing strategies, talks about an "oscillation between strategies of obstruction and exclusion on the one hand and the theme of desire for an ideally sympathetic and alert reader on the other."[51] Likewise, Cervantes plays with his readers—as the prologue clearly illustrates—pulling us in and out of the narrative and baiting the text with bits and pieces of classical sources to be discovered by the alert reader. Imitation for Cervantes becomes an imitation of pleasure, a game both for himself, the writer, and for the reader.

Several critics have commented on the idea that the prologue is a reflection of the main part of the text. Both are taken up by a surrogate reader; both contain interrupted narratives, stories within stories; both give weight to the metafictional aspects of writing, elaborating on the process of constructing the text; and both scrutinize current literary conventions. Of these conventions, the one that is both underscored and undermined is *imitatio*. More than just theorizing about the pros and cons of conventional imitation as the fictitious author and his anonymous friend do, the prologue is an example of Cervantes's imitative techniques. As Presburg has noted, Cervantes draws from and then transforms the dialectic traditions of Plato, the comic-serious rhetoric of Erasmus's *In Praise of Folly*, and the theoretical-fictional framework of López Pinciano's *Philosophia antigua poética*. In the main part of the text, Cervantes continues with his innovative and personalized imitation strategies. . . .

In *Don Quixote*, the polemical dialogue between the fictitious Cervantes and his friend offers the reader much more than a brief look at the supposed problems with which Cervantes struggles as he creates his novel. It delves into issues of literary convention, questions authority, and critiques the process of preserving ancient texts. Their dialogue exposes the ostentation and fraudulence of writers who have abused the precepts of imitation. It seeks to secure a richer understanding of artistic originality without fully rejecting imitation. This controversial writing strategy cannot be understood as a unified whole. Like the perspectivism that characterizes the novel, Cervantes's rewriting of sources is eclectic. It serves many purposes and suits the needs of a given context. Sometimes his imitation of sources is made obvious to the reader and is directly discussed in the text, as in Don Quixote's discussion of the Golden Age.[52] At other times, the imitation is more allusive and invites speculation, as with specific characterization and the models cited in the prologue. Gerli reminds us that Cervantes "reads works not as mere descriptions but as emblems, or evocations of themes and ideas, and in his rewritings of them allows us to theorize on the historical, social, political, and cultural conditions and consequences affecting the entire economy of textual production and consumption for the culture in which he moved."[53] *Don Quixote I* is, then, both a textual repository of collected fragments from a variety of sources and a marker that pushes on the borders defining standards of acceptable behavior and expectations. It is precisely within this amorphous terrain, stretched between imitation and originality, that the women of the prologue are conceived. Their names and sources ring of antiquity, yet their positioning in the prologue, their surfacing in the text, and their interface with some of the main characters of *Don Quixote I* proclaim Cervantes's originality.

NOTES

1. Miguel de Cervantes, *Prologue*, ed. B. W. Ife, vol. 1 of *Exemplary Novels* (Warminster, England: Aris & Phillips, 1992), 4.

2. Ibid., 5.

3. Cited in Curtius, *European Literature and the Latin Middle Ages*, 297.

4. Robert R. Edwards, *Ratio and Invention: A Study of Medieval Lyric and Narrative* (Nashville, Tenn.: Vanderbilt University Press, 1989), 81.

5. Miguel de Cervantes, *Viaje del Parnaso*, ed. Miguel Herrero García, vol. 5, Clásicos Hispánicos Serie 4 (Madrid: CSIC, 1983), 320.

6. All translations from *Viaje del Parnaso* are my own.

7. Alicia Ostriker, "The Thieves of Language: Women Poets and Revisionist Mythmaking," in *The New Feminist Criticism: Essays on Women, Literature and Theory*, ed. Elaine Showalter (New York: Pantheon, 1985), 314–38. Since Ostriker's seminal work, several critics have continued to explore revisionist mythmaking, a term coined by Adrienne Rich. For more on revisionist mythmaking and its relation to twentieth-century women artists and writers, see Estella Lauter, *Women as Mythmakers: Poetry and Visual Art by Twentieth-Century Women* (Bloomington: Indiana University Press, 1984); Susan Friedman, *Psyche Reborn: The Emergence of H. D.* (Bloomington: Indiana University Press, 1981); and Elizabeth Sakellaridou, "Feminist Heterologies: Contemporary British Women Playwrights and the Rewrite of Myth and History," in *English Studies in Translation: Papers from the ESSE Inaugural Conference*, ed. Robert Clark and Piero Boitani (New York: Routledge, 1993), 306–19. For feminist criticism and the uses of myth see Teresa de Lauretis, "Feminist Studies/Critical Studies: Issues, Terms, and Contexts," in *Feminist Studies Critical Studies*, ed. Teresa de Lauretis (Bloomington: Indiana University Press, 1986), 1–19; and Margret Brügmann, "Critical Resistance or Utopia? Questioning the Use of Mythical Protagonists to Explore Feminine Identity," in *Who's Afraid of*

Femininity? Questions of Identity, ed. Margret Brügmann, Sonja Heebing, Debbi Long, and Magda Michielsens (Atlanta, Ga.: Rodopi, 1993), 33–42. For revisionist mythmaking and feminist theology, see Angela West, *Deadly Innocence: Feminist Theology and the Mythology of Sin* (New York: Mowbray, 1995).

8. Lauter, *Women as Mythmakers,* 11.

9. Ostriker, "The Thieves of Language," 318.

10. Michael E. Gerli, *Refiguring Authority: Reading, Writing, and Rewriting in Cervantes* (Lexington: University Press of Kentucky, 1995), 4.

11. Ruth El Saffar, *Distance and Control in Don Quijote: A Study in Narrative Technique,* University of North Carolina Studies in the Romance Languages and Literatures 147 (Chapel Hill: University of North Carolina Press, 1975), 36–37.

12. In his chapter on *Don Quixote* Flores cites Leo Spitzer, Alban Forcione, F. W. Locke, and Mia Gerhardt as critics who have attributed omnipotent powers to Cervantes. Flores, *Rhetoric of Doubtful Authority,* 89–90.

13. Salvador Fajardo, "Instructions for Use: The Prologue to *Don Quixote I,*" *Journal of Interdisciplinary Literary Studies* 6, no. 1 (1994): 9.

14. Ibid.

15. The translation loses the nuance of the original Spanish but in a footnote Putnam—cited in Jones and Douglas (*DQ*)—gives the more literal translation: "Under my cloak, I kill [or I rule] the king" (9 n. 4).

16. E. C. Riley, *Cervantes's Theory of the Novel* (Oxford: Clarendon, 1962), 21.

17. Ibid., 27. Riley discusses Cervantes's sources for Don Quixote and the literary theory that he applies to his writing. In mentioning sources, Riley concentrates on those for Don Quixote and Sancho; he does not discuss those authors cited in the prologue that serve as sources for female characters. *Don Quixote* (London and Boston: Allen and Unwin, 1986), 42. He points to the possible influences on Cervantes's literary theories, including El Pinciano, Carvallo, Tasso, Giraldi Cinthio, G. B. Pigna, A. Piccolomini, and Mintumo (Riley, *Don Quixote,* 66), and discusses the importance of imitation theory for Cervantes. *Cervantes' Theory of the Novel,* 61–67. In his thorough study of the prologues to *Don Quixote,* Socrates treats the prologue as a function of literary criticism. Mario Socrates, *Prologhi al Don Chisciotte* (Padua: Marsilio, 1974).

18. Alban K. Forcione, *Cervantes and the Mystery of Lawlessness: A Study of El casamiento engañoso y El coloquio de los perros* (Princeton: Princeton University Press; 1984), 193.

19. Ibid., 191.

20. Sheila Fisher and Janet E. Halley, "The Lady Vanishes: The Problem of Women's Absence in Late Medieval and Renaissance Texts," in *Seeking the Woman in Late Medieval and Renaissance Writings: Essays in Feminist Contextual Criticism,* ed. Sheila Fisher and Janet E. Halley (Knoxville: University of Tennessee Press, 1989), 4. For more on the dialogue between male author and male reader and the role of the female character, see Nancy J. Vickers, "This Heraldry in Lucrece's Face," in *The Female Body in Western Culture: Contemporary Perspectives,* ed. Susan Rubin Suleiman, 209–22 (Cambridge: Harvard University Press, 1986); Anne J. Cruz, "Sexual Enclosure, Textual Escape: The *Pícara* as Prostitute in the Spanish Female Picaresque Novel," in Fisher and Halley, *Seeking the Woman in Late Medieval and Renaissance Writings,* 135–59; and Adriana Cavarero, *In Spite of Plato: A Feminist Rewriting of Ancient Philosophy,* trans. Serena Anderlini-D'Onofrio and Áine O'Healy (New York: Routledge, 1995), 4.

21. Edward Friedman, "Reading Redressed; or, The Media Circuits of *Don Quijote*," *Revista hispánica de cultura y literatura* 9, no. 2 (1994): 38–51.

22. Christine Gledhill, "Pleasurable Negotiations," in *Female Spectators: Looking at Film and Television*, ed. Deidre Pribram (London: Verso, 1988), 67.

23. Ibid.

24. I am reminded of Lope's "Arte nuevo de hacer comedias" [New art of writing plays] (1609), in which he too bids farewell to the ancients: "y, cuando he de escribir una comedia / encierro los preceptos con seis llaves" (and when I have to write a comedy I lock in the precepts with six keys). In *Significado y doctrina del Arte nuevo de Lope de Vega*, ed. Juan Manuel Rozas, Colección Temas 9 (Madrid: Sociedad General Española de Librería, 1976), v. 40–41. English translation from *The New Art of Writing Plays*, trans. William T. Brewster, in *Papers on Playmaking*, ed. Brander Matthews (Freeport, N.Y.: Books for Libraries, 1957), 13.

25. Américo Castro, "Los prólogos al *Quijote*," in *Semblanzas y estudios españoles*, ed. Juan Marichal (Princeton: Princeton University Press, 1956), 189–219; Juan Bautista Avalle-Arce, "Directrices del prólogo de 1605," in *Don Quijote como forma de vida* (Madrid: Castalia, 1976), 13–35.

26. For the former, see John J. Allen, *Don Quixote: Hero or Fool? (Part Two)* (Gainesville: University Press of Florida, 1979); and James A. Parr, *Anatomy of a Subversive Discourse* (Newark, Del.: Juan de la Cuesta, 1988). For the latter, see E. Friedman, "Reading Redressed."

27. Heiple points out that Lope de Vega's first sonnet in *Rimas humanas* (1602) is characterized by invention: "Lope goes much further and presents his poetry as children he has conceived and borne with pain." "Lope's Arte poética," in *Renaissance and Golden Age Essays in Honor of D. W. McPheeters*, ed. Bruno M. Damiani (Potomac, Md.: Scripta Humanistica, 1986), 118. Thus, for Cervantes who distances his relationship by claiming to be the stepfather, Lope's paternal claim would limit the reader's freedom of interpretation.

28. Kevin Dunn, *Pretexts of Authority: The Rhetoric of Authorship in the Renaissance Preface* (Stanford, Calif.: Stanford University Press, 1994), 14.

29. E. Friedman, "Reading Redressed," 50.

30. Michel De Certeau, *The Practice of Everyday Life*, trans. Steven Rendall (Berkeley and Los Angeles: University of California Press, 1984), 172.

31. Edwin Williamson, *The Half-Way House of Fiction: Don Quixote and Arthurian Romance* (Oxford: Clarendon, 1984), 82–83. While pointing out the complexities of Cervantes's irony, Williamson still concludes that the entire prologue is an acerbic attack of literary conventions and that Cervantes's aim is to dismiss them all.

32. John G. Weiger, *In the Margins of Cervantes* (Hanover, N.H.: University Press of New England, 1988), 33–34,

33. Porqueras Mayo argues that reflection on art is common to seventeenth-century artists. "Es típica del manierismo la reflexión intelectualista sobre el arte en general. Los prologuistas empiezan también a ensayar y reflexionar sobre los prólogos, y rompen antiguos moldes. Así se explica el prólogo al *Quijote I*, como una meditación manierista sobre el prólogo, para rebasarlo y desintegrarlo, y mostrar así el mismo proceso creativo del prólogo" [Typical of mannerism is the intellectual reflection on art in general. Prologue writers are also beginning to write about and reflect on prologues and are breaking old molds. So the prologue to *Don Quixote I* can be understood as a mannerist meditation on the prologue, to go beyond it and

break it up and, in this way, show the very creative process of the prologue]. "En torno a los prólogos de Cervantes," in Criado de Val, *Cervantes*, 77 (my translation). For an analysis of the prologue in Golden Age literature, see Alberto Porqueras Mayo, *El prólogo como género literario* (Madrid: CSIC, 1957), and for a more specific reading of Cervantes and the prologue, see Criado de Val, *Cervantes*. "En tomo a los prólogos de Cervantes," 75–84. J. M. Martínez Torrejón offers a thorough investigation on the prologue of *Don Quixote I*. He reads the prologue as an instrument of parody to mock established literary norms. "Creación artística en los prólogos de Cervantes," *Anales cervantinas* 23 (1985): 161–93. Elias Rivers is the first to offer a complete study of all of Cervantes's prologues. He focuses on the presence of Cervantes the artist and how he portrays himself through the years. "Cervantes' Art of the Prologue," in *Estudios literarias de hispanistas norteamericanos dedicados a Helmut Hatzfeld* (Barcelona: Ediciones Hispam, 1974), 167–71. George McSpadden classifies elements of the prologue in more than fifty groups. However, he does not go beyond the data stage nor explain how the elements function nor the differences among authors nor the importance of the usage of such an element. *The Spanish Prologue before 1700* (Potomac, Md.: José Porrúas Turanzas, 1979).

34. Fajardo, "'Instructions for Use," 11.

35. John Shawcross, "The Authority of the Writer and Readers of Renaissance Texts," *Literature Interpretation Theory* 5, no. 2 (1994), 111. I am also reminded of Howard Mancing's response to Henry Sullivan's article in which Mancing approaches the readers from the perspective of a cognitive scientist describing readers as "pragmatic beings who construct personally significant understandings of what they read; they are not abstract or implied entities that somehow exist within the text, as a function of the text, or as a textual norm; nor are they passive, empty spaces upon which language and/or ideology inscribes subjectivity." "Against Dualisms: A Response to Henry Sullivan," *Cervantes* 19, no. 1 (1999): 159.

36. Escudero and Martínez Torrejón argue that the prologue is an attack on how other writers use and abuse the prologue as a literary device. Carmen Escudero, "El prólogo al *Quijote* de 1605, clave de los sistemas estructurales y tonales de la obra," in *Actas del primer coloquio internacional de la Asociación de Cervantistas*, Alcalá de Henares 29/30 nov-1/2 dic, 1988 (Barcelona: Antropos, 1990), 181–85; Martínez Torrejón, "Creación artística en los prólogos de Cervantes." Others put forth that Cervantes's attack is directed at the *Arcadia*. Emilio Orozco Díaz, "Sobre el prólogo del *Quijote* de 1605 y su complejidad intentional: Notas para una close," *Insula* 35, no. 400–401 (1980): 7, 32–33; José S. López Navío, "Génesis y desarrollo del *Quijote*," *Anales cervantinos* 7 (1958): 157–235; *El ingenioso hidalgo don Quijote de la Mancha*, ed. Justo García Soriano and Justo García Morales, 12th ed. (Madrid: Aguilar, 1968). However, Palacín argues that Cervantes is not attacking Lope in his prologue. *En torno at Quijote: Ensayo de interpretación y crítica* (Madrid: Leira, 1965), 9.

37. Allen points out a double layer of irony in this passage. First, Cervantes's self-deprecation coincides with an assertion of his own self-sufficiency; second, Cervantes is not too lazy to "borrow" from Herrera's prologue in *Poesias de Garcílaso* (1580) for writing the dedication to *Don Quixote I*. Allen, *Don Quixote: Hero or Fool? (Part Two)*, 47.

38. Petrarca, *Letters on Familiar Matters*, 22.2.211.

39. Greene, *Light in Troy*, 45, 40.

40. Alban K. Forcione, *Cervantes and the Humanist Vision: A Study of Four Exemplary Novels* (Princeton: Princeton University Press, 1982), 191.

41. I borrow the term "immasculation" from Judith Fetterly, who discusses female audience response in/to American fiction. Judith Fetterly, *The Resisting Reader: A Feminist Approach to American Fiction* (Bloomington: Indiana University Press, 1978), xx. Feminist film critics also discuss immasculation of women in terms of the "male gaze." See Laura Mulvey, *Visual and Other Pleasures* (Bloomington: Indiana University Press, 1989), esp. 14–26.

42. Joan Wallach Scott, *Gender and the Politics of History* (New York: Columbia University Press, 1988), 42. For more on gender as a social construct, see Judith Butler, *Gender Trouble: Feminism and the Subversion of Identity* (New York: Routledge, 1990).

43. Lou Charnon-Deutsch, *Narratives of Desire: Nineteenth-Century Spanish Fiction by Women* (University Park: Pennsylvania State Press, 1994), 195 n. 16.

44. Ibid.

45. Sara Nalle, "Literacy and Culture in Early Modern Castile," *Past and Present* 125 (Nov. 1989): 65–96. Her tables on page 68 offer quantitative data on literacy rates in sixteenth- and seventeenth-century Spain. Nalle explains that the literacy rates for women are not very reliable because "women seldom appeared in any of the sources used except testaments." Ibid., 69.

46. Ibid., 77.

47. Ibid., 88–89.

48. Cruz, "Feminism, Psychoanalysis, and the Search for the M/Other in Early Modern Spain," 34–35.

49. Erasmus, *Collected Works*, 28:368.

50. Michael Riffaterre, *Text Production*, trans. Terese Lyons (New York: Columbia University Press, 1983), 111–12. D. Hamilton also draws from Riffaterre in her study of Virgil and *The Tempest*. She discusses both the artistry of concealing and revealing subtexts and the author's relationship with the reader in handling the displacement of the precursor text.

51. Cave, "Mimesis of Reading in the Renaissance," 157.

52. For further discussion on the Golden Age in *Don Quixote*, see Américo Castro, *El pensamiento de Cervantes, Revista de Filología Española* 6 (Madrid: Hernando, 1925); Luis Murillo, *Golden Dial: Temporal Configurations in Don Quijote* (Oxford: Dolphin, 1975); Peter N. Dunn, "Two Classical Myths in *Don Quijote*," *Renaissance and Reformation* 9 (1972): 2–10; Rudolph Schevill, *Ovid and the Renascence in Spain*, University of California Publications in Modern Philology 4, no. 1. (Berkeley and Los Angeles: University of California Press, 1913); Francisco Márquez Villanueva, *Personajes y temas del Quijote* (Madrid: Taurus, 1975); Mary Mackey, "Rhetoric and Characterization in *Don Quijote*," *Hispanic Review* 42 (1974): 51–66; Berndt-Kelley, "En torno a la 'maravillosa visión' de la pastora Marcela y otra 'ficción poética.'"

53. Gerli, *Refiguring Authority*, 8.

HOWARD MANCING

Cervantes as Narrator of Don Quijote

I. The Author

In this essay I would like to take a look at some questions often contemplated by literary scholars and casual readers alike: What is the relationship of the author to his or her text? Is the author or, at least, the author's voice, to be found in the text and, if so, where? Who tells the story; who is the narrator? As we try to identify the disembodied narrative voice that speaks to us from within the text, we might recall the image used by the Victor Talking Machine company, later RCA Victor, in the early days of sound recordings: Nipper the dog, sitting with head cocked, listening curiously to the bell-shaped speaker of a phonograph, as though wondering where his master is.[1] As has often been noted, it seems that when we read a novel we want to have the experience of communicating with another human being, with the author.[2]

But modern literary scholarship would seem to have banished the historical author from any role whatsoever in the text. Today most literary scholars labor under the influence of New Critical formalism, where the text stands alone and the author is irrelevant; or structuralism, where the text embodies culture and the author is irrelevant; and/or some form of poststructuralist theory, where the reader creates, or deconstructs, the text and the author is irrelevant. The author is dead, proclaims Roland Barthes; not quite dead, responds Michel Foucault, but merely a function of the text, and an eighteenth-century

From *Cervantes* 23, no. 1 (2003): 117–40. © 2003 by *Cervantes*.

invention, at that. It is often (condescendingly) assumed to be critically naïve to talk and write of authors in serious scholarly discourse.[3]

I would like to bring the author—in this case Cervantes—back into consideration as I look closely at the narrative structure of *Don Quijote*. Few issues in Cervantine scholarship have attracted more attention than the identification of the narrative voices in the novel and the clarification of relationships among them.[4] A high point of sorts is achieved by James A. Parr in his book Don Quijote, *An Anatomy of Subversive Discourse*, in which he describes no fewer than eleven "voices" and "presences" in Cervantes' novel and draws an elaborate chart to illustrate their relationships (30–36).

Without reviewing in detail the history of scholarly approaches to the subject of the narrative structure of *Don Quijote*, I would like to examine the issue in some detail, tracing the reader's perception of narrative voices from the beginning of the book to the end. In particular, I want to call into question the nearly universal assumption that the author himself, Miguel de Cervantes, is absolutely absent from the text. In doing this, I hope to illustrate the simultaneous simplicity and complexity of the narrative strategies in the text and to consider the nature of the narrative achievement of Cervantes. My method will be to take the book as it exists and read it from cover to cover, commenting in turn on each narrative element as it is perceived.

II. The Title Page

It would seem unnecessary to state the obvious: the fact that on the title page of the book it is announced that the work was "compuesto por Miguel de Cervantes Saavedra." It may be obvious, but one sometimes gets the impression that the poststructuralist assertion that authors do not exist is taken quite literally by some very sophisticated readers. There are times when one searches in vain for a reference to "Cervantes" in a great deal of current critical commentary. Parr, for example, constructs an elaborate, eleven-point "hierarchy" of what he calls "narrative voices and presences" in *Don Quijote*, beginning with "the extra-textual *historical author*, a presence." First of all, it would have been easier and more direct simply to say "Cervantes" than to utilize the somewhat awkward phrase "extra-textual historical author." More to the point, though Parr goes on to discuss the role and significance of each of the voices and presences he perceives in the text, he dismisses "the historical Cervantes" in a single sentence, while the ten others all receive at least a full paragraph of attention.

It is important, however, to recognize—explicitly—that Cervantes wrote *Don Quijote* and that this fact is acknowledged on the title page of the book, as well as elsewhere. As we will see, the claim—the fact—of authorship by the historical human being, Miguel de Cervantes, is significant in the narration of the fictional story of Don Quijote.

III. The Prologue to Part I

Susan Lanser's *The Narrative Act* (1981) is one of the most comprehensive, readable, and convincing of all studies of narration. In it, Lanser describes and evaluates better than any predecessor the role of what she calls the "extrafictional voice":

> In every text, ... even a fictional text, an authorial voice does communicate historical information. This authorial voice is an *extrafictional* entity whose presence accounts, for example, for organizing, titling, and introducing the fictional work. This extrafictional voice, the most direct textual counterpart for the historical author, carries all the *diegetic authority* of its (publicly authorized) creator and has the ontological status of historical truth. This is the voice of scientific and "utilitarian" discourse as well as cultural communication. It is a voice that, but for the degree to which literary criticism has removed the author's historical presence from the text, could simply be called the authorial voice. (122)

It seems clear that, as Lanser says, we routinely ascribe to the empirical human being called "the author" the words contained in texts of scientific or utilitarian discourse. When we read, for example, *The Origin of Species*, we do not ascribe the assertions in the text to any sort of narrative persona, but simply to Charles Darwin. We say that Toynbee and Prescott are the authors of the historical works that bear their names; we attribute to Hayden White or Jacques Derrida the statements in the critical texts they write. Even in autobiographical texts that consist of a mix of truth and fiction, such as Benjamin Franklin's *Autobiography* or Vladimir Nabokov's *Speak Memory*, there is no need to talk of the "narrator," the "textual persona," or the "implied author" of the text, but, simply, of Franklin or Nabokov. Similarly, if Isaac Asimov writes an introduction or a preface to a collection of his science fiction short stories, no one I have ever encountered attempts to distinguish between the voice of that preface and the voice of the historical figure of Asimov. No one routinely talks of anything like the "extrafictional voice of the introduction." There would be no point in it. Authors normally speak in their historically authorized "real" voice in order to introduce a fictional text.

In *Don Quijote*, the prologue of Part I is of particular interest to the reader, even though its function in the narrative scheme of *Don Quijote* is very often overlooked. Many literary scholars do not—indeed, feel that they must not—assume that the voice of the prologue of Part I of *Don Quijote* is that of the historical man, Miguel de Cervantes. For example, Parr attributes the voice of the prologue to what he calls a "dramatized author" (33), a voice separate from all others in the text, while John Weiger identifies that voice as that of an unnamed fictional character whom he calls the "prologuist." But, as I have just suggested, most common readers (and some literary critics and theorists, such as E. C. Riley and Jay Allen) assume that this voice is that of the author, Cervantes. To make matters more complicated, this supposedly fictional voice of the prologue claims some of the historical truths known to be associated with the historical author of the work. Surely it is both easier and more consistent with human psychology to accept the voice of the prologue as that of an author (Cervantes) who sometimes fictionalizes himself, than it is to conceive of it as a fictional character who sometimes "factualizes" himself by claiming, for instance, to be the author of the book we are reading, whose author we know is Cervantes.

Alberto Porqueras Mayo has studied the prologue as a literary genre in sixteenth- and seventeenth-century Spain, where it was more important and more prominent than it was in other Renaissance literatures. Porqueras maintains that the prologue is the author's direct link to the reader, the place where the author justifies his or her writing of the text and transmits to the reader valuable information about, and important clues on how to read, the text that follows. Elias Rivers, too, has defined the prologue as a "well-defined semi-academic genre in which writers presented their works to readers" (*Quixotic Scriptures* 108). And this, in fact, is what most of us assume to be true of other prologues of the period. In the first part of *Guzmán de Alfarache*, for instance, there are two prologues to the first part, one addressed to the "vulgar" reader and the second addressed to the "discrete" reader. These, together with the single prologue to the second part of *Guzmán* (1604), are devices employed by the author, Mateo Alemán, in his explicit didactic aim and serve to instruct the reader on how to read the fictional text that follows.

It is worth noting some of the strategies used by Cervantes in the prologues to his other books:

* In the prologue to his *Ocho comedias y ocho entremeses*, Cervantes reminisces about having watched avidly the early theatrical productions of Lope de Rueda. I do not know anyone who does not attribute this claim to the historical Cervantes.

* In the prologue to his *Novelas ejemplares*, Cervantes describes his physical appearance in some detail. I do not know anyone who does not take this to be an authentic self-portrait of the historical Cervantes. He even identifies himself by his full name, Miguel de Cervantes Saavedra, in this text.

* In his prologue to Part II of *Don Quijote*, Cervantes announces the forthcoming publication of his allegorical novel *Persiles* and promises a sequel to his pastoral novel *La Galatea*. I do not know anyone who does not assume that the historical Cervantes makes these statements.

* In the prologue to *Los trabajos de Persiles y Sigismunda*, Cervantes tells of a recent meeting with a student who was overjoyed to be in the company of the famous writer Miguel de Cervantes. Is this a strictly factual account, some sort of mixture of fact and fantasy or wishful thinking, or a purely fictional (and self-serving) account? Whatever we take it to be, it is a statement made by the historical Cervantes (who may or may not be narrating a fiction).

It seems quite clear to me that the extrafictional voice of the prologues that the reader perceives is that of Miguel de Cervantes.[5] The text of the prologue to the first part of *Don Quijote*, in fact, contains some claims that only the historical Cervantes could make. The claim to be the author of the book—recall the title page—or the worry about how to introduce the work to the public in a prologue can—logically—only by made by Cervantes, since authors write prologues to books they have written. The *yo*, then, who frets about this last pre-publication hurdle, the prologue, is Cervantes.[6] The problem comes in with the "friend" who enters the picture to discuss the author's dilemma.

It is commonly assumed that the scene Cervantes describes—he sits at his desk with writer's block, unable to compose his prologue, when a good friend arrives and discusses the matter with him—is a fiction. Therefore, for scrupulous, hair-splitting, modern literary scholars addicted to absolute binaries (see the discussion below in section VII), the entity who utters these words must be a fictional character and not Cervantes. As John Weiger puts it: "Few doubt that the prologuist's friend is a fictional character. Virtually no one doubts that the conversation is fabricated. It follows that the fictitious friend's interlocutor, the prologuist, is equally fictitious" (135). Logically, however, this scene has no less formal claim to authority than the recollection of the days of Lope de Rueda in the prologue to the *Ocho comedias*. Who can say for a fact that Cervantes ever saw Lope de Rueda? Why could that autobiographical statement not be just as much an invention as this dramatic scene? And what if Cervantes and some clever friend really did have the conversation recorded here, or, at least, one something like it? How can we "know" the "truth" of any autobiographical text? In fact, contemporary theorists of autobiography all stress the fact that any re-creation of the past, inevitably dependant on fallible memory, is ultimately an inseparable mixture of fiction and fact.[7]

Logically, then, the *yo* of all of Cervantes' prologues are either fictional entities and what they claim cannot be ascribed to the historical author, or all of them are extratextual voices—authorial voices—of substantial (but never absolute) diegetic authority. Why do we have so much trouble dealing with adjacent factual and fictional statements? Why do we have to resort to the invention of new narrative entities, personae, or masks, in an attempt to separate fictional and factual voices?

When I explain a scar on my arm by telling my daughters about the time the rustlers nearly stole the herd of cattle and how, in the ensuing gunfight, I was lightly wounded but we managed to fight off the bad guys, they have—especially now that they are older and more schooled in narrative conventions—no difficulty in distinguishing among a real scar, their real father, and a fictional tale. When I speak facetiously, sarcastically, or ironically to a group of my departmental colleagues, they do not need to resort to any concept of narrative masks or implied department heads in order to distinguish between truth and fiction and understand what I have to say. We all know (at least most of the time) how to interpret a wink, a smile, a nod, a tone of voice, or a posture, in order to separate fact from fiction in oral discourse. And we can interpret a wide variety of contextual cues in order to do the same in many written texts (although some, such as *Lazarillo de Tormes*, present more difficult and perplexing problems than *Don Quijote*).

In the world outside the realm of literary theory there is no pretense that we need a special term for talking or writing about our concepts of real people, historical figures, or authors of books. No one speaks of an "implied president" in political discourse, even when we know that what a Bill Clinton or George W. Bush says or writes may be quite different from what the "real" person thinks. By the same token, I know Jay Allen very well, but the version of him that I understand cannot be the version of himself that holds, nor is it identical to that held by any other individual. "My" Jay Allen is not "the" Jay Allen. Yet I can say "Jay Allen" (and not "the implied cervantista") and everyone knows that I am making no claim to essentialist knowledge but am simply referring to the person I know. As Michael Toolan says specifically of authors, "Even if we know an author personally, we still perform the same process of forming a mental picture or representation (itself a kind of narrative) of that author to ourselves as an integral part of the activity of knowing a person. In short, the pictures we have of authors are always constructions, so that all authors are, if you like, 'inferred authors'" (78). The conflict between reality and illusion has perhaps been the main theme of the novel since *Don*

Quixote, and it is nothing if not ironic if we should fail to see that narrative theory deals centrally with the same problem. Do we really have to work so hard to convince students that a speaker's, writer's, or narrator's words are to be taken with a grain of salt in many—even most—contexts? Is skepticism in general, and textual skepticism in particular, really so difficult to convey? Surely we teachers and professors of literature should be able to do that job without recourse to an arcane vocabulary and a set of imprecise concepts that *no one else in any other discipline* needs to employ when dealing with precisely the same issues. In effect, all of us are versions of ourselves, both to ourselves and to everyone else. As Bakhtin says, "It is customary to speak about the authorial mask. But in which utterances (speech acts) is there a *face* and not a mask, that is, no authorship?" (*Speech Genres* 152).

In the prologue to Part I, then, Cervantes pretends to discuss the nature of literary prologues with his friend.[8] He also states that he is not the *padre* but the *padrastro* of the book. The latter assertion is usually, and logically, linked with his claim to have searched the archives of La Mancha for the raw data he assembled into his account, just as historians, reporters, or editors assemble information from a variety of sources and write their versions of some events. For all we (absolutely) know, maybe there were some sort of local archives in La Mancha that Cervantes actually investigated. Formally, this statement has every bit as great a claim to being factual as his claim of having seen Lope de Rueda in his youth. Much more likely, however, and as is generally assumed by those who have written on the subject, this statement is presented with another textual wink, evoking the convention of the books of chivalry that were traditionally written in the guise of historical documents. So Cervantes says in effect: "I consulted all the sources and wrote this version of the story of *Don Quijote*; though I seem to be the author (*padre*), I am really only the editor (*padrastro*) of the text."

What this ironic posturing, intertextual allusion, and clever metatextual play does is establish the tone for the work: festive, satiric, intellectually subtle. The extrafictional voice—the voice of Miguel de Cervantes—may be engaging in a bit of fiction of its own, but it accomplishes the aims that Porqueras says prologues traditionally set out to accomplish. It prescribes the readers' horizon of expectations and contextualizes the story that is to follow, suggesting how readers might approach the text.

IV. Part I, Chapters 1–8: The Editor and His Text

Susan Lanser distinguishes between "public" and "private" narrators (basically the same as Genett's "extradiegetic" and "intradiegetic" narrators) in a fictional text. The latter, the private narrator, is usually a fictional character and is always subordinate to the former, the public narrator. The public narrator "generally defines for the reader the story world in which s/he will function as creator and authority" (137–38). Then, breaking with the scholars and theoreticians who would insist on a mandatory and absolute separation between the public narrator and the author, Lanser proceeds to make the following assertion:

> Ordinarily, the unmarked case of narration for public narrators is that the narrating voice is equated with the textual author (the extrafictional voice or "implied author") unless a different case is marked—signaled—by the text. In other words, in the absence of direct markings which separate the public narrator from the extrafictional voice, so long as it is possible to give meaning to the text within the equation author = narrator, readers will conventionally make this equation. This does not mean there are numerically more cases where author and narrator are equivalent than cases where they are not; it merely means that the separation between the two voices must be marked. (151)

What is particularly significant here is Lanser's insistence that there must exist a textual marker in order to distinguish between the author and the narrator. Again, in "nonfiction" texts, this presents no problem: we never need, nor are we given a signal, to distinguish between the historical Roland Barthes and the voice of *The Pleasure of the Text*, or between the historical Jay Allen and the voice in *Don Quixote: Hero or Fool?* But in fictional texts the problem is more complex. Normally, the textual marker is perfectly obvious. For example, Mark Twain is the author of *The Adventures of Huckleberry Finn*, but there is no temptation whatsoever to call him the narrator of the fictional text because there is an obvious and unavoidable textual marker: the narrator's name, Huck Finn. Or, again, Francisco de Quevedo is the author of *El buscón* but the narrator is identified as Pablos, an entity clearly distinct from Quevedo. In Daniel Defoe's *Moll Flanders* the narrator is Moll, not Defoe; in J. D. Salinger's *The Catcher in the Rye* the narrator is Holden Caulfield, not Salinger; in Ernesto Sábato's *El túnel* it is Juan Pablo Castel, not Sábato; and so forth. This, in fact, is the normal case: narrators explicitly have names or, at least, some characteristics that clearly distinguish them from their authors. Only in the absence of this sort of signal or marker (as is the case with the narrator "Marcel" in Marcel Proust's *Remembrance of Time Past* and the narrator "Carmen" in Carmen Martín Gaite's *El cuarto de atrás*[9]) do we have a problem.[10]

I believe that Lanser's distinctions here are clear, logical, and convincing, and that they have significant implications for *Don Quijote*. The greatest single stumbling block for overly sophisticated readers of the text has been the mind-set that says: public narrator [does not equal] author. Thus, the invention of a number of terms to assume the function of the author: a "persona," a "mask" or—most commonly—an "implied author." The classic articulation of this doctrine is that of the exemplary theorist, Wayne Booth, who, in his famous study *The Rhetoric of Fiction* (1961), asserts unequivocally that the "implied author is always distinct from the 'real man'—whatever we may take him to be—who creates a superior version of himself, a 'second self,' as he creates his work" (151).[11]

When a reader moves from the extrafictional prologue of any text to the fictional chapter 1, typically there is, according to both Rivers and Porqueras, some degree of uncertainty. In the fictional text of *Don Quijote*, the first words encountered are: "En un lugar de la Mancha, de cuyo nombre no quiero acordarme" (I, 1; 97). Quite clearly, there is no textual marker, no signal, at this point that distinguishes the *yo* narrating here from the *yo* of the prologue. In fact, the references in the first chapter to "los autores que deste caso escriben" (98) and "los autores desta tan verdadera historia" (102) tend to reinforce the equation. The identification of the public narrator of the fictional text and the Cervantes of the prologue is then made explicit in the following passage from chapter 2:

> Autores hay que dicen que la primera aventura que le avino fue la del Puerto Lápice; otros dicen que la de los molinos de viento; pero lo que yo he podido averiguar en este caso, y lo que he hallado escrito en los anales de la Mancha, es que ... (107)

It seems clear and consistent, then, to read the text in such a way as to identify the *yo* who reconstructs the "history" of Don Quijote, searches the archives of La Mancha, takes note of oral tradition, and pieces together a coherent story—the editor (the voice from the prologue, the *padrastro*) of the story—as Cervantes. Both in the prologue and in the fictional text the whole matter is treated lightly, obviously a spoof on the explicit literary models of the books of chivalry. Readers are invited to join in the fun and smile as they read the text, confident in the guidance provided by the author-editor-historian-narrator Cervantes.

The only passage that clouds the issue, and the one that has caused the greatest variety of responses in modern critical readers, is the final paragraph of chapter 8 where "el autor desta historia" breaks off his narration in the midst of the battle between Don Quijote and the Basque squire, claiming to have found nothing more written about the subject. Commenting on this, "el segundo autor desta obra" says that he finds it hard to believe that there is not more material available in the writings of "los ingenios de la Mancha" (153).

The problem comes in identifying and distinguishing between the *autor* and the *segundo autor*. Some (such as George Haley) have seen in the figure of this "second author" a shadowy presence that ultimately controls the text; others perceive him as the translator of the Arabic text; and still others (like Parr) view him as an independent transitional figure between the archival narrator of Chapters 1–8 and the "supernarrator" of the remainder of the text from I, 9 to the end of Part II.

Much simpler and more consistent, it seems to me, is to read this passage so that *el autor* refers to the most recently employed historical source from the annals of La Mancha, while the term *el segundo autor*—who, among other things, searches again the archives of La Mancha—refers to the author/editor of the text we are reading, i.e., Cervantes. There is a shift in person from first to third, but this narrative strategy is extremely common in Renaissance texts (e.g., in *Lazarillo de Tormes*) and should cause no reader, whether from the seventeenth or the twenty-first century, any conceptual problem. The text, though, is ambiguous. It invites—and obviously has received—a multiplicity of readings. In accord with Occam's razor, I believe that a simple consistent answer is superior to a complex consistent answer. It is simpler—and perfectly consistent with the other evidence of the text—to read this passage as another reference to the public narrator Cervantes and his playful, metafictional search for sources.

V. Part I, Chapters 9–52: The Manuscript of Cide Hamete Benengeli

In I, 9 Cervantes tells the (fictional) story of his quest for more information about Don Quijote in order to continue beyond the point where the text was truncated in mid-adventure at the end of the previous chapter. This fictional search results in the discovery of the manuscript written in Arabic by Cide Hamete Benengeli, which, after its translation by the *morisco* hired to do the job, forms the main text of the remainder of Part I. The public narrator remains the same Cervantes as before; there is no textual signal that there has been a change in narrative voice, no marked indication that a new voice has assumed this role, and therefore there is no reason to assume that this is a new narrative voice.

From now on Cervantes's primary source is the translated manuscript of Cide Hamete Benengeli, but occasionally he consults other sources and/or hearsay, and from time to time includes in his edited version of the translation some marginal comments by the Muslim historian or the translator. The definitive narrative hierarchy, then, is as follows:

*   The adventures of Don Quijote and Sancho Panza,

* as written in Arabic by the historian Cide Hamete Benengeli,

* as translated into Spanish by the unnamed *morisco*,

* as edited and written by Miguel de Cervantes,

* as read by the Reader.

There is again some difficulty in the final paragraphs of the last chapter of Part I when we read the following: "Pero el autor desta historia, puesto que con curiosidad y diligencia ha buscado los hechos que don Quijote hizo en su tercera salida, no ha podido hallar noticia de ellas, a lo menos por escrituras auténticas" (I, 52; 591). The narration goes on to talk again about other sources such as the Manchegan archives, hearsay evidence, oral tradition, conjecture, and so forth, and ends by reproducing some festive poetry, mostly in praise of a defunct Don Quijote. Along the way, the translator adds interpretive comments and, paradoxically, Cide Hamete even complains about the fidelity of the translation. The truth of the narrative is subverted when Cervantes, the main characters, and the translator call Cide Hamete's honesty into question, leaving the reader to contemplate a true history written by a congenital liar.

Although the term *el autor* has usually been employed in the text to refer to Cide Hamete, it seems clear that he is not the referent here in I, 52, for that normally omniscient historian would have no reason to search the archives of La Mancha for source material nor is it ever recorded that he had recourse to such archival sources. More reasonable is the reading that the editor—Cervantes—carried out yet again such a search after Cide Hamete's manuscript came to an end. We have seen before that Cervantes has been careless or, at least, inconsistent, in his use of terms, referring to himself as father, stepfather, author, second author, and so forth. Assuming that *el autor* here refers again to Cervantes as editor of the text is, I believe, both the simplest and the most consistent reading.

VI. Part II: Miguel de Cervantes vs. Cide Hamete Benengeli

Again, the title page of Part II of the novel includes an affirmation of authorship: "por Miguel de Cervantes Saavedra, autor de su primera parte." The extrafictional prefatory material this time contains the uncharacteristically long approval to print the book by the Licentiate Márquez Torres, a text that has been considered a fiction by some, and the witty and charming dedication—which consists of yet another fiction—by the historical author, Miguel de Cervantes, to his historical patron, the Count of Lemos. Since the voice of this dedication and the voice of the subsequent prologue both claim to be in the final stages of composition of *Los trabajos de Persiles y Sigismunda*, Cervantes' posthumous allegorical romance, it is quite clear that both belong to Cervantes. Since in the prologue Cervantes assures the reader that "esta segunda parte de *Don Quijote* que te ofrezco es cortada del mismo artífice y del mesmo paño que la primera" (26), it is quite clear that he again proposes himself as the public narrator of the text to follow.

In fact, all of Part II maintains the same narrative structure as was outlined above for the bulk of Part I: Cide Hamete narrates, in Arabic, the events of Don Quijote and Sancho; the *morisco* translates this into Spanish; and Cervantes edits the translation and actually writes the version that we read. As before, there are times when other sources and hearsay are consulted; there are more direct citations of Cide Hamete's words and the translator's opinions are recorded more frequently than in the first part. Allen ("The Narrators") and Mancing ("Cide Hamete") have traced the growing tension between the public narrator, Cervantes, and the private narrator, Cide Hamete Benengeli, showing how the latter misunderstands and misinterprets characters and events and becomes himself an increasingly comic character, while the former calls the reader's attention to the historian's shortcomings and manipulates the metatextual narrative humor.

There is still one difficult and confusing passage that must be addressed; characteristically, it comes at the end of Part II, in the very last chapter of the entire novel. Having just narrated the death of Don Quijote and having just brought his story to a conclusion, Cide Hamete turns to his pen and, symbolically hanging up this tool of his trade, instructs it—the pen—to proclaim: "Para mí sola nació don Quijote, y yo para él; él supo obrar y yo escribir; solos los dos somos para en uno" (II, 74; 578). Since this passage goes on with no apparent shift in narration, we must assume that the *pluma* also says the following, the last words of the book: "yo quedaré satisfecho y ufano de haber sido el primero que gozó el fruto de sus escritos eternamente, como deseaba, pues no ha sido otro mi deseo que poner en aborrecimiento de los hombres las fingidas y disparatadas historias de los libros de caballerías, que por las de mi verdadero don Quijote van ya tropezando, y han de caer del todo, sin duda alguna. *Vale*" (II, 74; 578). Evidently some sort of change or blurring has taken place here. Since *satisfecho*, *ufano* and *primero* are all masculine, it is clearly not the feminine pen, *la pluma*, speaking at this point (as it was earlier in the paragraph when the pen was instructed to say sola, a feminine adjective). As Allen (*Hero or Fool?* II) has observed, there seems to be some kind of grammatical and narrative collapse at this point and all the voices—the pen, Cide Hamete, Cervantes—fuse together (see also Anderson). Some have made much of the role of the pen, but since its appearance is so brief, at the very end of a long book, and in such an ambiguous passage, I cannot see how it has any substantial significance at all in the narrative scheme of things.

VII. Theoreticism

One of the main reasons why scholars have had so much difficulty with the narrative structure of *Don Quijote* is that they have too often fallen into the trap of binary thinking[12]: something must be either fact or fiction; you can be either a human being in real life or a fictional character or textual narrator; but you can never be something between these mutually exclusive extremes or some combination of both of them. Those scholars—formalists, structuralists, semioticians, and poststructuralists alike—who take it as a matter of faith, or as some sort of absolute and universally accepted law, that the historical author can never, under any circumstances, enter into his or her own fictional narrative are the ones who are forced by their theory to go to the greatest extremes in separating and multiplying narrative voices, always exiling Cervantes himself.[13] The binary assumption is what forces some to insist that the *yo* of the prologue cannot be Cervantes, because the prologue is a fiction and the historical human being of flesh and bone cannot be part of a fiction. It is then further assumed and asserted as fact that the "friend" of the prologue is a fiction, and if the friend is a fiction the person he talks to must also be a fiction: fiction with fiction, and fact with fact; never the twain shall meet. So it is suggested that the prologue is written not by Cervantes but by an unnamed and totally fictional entity of some kind. The voice perceived in the prologue in turn cannot be the narrator of the fictional text (although the reason why is not clear), and so the narrators (or narrative voices) begin to multiply. In all this we have an example of what Bakhtin (*Towards a Philosophy*) calls "theoreticism": the condition that exists when one's beautiful abstract theory is more important than dealing realistically and pragmatically with life, and so life is sacrificed to theory.

VIII. The Achievement of Cervantes

In conclusion, let me recall the words of one of the more famous fictional narrators of the twentieth century: Holden Caulfield, in Salinger's *Catcher in the Rye*. At one point in his narrative, as Holden reflects on a book he has particularly enjoyed reading, he says, "What really knocks me out is a book that, when you're all done reading it, you wish the author that wrote it was a terrific friend of yours and you could call him up on the phone whenever you felt like it" (19).

What is, I believe, so wonderful about the narration of *Don Quijote* is the diabolical complexity of the simple narrative scheme Cervantes employs. The increasingly complicated structures and relationships that scholars have contrived to see in the text, culminating in Jim Parr's eleven-level schema and complex conceptual graph, do not seem justified, as I have attempted to demonstrate here. *Don Quijote* is not a text with multiple public narrators, and its many private narrators are easily perceived for what they are.

Much more intriguing, I believe, is the magical way in which Cervantes moves us from the title page and its empirical claim of authorship, through the clever extratextual prologue that is clearly his, and into the fictional text without skipping a beat and without changing narrative voice. The ease with which he transforms himself from a historical person into a narrator of fiction, and the inevitability of the reader's making this smooth transition from fact to fiction, is a stunning achievement. We move with Cervantes through the looking-glass into a narrative wonderland of unrivaled genius. I suggest that Cervantes's personal intimacy with readers, as he accompanies and guides us on a magical narrative adventure through the text, is one of the reasons why Cervantes has had such an appeal. The historical Cervantes, the author and the narrator of *Don Quijote*, enchants not only general readers such as Holden Caulfield, but also some of the finest scholars who have dealt with the text.[14]

Notes

1. Nipper, a Jack Russell terrier whose image appeared on the labels of all RCA Victor recordings and in most of its advertisements, is the most famous dog who ever lived, if one takes as criterion the number of times his likeness has been reproduced. For an introduction, http://www.nipperhead.com/nipper.htm and http://www.tvacres.com/adanimals_nipperrca.htm (6 March 2003).

2. This observation is often made merely in passing, but it is effectively argued by Schippers, Booth (*The Company*), and Turner.

3. Barthes' dead author statement ranks as one of the three most famous and most absurd proclamations of contemporary French-based literary theory. (The other two are Derrida's statement that there is nothing outside the text, and Lacan's affirmation that the unconscious is structured like a language.) Foucault suggested that the concept of "author" did not exist before the eighteenth century, an idea enthusiastically endorsed by Martha Woodmansee and others (see particularly Woodmansee and Jaszi). The reality of Spanish Renaissance literature refutes such an ahistorical position, as is clear from the interest in the contemporary theories of authorship of the original *Celestina*, *Amadís de Gaula*, and *Lazarillo de Tormes*; the canonization of Garcilaso de la Vega as a great author; the institution of the pre-copyright in the *privilegio*; and the reactions of Mateo Alemán and—above all—Cervantes to the appropriation of their works by others. For more reasoned consideration of the relationship between author and work, see Burke, Close, Hix, Keefer, and Kerr.

4. I will make no attempt to include here a complete bibliography on the subject or to trace in detail the ebb and flow of the debate, but some of the most significant studies on the subject are by Allen, El Saffar, Fernández Mosquera, Flores, Haley, Lathrop, López Navia, Mancing ("Cide Hamete"), Martín Morán, Parr, Paz Gago, Presberg, and Weiger.

5. Not in the prologue to his *Viaje del Parnaso*, but in chapter 4, Cervantes describes himself in terms that are simultaneously self-depreciating and self-promoting (see also the "Adjunta" to the poem). The narrator of the poem, Cervantes, is simultaneously a fictional character who makes a trip to the mythical Mount Parnassus and defends it against bad poets and the historically real ex-soldier who was maimed in the battle of Lepanto, the author of *La Galatea, Don Quijote,* and other works. The fact that in *Parnaso* the author and the narrator are both named Cervantes has caused a problem for those critics who insist on the absolute exclusion of the historical author from a fictional account. See the important essays by Canavaggio, Riley (*"Viaje"*), and Rivers ("Cervantes' Journey").

6. Note that whatever "truth claim" might be involved in the prologue is clearly contextualized as ironic and not literal. Cervantes here is "fictionalized," but only in the sense that we all fictionalize ourselves when telling a fictional story, especially if it is about ourselves.

7. For the inevitably fictional, self-creating nature of the autobiographical project, and the fine lines separating autobiography, autobiographical fiction, and fictional autobiography, see Bruner, Couser, Eakin, Freeman, Herman, Spacks, and Stanley.

8. Vindel and, citing him, Eisenberg (96 n. 81) identify the friend as Cervantes' publisher, Francisco de Robles.

9. This is a particularly interesting example, as this narrator has the same initials as the author, is the author of novels with the same titles as Martín Gaite's own books, and shares many of the facts of her life with Martín Gaite. This brilliant novel is as good an example as one can find of the metafictional blurring of the line between historical author and fictional narrator/character.

10. Lanser's approach also suggests that the unnamed "omniscient narrators" of the majority of novels can be associated with the author. And why not? Isn't it in fact Tolstoy who tells us the story of *Anna Karenina?* That's what novelists are: storytellers. Some novelists, like Henry Fielding and Benito Pérez Galdós, explicitly make it clear that they are telling the stories: that they are the narrators of their novels.

11. The concept of the implied author adds nothing to any consideration of the narrative structure of a work of fiction. This is not the place to elaborate on the subject, but since it is Booth who is most responsible for the concept of the implied author in the place of the historical author, I felt compelled to state in passing my objection. For representative criticism of the concept, see Bal, Genette, Ferguson, Juhl, Killham, Stecker, and Toolan.

12. Since Aristotle's dictum that something cannot be A and not-A at the same time, binary thought has been prevalent in western intellectual discourse. And since Saussure made binaries essential to his structural linguistics, the basis for all French-based literary theory, it is essential to all forms of structuralism, semiotics, and poststructuralism. For critiques of binarism (and dualism in general), see Kosko, Tavris, and Mancing ("Against Dualisms").

13. Presumably those scholars who deny the possibility of a historical personage within the confines of a fictional text are forced by their theories to deny that the references to Cervantes in the text (as author of *La Galatea* in I, 6, or as the soldier referred to as "tal de Saavedra" in I, 40; 476) are to the historical Cervantes, because the author cannot be permitted any entry into his fiction. If the historical person of flesh and blood cannot be in the text, these textual figures must, by definition, be complete fictions.

14. I have read versions of this essay on various occasions, starting with the annual Cervantes Lecture at Fordham University in 1991. Other versions have been read at the University of Vermont, Drew University, the University of Kentucky, and my own Purdue University. I would like to thank the many friends and colleagues—particularly Leo Hoar of Fordham University—whose comments have helped me make my presentation more precise.

Works Cited

Allen, John Jay. "The Narrators, the Reader and Don Quijote." *MLN* 91 (1976): 201–12.

———. *Don Quixote: Hero or Fool? A Study in Narrative Technique.* Gainesville: U of Florida P, 1969.

———. *Don Quixote: Hero or Fool? Part II.* Gainesville: U Presses of Florida, 1979.

Anderson, Ellen M. "His Pen's Christian Profession: Cide Hamete Writes the End of *Don Quixote*." *RLA: Romance Languages Annual* 6 (1994): 406–12.

Bakhtin, M. M. *Speech Genres and Other Late Essays.* Ed. Caryl Emerson and Michael Holquist. Trans. Vern W. McGee. Austin: U of Texas P, 1986.

———. *Towards a Philosophy of the Act.* Ed. Michael Holquist and Vadim Liapunov. Trans. and notes by Vadim Liapunov. Austin: U of Texas P, 1993.

Bal, Mieke. *Narratology: Introduction to the Theory of Narrative.* Trans. Christine van Boheeman. Toronto: U of Toronto P, 1985.

Barthes, Roland. "The Death of the Author." In *Image, Music, Text.* Trans. Stephen Heath. New York: Hill and Wang, 1977. 142–48.

Booth, Wayne C. *The Company We Keep: An Ethics of Fiction.* Berkeley: U of California P, 1988.

———. *The Rhetoric of Fiction.* Chicago: U of Chicago P, 1961.

Bruner, Jerome. "The Autobiographical Process." In *The Culture of Autobiography: Constructions of Self-Representation.* Ed. Robert Folkenflik. Stanford: Stanford UP, 1993. 38–56.

Burke, Seán. *The Death and Return of the Author: Criticism and Subjectivity in Barthes, Foucault and Derrida.* Edinburgh: Edinburgh UP, 1992.

Canavaggio, Jean. "La dimensión autobiográfica del *Viaje del Parnaso*." *Cervantes* 1.1–2 (1981): 29–41.
    8 April 2003. http://www2.h-net.msu.edu/~cervantes/csa/articf81/canavagg.htm

Cervantes Saavedra, Miguel de. *El ingenioso hidalgo Don Quijote de la Mancha.* 2 vols. Ed. John J. Allen. Madrid: Cátedra, 1977.

Close, Anthony. "The Empirical Author: Salman Rushdie's *The Satanic Verses*." *Philosophy and Literature* 14 (1990): 248–67.

Couser, G. Thomas. *Altered Egos: Authority in Autobiography.* New York: Oxford UP, 1989.

Eakin, John Paul. *Fictions in Autobiography: Studies in the Art of Self-Invention.* Princeton: Princeton UP, 1985.

Eisenberg, Daniel. *La interpretación cervantina del Quijote.* Trad. Isabel Verdaguer. Madrid: Compañía Literaria, 1995. March 6, 2003. http://bigfoot.com/~daniel.eisenberg.

El Saffar, Ruth. *Distance and Control in Don Quixote: A Study in Narrative Technique.* North Carolina Studies in the Romance Languages and Literatures, 147. Chapel Hill: U North Carolina P, 1975.

Ferguson, Suzanne. "The Face in the Mirror: Authorial Presence in the Multiple Vision of Third Person Impressionist Narrative." *Criticism* 21 (1979), 230–50.

Fernández Mosquera, Santiago. "Los autores ficticios del *Quijote.*" *Anales Cervantinos* 24 (1986): 47–65.

Flores, R. M. "The Rôle of Cide Hamete in *Don Quixote.*" *Bulletin of Hispanic Studies* 59 (1982): 3–14.

Foucault, Michel. "What Is an Author?" In *Language, Counter-Memory, Practice.* Ed. Donald F. Bouchard. Trans. Bouchard and Sherry Simon. Ithaca: Cornell UP, 1977. 113–38.

Freeman, Mark. *Rewriting the Self: History, Memory, Narrative.* London: Routledge, 1993.

Genette, Gérard. *Fiction and Diction.* Trans. Catherine Porter. Ithaca: Cornell UP, 1993.

———. *Narrative Discourse Revisited.* Trans. Jane E. Levin. Ithaca: Cornell UP, 1988.

Haley, George. "The Narrator in *Don Quijote*: Maese Pedro's Puppet Show." *MLN* 80 (1965): 146–65.

———. "The Narrator in *Don Quixote*: A Discarded Voice." In *Estudios en Honor a Ricardo Guillón.* Ed. Luis T. González-del-Valle and Darío Villanueva. Lincoln, NE: Society of Spanish and Spanish-American Studies, 1984. 173–83.

Herman, David. "Autobiography, Allegory, and the Construction of the Self." *British Journal of Aesthetics* 35 (1995): 351–60.

Hix, H. L. *Morte d'Author; An Autopsy.* Philadelphia: Temple UP, 1990.

Juhl, P. D. *Interpretation: An Essay in the Philosophy of Literary Criticism.* Princeton: Princeton UP, 1980.

Keefer, Donald. "Reports of the Death of the Author." *Philosophy and Literature* 19 (1995): 78–84.

Kerr, Lucille. *Reclaiming the Author: Figures and Fictions from Spanish America.* Durham, NC: Duke UP, 1992.

Killham, John. "The 'Second Self' in Novel Criticism." *British Journal of Aesthetics* 6 (1966): 272–90.

Kosko, Bart. *Fuzzy Thinking: The New Science of Fuzzy Logic.* New York: Hyperion, 1993.

Lanser, Susan Sniader. *The Narrative Act: Point of View in Prose Fiction.* Princeton: Princeton UP, 1981.

Lathrop, Thomas A. "Cide Hamete Benengeli y su manuscrito." *Cervantes: Su obra y su mundo. Actas del I Congreso Internacional sobre Cervantes.* Ed. Manuel Criado de Val. Madrid: EDI-6, 1981. 693–97.

———. "Who Is the Narrator in *Don Quijote*?" *Hispanic Studies in Honor of Joseph H. Silverman.* Ed. Joseph Ricapito. Newark, DE: Juan de la Cuesta, 1988. 297–304.

López Navia, Santiago Alfonso. *La ficción autorial en el "Quijote" y en sus continuaciones e imitaciones.* Madrid: U Europea de Madrid–CEES, 1996.

Mancing, Howard. "Against Dualisms: A Reply to Henry Sullivan." *Cervantes* 19.1 (1999): 158–76.8 April 2003. http://www2.h-net.msu.edu/~cervantes/csa/artics99/mancing.htm.

———. "Cide Hamete Benengeli vs. Miguel de Cervantes: The Metafictional Dialectic of *Don Quijote.*" *Cervantes* 1.1–2 (1981): 63–81.8 April 2003. http://www2.h-net.msu.edu/~cervantes/csa/artics99/mancing.htm.

Martín Gaite, Carmen. *El cuarto de atrás.* Barcelona: Destino, 1978.

Martín Morán, José Manuel. "La función del narrador múltiple en el *Quijote* de 1615." *Anales Cervantinos* 30 (1992): 9–64.

Parr, James A. Don Quixote: *An Anatomy of Subversive Discourse.* Newark, DE: Juan de la Cuesta, 1988.

Paz Gago, José María. *Semiótica del "Quijote": Teoría y práctica de la ficción narrativa.* Amsterdam: Rodopi, 1995.

Porqueras Mayo, Alberto. *El prólogo como género literario: Su estudio en el Siglo de Oro español.* Madrid: Consejo Superior de Investigaciones Científicas, 1957.

Presberg, Charles D. *Adventures in Paradox: Don Quijote and the Western Tradition.* University Park: Penn State UP, 2001.

Riley, E. C. "El *Viaje del Parnaso* como narración." *Cervantes: Estudios en la víspera de su centenario.* Ed. Kurt Reichenberger. 2 vols. Kassel: Reichenberger, 1994. 2: 491–507.

———. "Three Versions of *Don Quixote*." *Modern Language Review* 68 (1973): 807–19.

Rivers, Elias L. "Cervantes' Journey to Parnassus." *MLN* 85 (1970): 243–48.

———. *Quixotic Scriptures: Essays in the Textuality of Hispanic Literature.* Bloomington: Indiana UP, 1983.

Salinger, J. D. *Catcher in the Rye.* New York: Signet, 1953.

Schippers, J. G. "On Persuading (Some Notes on the Implied Author in Critical Discourse)." *Dutch Quarterly Review of Anglo-American Letters* 11 (1981): 34–54.

Spacks, Patricia Meyer. *Imagining a Self: Autobiography and Novel in Eighteenth-Century England.* Cambridge: Harvard UP, 1976.

Stanley, Liz. *The Auto/biographical I: The Theory and Practice of Feminist Auto/biography.* Manchester: Manchester UP, 1992.

Stecker, Robert. "Apparent, Implied, and Postulated Authors." *Philosophy and Literature* 11 (1987): 258–71.

Tavris, Carol. *The Mismeasure of Woman.* New York: Simon & Schuster, 1992.

Toolan, Michael J. *Narrative: A Critical Linguistic Introduction.* London: Routledge, 1988.

Turner, Mark. *Reading Minds: The Study of English in the Age of Cognitive Science.* Princeton: Princeton UP, 1991.

Weiger, John G. "The Prologuist: The Extratextual Authorial Voice in *Don Quixote*." *Bulletin of Hispanic Studies* 65 (1988): 129–39.

Woodmansee, Martha. *The Author, Art, and the Market: Rereading the History of Aesthetics.* New York: Columbia UP, 1994.

Woodmansee, Martha, and Peter Jaszi, eds. *The Construction of Authorship: Textual Appropriation in Law and Literature.* Durham, NC: Duke UP, 1994.

EDWARD H. FRIEDMAN

Books Errant:
The Objects of Invention in Don Quixote

Y ¿por ventura, . . . promete el autor segunda parte?

My focus in this essay will be on the role of objects—and, in particular, the book as object—in the two parts of *Don Quixote*. In Part 1, of 1605, Cervantes presents Alonso Quijano, the reader of romances of chivalry, as a character who seeks to actualize verbal signifiers. Don Quixote finds, and at times assembles, a range of objects that will validate both chivalry and his own chivalric identity. The knightly trappings, the idealized love "object", Mambrino's helmet, the objects refashioned into enemies, and the manuscript of "The Tale of Ill-Advised Curiosity", among numerous examples, indicate a dual (and perhaps dueling) rhetoric between author and protagonist. Each strives to forge a signature by rewriting the literary past, and the objects chosen underscore competing conceptions of synecdoche and metonymy. This rhetoric changes in Part 2, of 1615, in which the overpowering object is Part 1, the book that belongs conjointly to the Arab historian Cide Hamete Benengeli and Miguel de Cervantes. By a marvelous coincidence, life imposes itself upon art in the form of a spurious sequel by the pseudonymous Alonso Fernández de Avellaneda, and this phenomenon affects the tone and direction of the narrative, as well as the rivalry between the writer of fiction and the historian[1]. The obsession with books takes a

From *Anuario de Estudios Cervantinos* 1 (2004): 41–55. © 2004 by Mirabel Editorial.

brilliant and ironic turn in the 1615 *Quixote*, as the knight-errant and his creator contemplate defensive strategies. In Part 2, the objects of Part 1 coalesce into a single book and its evil twin, its significant other. At the same time, Don Quixote—having been immortalized in print—becomes the object of the metafictions of readers within the text. Marshalling this modified rhetoric, Cervantes redefines conventional tropes and projects new narrative paradigms.

The prologue to Part 1 of *Don Quixote* features an author bearing a heavy document. The most significant physical object is, of course, this unpublished manuscript, whose fate is left to the writer's alter ego, the friend. The friend is a crucial figure in the scheme of things, for he expands the distance between the historical Cervantes and the fictional prologuist. He is an agent of deferral, precociously a poststructuralist's dream. Equally symbolic is the manuscript, which will become the book. Cervantes's prologue has points of contact with the prologue to *Lazarillo de Tormes*, in which an author refers to a book in the marketplace and an implied readership and a narrator/protagonist offers the lead-in to the explanation of a case. There is, at best, only a light transition between one presence and another, and no acknowledged change of "voice" (see Friedman, 1987: 15–34). In the first part of the *Quixote*, Cervantes cedes authority first to his fictional "other" and then to "another", and finally to a narrator whose product, manifested in a playful yet highly complex fashion, is only negligibly differentiable from the manuscript—in its translated form and with a degree of editorial commentary—of Cide Hamete Benengeli[2]. These are certainly books as objects, and they are essential elements of Part 1. So are the literary contributions of characters such as the dead poet Grisóstomo, the picaresque work-in-progress of the galley slave Ginés de Pasamonte, the "book of memories" of Cardenio, and the manuscript of *El curioso imperti-nente*, not to mention the scrutiny of the library—brilliant as critique and as allegory—and the discussion of books at the inn in chapter 32 and with the canon from Toledo in chapter 47. Hardly has Don Quixote set out on his first sally when he begins to imagine the description of his exploits, a book, one might say, under advance contract. And before that, the narrator of chapter 1 begins to express concern about the status of the book, the "true history" of the adventures of Don Quixote.

Cervantes's literary and metaliterary aims are evident from the opening, from the prologue and the first chapter. The prologue is not just about narra-tive deferral or narrative polyphony and the play of perspectives, but—perhaps primarily—about the object in hand—the manuscript—and the books that motivated its composition. Juxtaposed with the fictional Cervantes and his pages of text are the romances of chivalry and idealistic narrative in general. The prologue is the first of many lessons in intertextuality in the *Quixote*. It is, simultaneously, the first lesson in negative hermeneutics, in which the text shows itself not so much ripe for interpretation as difficult, or nearly impossible, to interpret[3]. The friend has all the answers with respect to intentionality, but he is at least twice-removed from the source. He highlights the destruction of a literary genre, but note that four centuries after the publication of Part 1 we care very much about *Don Quixote* while our interest in chivalric romance may be negligible. It is what could be termed "the new art of writing narrative" that interests and even consumes us, which means that the book is the object in the center. As the reader enters the text proper, it would seem that reading and writing cast themselves as the all-encompassing preoccupations of the protagonist and of the narrator, respectively. The negative hermeneutics, as it were, emphasize history, since the narrator categorizes the text as a "true history", therein relishing the double meaning of the Spanish *historia* and entering the territory of "fictional truth". The Cervantes *contemplativo*, *metafísico*, aligns himself to the professional entity, Cervantes the writer, to discuss a variety of issues that could be grouped under the rubric of "perceiving reality": subjectivity versus objectivity, perspective, the capturing of vision and thought through words, hierarchies, and bases of authority, etc. All this, appears, will come into "the book", and it already seems to have done so.

In the first chapter, Cervantes complements the book with other objects of practical and emblematic value, derived, of course, from reading: armor, a helmet, a worthy steed, and a lady to serve. That the accoutrements of knight errantry are less than elegant does not impede the forward movement. That the final and most precious object is nonexistent becomes a positive element, a guiding force, for the author and a variety of characters. Don Quixote's preparation for the first sally offers a look at key objects and a key to Part 1. Alonso Quijano—or whatever that elusive name may be—refashions himself as Don Quixote, certifying the process by adopting a new name, a new identity, and a new set of signifieds. The dichotomy of the name establishes a formula for the 1605 *Quixote*. Objects are reproduced in chivalric terms, as a function of the imagination and/or the dementia of Don Quixote. The narrative, in many ways, is about how the protagonist interprets the signs that surround him, how he re-envisions, renames, redirects, and recontextualizes the objects with which he comes into contact. The consummately ingenious Cervantes, whose imagination never sleeps, has the friends and family of Don Quixote push the "enchanter" onto the knight, so that there is an internal logic to the double discourse, a factor in the dual approach to perception. Part 1 of the novel abounds in adventures, each of which is generally associated with objects that can be assessed as to their "real" and "fictional" worth. One could summarize the structure of Part 1 as the search for a mediating space between the mad knight and the people and objects that confront him on the road.

The second sally, which marks the intervention of Sancho Panza, begins with the *archiconocido* episode of the windmill, contains objects galore, frequently dichotomous: an inn with women such as Maritornes or a castle full of exemplary damsels, a herd of sheep or attacking troops, fulling mills or mysterious enemies, a barber's basin or helmet of Mambrino, and so forth. These sections reveal Don Quixote at his metatheatrical prime. True to the spirit of doubling, the knight is in control and, in a double sense, out of control. His misreadings take center stage, and other characters enter his fantasy world when he refuses to recognize their "real-world" options. Objects are fundamental here, because they are components of the semiotics of his madness, or of his impressive faculty for creativity. This is Don Quixote's character formation, whereby he establishes the persona that will make him famous, and, at the same time, that will allow readers of the book written to honor his illustrious deeds to know him and hence to preempt his responses. These are his chivalric battles, his victories and defeats, concrete evidence of his status, his stature, his "being in the world". He is both actor and rhetorician, for he participates in an event and interprets that event for onlookers who seem to process data in a different manner. The narrator of the early part of the novel seeks informants and archival information until he stumbles across Cide Hamete Benengeli's chronicle. This is the object that generally embraces the others. The book as object—in the prologue, in the library tomes that dried up the *hidalgo*'s brain, in Don Quixote's anticipation of the document that will record his life on the road, in the Arab historian's version of the knight's "fortunas y adversidades", and later in the pages on which *El curioso impertinente* is written—enters into a dynamic relationship with action. Don Quixote talks and acts, acts and talks. Like the faithful—we hope—*morisco*, he is a translator. At Juan Palomeque's inn, for example, we overhear him describing events with which we have previously been acquainted, retold with added flourishes and self-congratulation, that is, with chivalric retooling.

In the lengthy Sierra Morena sequence—from the meeting with an *enraged* Cardenio to the final exit from the inn by an *encaged* Don Quixote—the narrative pattern changes dramatically. The singular adventures of Don Quixote become adventures in storytelling: by Cardenio, by Dorotea, by the princess Micomicona, by Luscinda, by an unnamed but undisguised Cervantes, and by the captive, among others. At certain critical moments in this section of the narrative, the knight errant is conspicuous by his absence, but the recourse of doubling remains. Cardenio's explanation of his emotional undoing proceeds from the discovery of the *librillo de memorias* (and mirrors Don Quixote's madness, as well). Dorotea the jilted woman becomes an actress with a (hi)story of her own. Luscinda completes (and drastically revises) Cardenio's story. *El curioso impertinente* embeds itself in pseudo-chivalric scheme of Cide Hamete's chronicle, as Cervantes effects a redoubling of his own authorial role. He is also "in the picture" of the captive's tale, as a former captive and as an allusion within the narration. The two sustained narratives directly follow the debate on the fiction versus non-fiction between Juan Palomeque and Pero Pérez. Cervantes challenges the reader to reflect on the points of contact and the points of contrast between the oral tradition and the printed word, between story and history, and between the objective and the subjective, but one cannot help but notice the ever-weakening dividing lines in all cases. As the doubling devices suggest, speech always stands in the shadow of writing, story in the shadow of history, the objective in the shadow of the subjective, and vice versa. The book is alternately in the foreground and in the background, in continual motion and continual transformation.

To recapitulate, briefly: *Don Quixote* starts with a book awaiting publication. The prologue addresses the range and limits of literature and looks at questions of authority in a historical moment in which the new science, a new geography, and new philosophies inflect the most stable—and the most sacred of institutions. The motif of the double or alter ego finds an analogue, most appropriately, one might submit, first in chivalric episodes; with Don Quixote, alter ego of both Alonso Quijano and Amadís de Gaula, fighting the objects that arise before him, poised to convert themselves into the raw material of knightly feats of valor, and then (when Don Quixote and Sancho leave the beaten path) in shadow narratives, the reduplication of the strategies and topoi of reading and writing.

In the 1615 *Quixote*, many extraordinary things happen, but I would like to isolate two elements—one carefully calculated and the other absolutely unplanned—which will have an impact on the progression and on the cumulative impact of the story and on the history of Don Quixote. Neither will come as a surprise to readers of the novel. The first is the publication of Part 1, and the second is the publication in 1614 of the "false" *Quixote*. The result of these phenomena is that the "authentic", "legitimate" Part 2 subordinates all other objects, much more emphatically than in Part 1, to *the book*, understood in the narrowest and broadest sense. There is an allegorical edge to the 1605 *Quixote*, not just of the burning of books and souls but of the literary enterprise itself, through Cervantes, as an individual writer who evokes the act and art of writing, and Alonso Quijano, as an individual reader who evokes the act and craft of reading. Cervantes sets the stage for the radical revisionism—revisionist history, so to speak—that will come about in Part 2[4].

We seem to have the opportunity to see Cervantes's plan for the second part in place, with the notable exception of the prologue of 1615, until the Avellaneda sequel intrudes when Cervantes had finished about two-thirds of the text. The book—the chronicle—has made its entry into the world and allows the world to enter the text in exciting and innovative ways. The "shadow texts" of Part 1 converge in Part 2 as a real property. The content of Part 2 is predicated on the existence of the book, and Don Quixote takes a back seat to his immortalized self, or other. Sansón Carrasco, the duke and duchess, and countless citizens are familiar with the modus operandi of the knight. The illiterate Sancho Panza, who constantly has been at the side of Don Quixote, enjoys the same perks as these readers and, in effect, becomes one of them, one step ahead of his master. Cervantes would seem to appreciate the reciprocal attachment—the interdependence—of life and art. As the world more palpably informs the text, the text, in turn, reaches advanced heights of metafiction, metacriticism, and metatheory. Then comes the bolt from the blue, in the form of a pseudonymous counternarrative. This hellish intrusion is a gift from heaven, as well. Don Quixote is animated to fight for his literary and chivalric credentials. The ludicrously proposed "true history" becomes the *true history*, and Cide Hamete, whose veracity has been called into question, becomes perforce the *true historian*. The rivalry between the historical author and the fictional chronicler gains in intensity when life magnificently encroaches upon art. The Cervantes–Don Quixote–Cide Hamete Benengeli triumvirate—formerly a ground for contention—is now a collaboration, in the battle for legitimacy, respectability, and bragging rights. There may be other objects in Part 2—the *retablo* of Maese Pedro, the divining ape, the enchanted head, theatrical productions and dramatic stagings, poems, and other items—but these objects, far more often than not, have their origins in books, especially in *Don Quixote*, Part 1.

A major paradox of the comprehensive Quixote—the two, or three, Quixotes—is that as the text becomes more worldly, more *out* in the world, it becomes more self-contained, more self-sustaining. The romances of chivalry all but disappear in Part 2; Part 1 and the false continuation have replaced them. They are the stuff of drama (in the duke and duchess's spectacles) and the stuff of dreams, vehicles of the past (in the Cave of Montesinos). Don Quixote's most threatening enemies are Sansón Carrasco, avid reader and critic of Part 1, and the elusive and insidious "Avellaneda". Alternatively, Don Quixote goes to Barcelona, where he sees the Avellaneda volume, but in the "real" or historical Barcelona, another volume has preceded them both. And from yet another angle of vision, the text transports us to hell (in 2, 70), where Altisidora describes a diabolical game in which copies of the false second part substitute for balls. Where does this lead the reader? Inward and outward. The book is the intrinsic object par excellence and the extrinsic object par excellence, the object as subject, the subject as object, self and circumstance inseparably and indistinguishably linked. I would deny, with vigor, that it is overly quixotic to discern in—to *read into*—*Don Quixote* the most profound and engaging questions of current theoretical debate, along with some answers. Taken aback by an unwelcome literary object, Cervantes mounts an attack that completes his vision, which is not synonymous with saying that the vision is complete. Even closure is ambiguous and, arguably, mutable. After all, the very last object in the novel is not Alonso Quijano's will but Cide Hamete's pen.

The articulate pen is a metonym for the writer—Cide Hamete Benengeli, Miguel de Cervantes, and writers in general—and the centerpiece for a series of metonymic instances. The moving passages that bring closure to *Don Quixote* render verbally what Diego Velázquez will render visually around twenty years later in *Las meninas*. Having represented the artist in the work of art (from the prologue of Part 1 onward) and having inhabited the book with other books and framings of the narrative process, Cervantes glorifies the act of literary creation and, by extension, the creator. The authorial intervention at the end is a fitting conclusion to the events of the final chapter, which culminates in the rejection by Alonso Quijano of Don Quixote's chivalric identity. Throughout the text, Don Quixote argues for the superiority of arms over letters. Here, arms are retired, and letters prevail, if ironically. Don Quixote, the supreme advocate of arms is, of course, also the supreme advocate of the romances of chivalry. Books drive him to become a knight errant, and although, once converted, he professes to dismiss words in favor of deeds, the text into which he is inscribed places him in situations in which words—the written word—take over, to subsume actions. The declaration of the pen in 2, 74, is directed neither to chivalry nor to chivalric romance, as things of the past, but to the authority of writing and thus of the writer. The concluding statement bears on the present and on the ability of the literary artist to progress, to generate change, to reconfigure, and to stretch the imagination. The pen is anything but an independent agent; it relies on another, on its wielder. It signals invention, ingenuity, and continuity. In the final chapter, the chronicle of a death foretold, the predominant image is of birth: "Para mí sola nació don Quixote, y yo para él". The death is symbolic, and the birth may be more so.

Cervantes is a master at combining the syntagmatic and the paradigmatic. He builds new models from old, but he always leaves traces of precedent, of his predecessors. Like many others, I find myself regularly juxtaposing *Don Quixote* and *Las meninas*, because Velázquez paints a companion piece and counterpart to Cervantes's novel, or, more properly in this context, novels. The painter at work, the mirror image of the king and queen, the door frame, and the light that enters from the window to the side depict the crossroad of life and art. The *infanta* Margarita and her companions vie to an extent with the monarchs and with the artist—and one might contend, with the literal and figurative spectators—for centrality, but Velázquez includes in his painting other works of art, which hang on the wall, dark and decidedly off-center, but intimately related to the proceedings and to the messages of *Las meninas*. As Jonathan Brown has shown, Velázquez struggles to elevate himself and his fellow artists through the power of association. He places himself alongside the royal family and implies that he belongs with them. At the same time, he places them in his milieu, wherein he imitates—and supplies his own version of—reality. He blends artistic self-consciousness with a sense of history, and he refuses to see the two elements as mutually exclusive. Velázquez thereby reenacts visually what Cervantes demonstrates in *Don Quixote*, namely, that the creative impulse is inextricably bound to reality, to history. The book replicates aspects of life through the instrument of its medium, yet it resides in the world, as well. At a given point, reality may be the macrocosm and fiction the microcosm, or the relationship may as easily be reversed. The art object—in this case, the book as object—becomes the basis for a theory of realism, conveyed, paradoxically through narrative praxis.

The prologue to Part 1 invites the reader to classify the text as satire directed at the romances of chivalry, but only an idle reader could fail to observe the intricacies of the undertaking. The loquacious friend causes a communicative displacement, a gap between the (fictionalized) author and the target audience. The first prologue is about recognizing the rules that govern literary compositions (and, by extension, the rules that govern behavior, social interaction, and spiritual protocol) and about devising strategies for breaking those rules. Cervantes seems to be aware of the delicate balance between dependence and renunciation. Chivalry as an institution and, more relevantly, as intertext gives rise to the actions of author and protagonist. If the novel ultimately is not about chivalry, chivalry is its reigning motif, its backbone. It is the cultural past that must be respected and purged, or flushed out (in its multiple meanings). Centuries before Mikhail Bakhtin, Cervantes accentuates the dialogical aspects of literature; *Don Quixote* enters into dialogue with art, history, politics, philosophy, and theology[5]. Chivalric romance serves as pretext and, correspondingly, as the ungainly but necessary other in a work that deftly interrogates alterity. (Consider Cide Hamete Benengeli, for example). Chivalry as a social and literary phenomenon evokes glory days and illustrious comportment, as well as books deemed to be harmful to the "republic", in this case a republic that unites Church and State. The prologue initiates the decentering and the disruption of antitheses that will characterize the narrative as a whole. A portion of this project involves a disapproving evaluation of idealistic fiction, less pronouncedly for its idealism than for its escapism. Cervantes's solution may be in line with the sensibility of the

Counter Reformation, but only as deflected through secular humanism. A theme of the prologue is authority; a focal point is the eye of the beholder.

That beholder may be a historian or a writer of fiction, or a writer of fiction who pretends to be a historian or who grafts a problematic historian onto the fictional narrator. Flouting the conventions of idealistic narrative, Cervantes enters the realm of realism, but the realism of *Don Quixote* must be qualified on a number of levels. Realism may be said to stand in opposition to both idealism (romance) and metafiction. Whereas idealistic forms of fiction tend to embellish their subjects, to gloss over the undesirable, and to stray from the laws of verisimilitude, those labeled realistic endeavor to remain faithful to—to emulate—details of reality and of logic. The picaresque underside or lower depths contrast with the glamorized and antiseptic countryside of pastoral, for example, and Don Quixote is, analogously, Amadís de Gaula without the aura of invincibility, warts and all, seeking the purity and the integrity of romance in the real world. Although Cervantes was clearly influenced by the Italian *novella* and by the picaresque, the result has stronger ties to baroque disillusionment than to what would come to be known as psychological realism. As dramatized in the pages of the text, the fantasy world of Don Quixote opposes the real world of *Don Quixote*; romance and anti-romance share the stage. Cervantes makes the reader conscious of questions of disposition (*dispositio*) through references to "the true history" and historiography from chapter 1 forward, and thus the dichotomy of history and poetry comes into the equation. Because Cervantes is not just writing history or writing fiction, but combining the two and commenting on the process, metafiction becomes the outer circle, the decisive frame. The matter of fabrication is essential to *Don Quixote* because of the obvious correlation between creation and perception. The travails of the author and the various authorial surrogates occupy much of the narrative space in *Don Quixote*, which gives prominence to writing and the writer, but these efforts are aimed at reading and the reader, from Don Quixote and his brethren within the text to the narratee(s) to the implied reader(s) to generations of real readers, who feel the impact of fiction, history, and reception history. Velázquez's artist and subjects yield to the spectator. Cervantes's poet/historian yields to the reader. When Avellaneda flagrantly yet fortuitously invades the frame (not unlike Pablo Picasso's and Richard Hamilton's usurpation of Velázquez's space, but with a reverential air and, naturally, without an avenging rejoinder), the veiled author further privileges the reader.

The friend of the prologuist of Part 1 lobbies for creative freedom. The departure from the norm is a liberating experience for the author and for the reader, who becomes a collaborator in the design of the (hi)story. The paradigm of imitation as ironic re-creation applies to Cervantes and to Don

Quixote. Both writer and knight diminish the reader's horizon of expectations; it is difficult to predict what will happen next (see Iser, 1978: 107–134). That is why the disputable reliability of Cide Hamete Benengeli befits the narrative scheme. The Arab historian relocates the sense of wonderment—the *admiratio* that Don Quixote inspires in those whose path he crosses—to the reader. Traditional oppositions do not hold, and one anticipates not the known but the unknown. The process described, or undergone, in Part 1 has reached fruition as Part 2 begins. There is a book to read and to comment upon. While the sweeping collection of narrators in the first part has a complement in the second, the more valid analogue might join the storytellers of the 1605 *Quixote* with the collection of readers of the 1615 text, consumers of—one is never quite sure—Cide Hamete's chronicle or Cervantes's fiction. The play of writer and reader acquires a new cast when the Avellaneda sequel is published.

The two parts of *Don Quixote* are about the significance of books in the world. Part 1 allegorizes the transition from oral to print culture and the shifting centers of authority in early modern society. The adventures of the knight, the variations on the theme of narration, and what Miguel de Unamuno centuries later would call "cómo se hace una novela" stimulate and balance each other, as do history and poetry[6]. In Part 2, books cede to *the* book, to the publishing event that would seem to erase the dividing line between life and art. *Don Quixote* displays reader-response as plot device and as practical criticism. Books instruct and mold us. They are components of our world. They act upon us and we upon them. Cervantes and Cide Hamete Benengeli show that Alonso Quijano fashions Don Quixote from books. Their book(s) will affect the commerce between the literary subject, along with those who encode him in the text, and a discriminating, fickle, and critical public. This engagement empowers the reader as arbiter of taste and, within the narrative, as metadramatist. Don Quixote's role changes noticeably when he ceases to be the reader, when book buyers (or listeners) have read him (or have been read to) in advance. He is a scapegoat or sacrificial victim of the printing phenomenon, which puts his future in the hands of others. He is no longer a private citizen; fame has left him exposed, and his fame now precedes him as he takes to the road. Stated succinctly, Part 2 adds an important dimension to the metaliterary thrust of the text. The book-in-the-making has been completed, it has attracted the attention of readers, and the foundation for critique has been laid. In Part 1, Cervantes entices the reader to fill in gaps and to think about ways of restoring order to the narrative chaos. The aftermath of Alonso Quijano's obsessive reading merges with the gathering and processing of information, so that the writer(s) can compose an account of the neo-chivalric exploits. In Part 2, the book supersedes its subject, and reading enters a new phase. Don Quixote is caught off guard, and so, finally, is Cervantes.

Early in Part 1, prior to his first adventure, Don Quixote meditates on the chronicle that will glorify his name. On learning at the beginning of Part 2 that such a book exists, Don Quixote is concerned about the accuracy of the document. Cervantes incorporates criticism and the aesthetics of reception into the second part in an intriguing way, since they now refer to his own narrative. He serves up a full meal, from soup to nuts, from the seeds of a narrative to criticism and the theoretical implications of said criticism. Readers have digested the material, and they have expressed their opinions. Furthermore, reader-response becomes the catalyst or motivating factor—the basic apparatus of the plot—in Part 2. Even the illiterate Sancho Panza has learned how to "read" *Don Quixote*, which makes him an able, if not always willing, collaborator of Sansón Carrasco and the duke and duchess. When the Avellaneda continuation invades Cervantes's life and text, the question of which knight is the legitimate Don Quixote is relegated to the question of which narrative is the legitimate *Don Quixote*. Avellaneda distracts Cervantes, but the spurious sequel invigorates the "true" second part, made more genuine by the real-life struggle of the authors and by the inferior credentials of the false *Quixote*. If the deep structure of the 1615 text is defined through the status of the book—the 1605 book—in multiple and shifting frames, Avellaneda compels Cervantes and Don Quixote to assert their territorial rights, and the territory involved brings together the fictional and the real. As irony builds, Don Quixote, having lost to the Knight of the White Moon, scores a victory over his literary rival, as certified by Don Álvaro Tarfe (2, 72), and Cide Hamete Benengeli is suddenly the reliable narrator. Thanks to Avellaneda, Cervantes is able to broaden the metafictional base of *Don Quixote*. Reception and reception history are modified within the text.

The most evident consequence of the Avellaneda *Quixote* is Cervantes's decision to bring closure to the narrative, through the death of Alonso Quijano. Even for the romantically inclined who would insist that Don Quixote lives, the story is, for all intents and purposes, over. *Don Quixote*, however, tells another story, which translates into a unique intellectual autobiography. Mutable in its rhetoric, "the book" is all books and the one alone. From the dialectics of poetry and history—and of Part 1, Part 2, and Part 2 bis—there emerges a poetics of narrative, a template for the novel. Cervantes's two volumes, aided by Avellaneda's imposing tome, break away from idealism, to temper realism with metafiction and to foresee, with a rare prescience, the novels (and the theory) to come. Don Quixote epitomizes bookishness. His psyche, not without its desires and individual foibles, has literature at its center[7]. He exhibits traits associated with the real world in his own manner, obliquely. The novel in which he speaks and acts adopts an equivalent discursive technique, defamiliarizing rather than mimetic. Would it be correct to say that, in *Don*

Quixote, the medium is the message? I would say yes, but by no means in a limited or limiting sense, and that is the point. Cervantes disguises his fiction as history, but he knows that readers will see through the disguise. As he lays bare his recourses—the tools of the trade—he would seem to ask the reading public to identify his personal approach to representation and to ponder the challenges that face the writer. Time and again, he confirms that narrative is rarely static and rarely stable. Cervantes toys with history, and history toys with Cervantes, most egregiously in the form of an unauthorized sequel. Cervantes has to suffer the insult, but, through irony heaped upon irony, *Don Quixote* is enriched by the unwelcome presence, which substantiates the rule of inconsistency. In the last analysis, then, history proves Cervantes to be correct about his story and about history.

Notes

1. The most sustained study on the Avellaneda sequel is that of James Iffland. See also Aylward, Maestro, and Friedman (2000).

2. On the topic of narrative discourse in *Don Quixote*, I am indebted to Ruth El Saffar, James A. Parr, John G. Weiger, José Manuel Martin Morán, Alan J. Burch, Charles D. Presberg, and many other scholars of Cervantes, as well as to Wayne C. Booth and those who have followed him in examining "the rhetoric of fiction". Currie offers a solid overview of the theoretical issues.

3. In the section on negative hermeneutics in the first edition of *Twentieth-Century Literary Theory* (included in the second edition under the rubric of hermeneutics), K. M. Newton accentuates the debate "between the tradition of Schleiermacher and Dilthey in which the hermeneutic enterprise was to enable texts written in the past to be understood in their own terms by a later age and the Heidegger influenced method of H.-G. Gadamer in which the interests of the present-day interpreter and the text as the product of the past are kept in balance". He continues, "Some more recent theorists have, however, gone much further than Gadamer and have argued that hermeneutics should not only reject the view that the purpose of hermeneutics is to restore a text's past meaning in its own terms but should use modern concepts to question and undermine that meaning" (192). Newton uses texts by Paul Ricoeur and William V. Spanos to illustrate his point.

4. See Friedman (2002). I would like to acknowledge the work of Hayden White, Michael Riffaterre, Claire Colbrook, and Diana de Armas Wilson—to cite but four scholars whose research has influenced my own—on the interplay of history and fiction.

5. For a concise presentation, see "Discourse Typology in Prose". See also Todorov esp. 60–74 and Spadaccini and Talens 109–67 ("Narrativity and the Dialogic"). The concepts of *defamiliarization* and *laying bare the devices*, alluded to in this essay, refer, as well, to Russian Formalism. See Lemon and Reis, esp. Victor Shlovsky's "Art as Technique" (3–24).

6. In addition to *Cómo se hace una novela*, see Unamuno's prologue to the three exemplary novels, for a commentary on narrative realism.

7. On the psychology of Don Quixote, key studies include Johnson and the essays in El Saffar and Wilson.

WORKS CITED

Avellaneda, Alonso Fernández de [pseud.] (1987), *El ingenioso hidalgo don Quijote de la Mancha, que contiene su tercera salida y es la quinta parte de sus aventuras*, ed. Fernando García Salinero, Madrid, Castalia.

Aylward, Edward T. (1989), *Toward an Evaluation of Avellaneda's False 'Quijote'*, Newark, DE, Juan de la Cuesta.

Bakhtin, Mikhail [Mixail Baxtin] (1978), "Discourse Typology in Prose", *Readings in Russian Poetics: Formalist and Structuralist Views*, ed. Ladislav Matejka and Krystyna Pomorska, Ann Arbor, University of Michigan Slavic Publications (176–196).

Booth, Wayne C. (1961), *The Rhetoric of Fiction*, Chicago, University of Chicago Press.

Brown, Jonathan (1978), "On the Meaning of *Las Meninas*", *Images and Ideas in Seventeenth-Century Spanish Painting*, Princeton, Princeton University Press (87–110).

Burch, Alan J. (1995), "*Don Quijote* and Narrative Theory: A Critical and Metacritical Reading", Diss. Indiana University.

Cervantes, Miguel de (1998), *Don Quijote de la Mancha*, ed. del Instituto Cervantes, dir. Francisco Rico, 2 vols., Barcelona, Crítica.

Colebrook, Claire (1997), *New Literary Histories: New Historicism and Contemporary Criticism*, Manchester and New York, Manchester University Press.

Currie, Mark (1998), *Postmodern Narrative Theory*, New York, St. Martin's.

El Saffar, Ruth (1975), *Distance and Control in 'Don Quixote': A Study in Narrative Technique*, Chapel Hill, University of North Carolina Department of Romance Languages.

El Saffar, Ruth Anthony, and Diana de Armas Wilson, eds. (1993), *Quixotic Desire: Psychoanalytical Perspectives on Cervantes*, Ithaca and London, Cornell University Press.

Friedman, Edward H. (1987), *The Antiheroine's Voice: Narrative Discourse and Transformations of the Picaresque*, Columbia, University of Missouri Press.

Friedman, Edward H. (2000), "Insincere Flattery: Imitation and the Growth of the Novel", *Cervantes* 20.1 (99–114).

Friedman, Edward H. (2002), "The Muses of the Knight: *Don Quixote* and Revisionist History", *'Never-ending Adventure': Studies in Medieval and Early Modern Spanish Literature in Honor of Peter N. Dunn*, ed. Edward H. Friedman and Harlan Sturm, Newark, DE, Juan de la Cuesta (175–192),

Iffland, James (1999), *De fiestas y aguafiestas: risa, locura e ideología en Cervantes y Avellaneda*, Madrid, Iberoamericana, Frankfurt am Main, Vervuert.

Iser, Wolfgang (1978), *The Act of Reading: A Theory of Aesthetic Response*, Baltimore and London, Johns Hopkins University Press.

Johnson, Carroll B. (1983), *Madness and Lust: A Psychoanalytical Approach to Don Quixote*, Berkeley, University of California Press.

Lazarillo de Tormes (2000), ed. Robert Fiore, Asheville, NC, Pegasus.

Lemon, Lee T., and Marion J. Reis, eds. (1965), *Russian Formalist Criticism: Four Essays*, Lincoln and London, University of Nebraska Press.

Maestro, Jesús G. (1994), "Cervantes y Avellaneda: Creación y transducción del sentido en la elaboración del *Quijote*", *Cervantes: Estudios en la vispera de su centenario*, 2 vols., Kassel, Germany, Reichenberger, 1 (309–341).

Martín Morán, José Manuel (1990), *El 'Quijote' en ciernes*, Torino, Edizioni dell'Orso.

Newton, K. M. (1988), *Twentieth-Century Literary Theory: A Reader*, London, Macmillan; 2nd ed., 1997, New York, St. Martin's.

Parr, James A. (1988), *Don Quixote: An Anatomy of Subversive Discourse*, Newark, DE, Juan de la Cuesta.

Presberg, Charles D. (2001), *Adventures in Paradox: Don Quixote and the Western Tradition*, University Park, Pennsylvania State University Press.

Riffaterre, Michael (1990), *Fictional Truth*, Baltimore, Johns Hopkins University Press.

Spadaccini, Nicholas, and Jenaro Talens (1993), *Through the Shattering Glass, Cervantes and the Self-Made World*, Minneapolis and London, University of Minnesota Press.

Todorov, Tzvetan (1984), *Mikhail Bakhtin: The Dialogical Principle*, trans. Wlad Godzich, Minneapolis, University of Minnesota Press.

Unamuno, Miguel de (1977), *Cómo se hace una novela*, ed. Paul R. Olson, Madrid, Guadarrama.

Unamuno, Miguel de (1987), *Tres novelas ejemplares y un prólogo*, ed. Demetrio Estébanez Calderon, Madrid, Alianza.

Weiger, John G. (1988), *In the Margins of Cervantes*, Hanover, University Press of New England.

White, Hayden (1987), *The Content of the Form: Narrative Discourse and Historical Representation*, Baltimore and London, Johns Hopkins University Press.

White, Hayden (1978), *Tropic of Discourse: Essays in Cultural Criticism*, Baltimore and London, Johns Hopkins University Press.

Wilson, Diana de Armas (2000), *Cervantes, the Novel, and the New World*, Oxford, Oxford University Press.

MARIO VARGAS LLOSA

A Novel for the Twenty-first Century

*D*on Quixote de La Mancha, Cervantes' immortal novel, is first and foremost
an image: a fifty-something gentleman in anachronistic armor and as bony
as his horse, accompanied by a coarse and chubby peasant riding a donkey,
a sometime squire, frozen in winter, burning in summer, crossing the plains
of La Mancha in search of adventures. He is driven by a mad plan: to revive
a long-eclipsed era (one, in fact, that never existed) of knights-errant, who
traveled the world helping the weak, righting wrongs, and dispensing justice
to those who would otherwise never know it—a plan which seizes him after
reading chivalric romances to which he attributes the veracity of history.

This ideal is impossible to reach because everything in Don Quixote's
reality refutes it. There are no knights-errant, no one professes the ideas or
respects the values that once moved them, and war no longer consists of ritu-
alistic duels between knights. Now, as Don Quixote laments in his discourse
on arms and letters, war is no longer settled by swords and lances, that is, by
the courage and dexterity of individuals, but rather by the thunder of artillery
which, in the roar of death, has erased the codes of honor and heroic deeds
that forged the mythic figures of an Amadís of Gaul, a Tirant lo Blanc and a
Tristan de Leonis.

Does this mean that *Don Quixote de La Mancha* is a book focused on the
past, that Alonso Quijano's madness comes from a desperate nostalgia for a

From *Harvard Review* 28 (2005): 125–36. © 2005 by Mario Vargas Llosa.

world that is gone, from a profound rejection of modernity and progress? This would be true if the world for which Don Quixote yearns and which he is intent on reviving had ever had a place in history. In truth, it only ever existed in the imagination, in legends and utopias created by men to escape the insecurity and barbarism of their lives—societies of order, honor, principles, fair and redeeming citizens, which compensated them for the violence and suffering of life in the Middle Ages.

The books of chivalry that incite Don Quixote's madness are not realistic, and the delirious feats of their paladins do not reflect reality. Yet they are an authentic and imaginative response, filled with dreams and wishes and, above all, denial, to a very real world—a dream of ceremony and elegance, of justice triumphant and evil punished, so different from the real world in which those who avidly read the chivalric romances (or listened to them in taverns and plazas) lived. Thus, the dream that transforms Alonso Quijano into *Don Quixote de La Mancha* does not constitute a reenactment of the past, but rather something much more ambitious: the realization of a myth, the transformation of fiction into living history.

This fantasy, which seems insane to those around Alonso Quijano, especially to his friends and acquaintances in his village—the priest, the barber Nicolás, the housekeeper and her niece, the bachelor Sansón Carrasco— gradually infiltrates reality, thanks to the fanatical conviction with which the Knight of the Sad Countenance imposes it on his surroundings, fearless of the thrashings and blows he receives and the misfortunes that befall him everywhere as a result. In his splendid interpretation of the novel, *Para leer a Cervantes* (El Acantilado, 2003), Martin de Riquer insists that throughout his long adventure Don Quixote does not change, that he never loses his certainty that it is the enchanters who distort reality so that he appears mistaken when he attacks windmills, wineskins, sheep, or pilgrims, believing them to be giants or enemies. Undoubtedly, this is true. Yet, although Don Quixote does not change, imprisoned as he is in his rigid chivalric vision of the world, what does change are his surroundings, the people around him, and the very reality, which, as if infected by his powerful madness, becomes less and less real until—as in a Borges story—it becomes pure fiction. This is one of the most subtle and most modern aspects of the great Cervantine novel.

Fiction and Life

The central theme of *Don Quixote de La Mancha* is fiction, its raison d'être, and the way it infiltrates life, forming and transforming it. Thus, what would seem to many modern readers the Borgesian theme *par excellence* (from "Tlon, Uqbar, Orbis Tertius") is actually a Cervantine subject, which, centuries later, was revived by Borges, giving it his own personal twist.

Fiction is the main issue of the novel because the gentleman from La Mancha has been "unhinged"—his madness is also an allegory or symbol, ahead of a clinical diagnosis—by the fantasies of chivalric romance. Believing the world to be as it is described in the novels of Amadíses and Palmerines, Don Quixote rushes at it in search of adventures in which he will participate parodically, provoking and enduring minor catastrophes. He will not learn the lesson of realism from these unfortunate experiences. With the unmoving belief of a fanatic, Don Quixote blames on the evil enchanters the fact that his feats are transformed into farces. In fact, in the end, Don Quixote triumphs; fiction infects true life and reality gives way to his fantasies. Sancho Panza, who has been introduced as a materialist and pragmatist, at last succumbs to the delights of the imaginary and, as governor of Barataria, accommodates himself to the world of falsity and illusion. His language, which at the beginning of the story is earthy, direct and populist, becomes refined and occasionally as pretentious as that of his master.

The stratagem by which Basilio prevents the beautiful Quiteria from marrying the wealthy Camacho so as to marry her himself—isn't that fiction? Basilio "commits suicide" amid preparations for the wedding, stabbing himself with a sword and bathing in blood. In agony as he dies, he asks Quiteria for her hand in marriage or he will die without confession. As soon as Quiteria agrees, Basilio returns to life, revealing that his suicide was pure theater and that the blood he shed came from a hidden pipe. The fiction, nonetheless, is effective and, with Don Quixote's help, becomes reality as Basilio and Quiteria unite in marriage.

The friends from Don Quixote's town—so opposed to the passion for reading novels that they burn Don Quixote's library on the pretext of curing Alonso Quijano's madness—also appeal to fiction by scheming to return the Knight of the Sad Countenance to his sanity and the real world. They actually achieve the opposite, however. The bachelor Sansón Carrasco dresses up twice as a knight-errant, first as the Knight of the Mirrors and later in Barcelona as the Knight of the White Moon. The first time the deception turns out to be counterproductive and Don Quixote has his own way. But the second time it achieves its aim, forcing Don Quixote to renounce his arms for a year and return to his village, bringing the story to its denouement.

The ending is a rather staged and depressing anti-climax and consequently, perhaps, Cervantes completed his work in a few more pages. There is something abnormal and even unreal in Alonso Quijano's decision to return to reality, when reality has become to a great extent fiction, as a weepy Sancho Panza indicates when he proclaims to his master from his deathbed that they should "be off to the country dressed as shepherds" to act out the pastoral fiction that is the last of Don Quixote's fantasies.

The fictionalization of reality reaches its peak with the appearance of the mysterious duke and duchess, who increase the pace and number of theatrical and fabulous changes. The duke and duchess have read the first part of the story, as have many other characters, and when they meet Don Quixote and Sancho Panza they are as seduced by the novel as Don Quixote is by the romances of chivalry. In their castle they arrange for life to become fiction and for the unreality in which Don Quixote lives to be reproduced in real life. The duke and duchess do this with the intention of laughing at the crazy gentleman and his squire—or so they believe. But the game begins to corrupt them, for later, when Don Quixote and Sancho leave for Zaragoza, the duke and duchess round up their servants and soldiers to find the two and bring them back to the castle, where the fabulous funeral ceremony and supposed resurrection of Altisidora has been organized. In the world of the duke and duchess, Don Quixote is no longer an eccentric; he is right at home in these fictional surroundings, from the island of Barataria, where Sancho realizes his dream of being governor, to the flight aboard Clavileño, the artificial quadruped on which the great Manchegan gallops through the clouds of illusion.

Another wealthy and influential man, Don Antonio Moreno, who lodges, wines, and dines Don Quixote in Barcelona, also stages some spectacles which break down reality. For example, in his house he has an enchanted bronze head, which answers questions posed to it, appearing to know the future and past of the other characters. The narrator explains that this is an "artifice," and that the supposed fortuneteller is in fact a hollow machine with a student who sits inside and responds to questions. Isn't this yet another manifestation of living fiction, creating theater from life, as Don Quixote does, but with less ingenuity and greater malice?

During his stay in Barcelona, when his host Don Antonio Moreno is walking Don Quixote through the city, a Castilian emerges who calls out to the Ingenious Gentleman: "You are mad … [and] you have the quality of turning into madmen and fools those who meet and speak with you." The Castilian is right: Don Quixote's madness, his thirst for unreality, is contagious and has fostered in others the appetite for fiction that possesses him.

This explains the flowering of stories, the forest of tales and novels, which is *Don Quixote de La Mancha*. Not only the elusive Cide Hamete Benengeli, the other narrator of the novel, who boasts of being merely its transcriber and translator (although he is really its editor, annotator, and commentator as well), reveals this passion for the imaginary life of literature, incorporating occasional tales—"The Man Who Was Recklessly Curious" and the tale of Cardenio and Dorotea, for example—into the main story of Don Quixote and Sancho Panza. Characters like the beautiful Moorish woman, the Knight of the Green Coat, or the Princess Micomicona, also share this propensity or narrative vice, which leads them to tell tales, real or invented, creating in the course of the novel a landscape of words and imagination which comes before, even at times abolishes, the other natural but not very realistic one of clichés and conventional rhetoric. *Don Quixote de La Mancha* is a novel about fiction in which imaginary life is everywhere, in the vicissitudes, the words, even the very air that the characters breathe.

A Novel of Free Men

In addition to being a novel about fiction, *Don Quixote* is also a song to freedom. Let us pause for a moment to reflect on these very famous words of Don Quixote to Sancho Panza: "Freedom, Sancho, is one of the most precious of heaven's gifts. It cannot be compared to the treasures of the land or sea. For freedom, as for honor, one can and should risk one's life, while captivity is the worst evil which can come to men."

Behind these words, and the fictitious character who utters them, is the figure of Miguel de Cervantes, who knew well of what he spoke. The five years during which he was held captive by Moors in Algiers and the three times he was imprisoned in Spain for debt and mismanagement of his position in the purchasing bureaucracy of the Armada in Andalusia—these experiences must have whetted his appetite for freedom and spurred his horror of captivity, filling Don Quixote's words with authenticity and force and giving a libertarian slant to the story of our Ingenious Gentleman.

What, then, is Don Quixote's concept of freedom? Is it that of so-called European liberals from the eighteenth century onward: the sovereignty of the individual to choose his life, without pressures or limitations, according to his intelligence and his will? This is what, several centuries later, Isaiah Berlin would define as "negative freedom," freedom from interference and coercion to think, express oneself, and act. At the heart of this idea of freedom is a profound distrust of authority and of the crimes that those in power might commit.

Let us remember that Don Quixote pronounces this exalted praise of freedom as he leaves the domain of the anonymous duke and duchess, where he has been treated like royalty by the man of the castle, the very incarnation of power. Yet, even amidst this flattery and pampering, the Ingenious Gentleman perceives an invisible corset which threatens and diminishes his freedom—"because I did not enjoy it with the liberty that I would have if [the gifts and abundance heaped on me] were mine." The assumption is that the basis of liberty is private property and that pleasure is only complete when one's capacity for initiative, one's freedom of thought and action, is not constrained. "Fortunate is he to whom the heavens have given bread without obliging him to thank anyone but the heavens themselves!"

It cannot be made clearer: freedom is individual and requires a mini-
mum level of prosperity. He who is poor and depends upon charity to survive
is never entirely free. It is true that there existed a time many years ago, as
Don Quixote reminds the stunned goatherds in his speech on the Golden
Age, when "virtue and goodness reigned in the world" and, in this heavenly
era before private property, "those who lived did not even know the words
yours and *mine*" and "all things were common property." But time passed and
"our detestable centuries" arrived, wherein, so that there might be security
and justice, "the order of knights-errant was instituted to defend maidens, to
protect widows and to help orphans and the needy."

Don Quixote does not believe that justice, order, and progress are the
responsibility of authority, but rather that of individuals who, like the knights-
errant and himself, take it upon themselves to rid the world of injustice and
bring freedom and prosperity. This is the knight-errant: one who, inspired by
his calling, hurls himself out into the world to look for remedies for all that
ails it. Authority, when it appears, instead of easing the task, generally makes
it more difficult.

Where is authority in the Spain that Don Quixote crosses in his three
journeys? We must leave the novel to know that the king alluded to on several occasions is Philip III, because, in the fiction, except for a few fleeting
appearances, such as that of the governor of Barcelona during Don Quixote's
visit to that city's port, the authorities are notably absent. The institutions that
embody them, such as the Saintly Brotherhood or rural Spain's judicial corps,
which are mentioned during Don Quixote and Sancho's trips, are likewise
viewed as something far away, dark, and dangerous.

Don Quixote does not hesitate to confront authority and challenge the
law when it deviates from his own conception of justice. In his first sally
he confronts the wealthy Juan Haldudo, a neighbor from Quintanar, who is
beating one of his servants because he has lost some sheep—which, according to the barbarous customs of the era, he has every right to do. But for our
Manchegan this is intolerable and he rescues the servant, righting what he
sees as a wrong. (As soon as he departs, Haldudo flogs the servant to death,
despite his promises not to mistreat him.) The novel is filled with episodes
like this, in which the individualist vision of justice leads the bold gentleman
to disrespect authority, law, and custom in the name of what is for him a
superior moral imperative.

The adventure in which Don Quixote takes this libertarian spirit to a
nearly suicidal extreme—suggesting that his idea of freedom also anticipates
in some respects the anarchist thinkers of two centuries later—is one of the
most celebrated in the novel: the liberation of the twelve delinquents, among
them the sinister Ginés de Pasamonte, the future Master Pedro who forces

the Ingenious Gentleman, despite being perfectly aware that they are dealing with ruffians condemned for their misdeeds, to row the galleys of the king. The reason for his open challenge to authority—"it is not right that honorable men are the hangmen of others"—hardly conceals Don Quixote's love of liberty, which, if he had to choose, he would place ahead of justice, or his profound mistrust of authority, which for him is no guarantee of what he ambiguously refers to as "distributive justice," an expression that implies an egalitarian counterweight to his libertarian ideals.

In this episode, in order to reiterate how insubordinate and free his thought is, Don Quixote praises the "trade of the procurer," as "very necessary in an orderly republic," and indignantly suggests that an elderly man who was sentenced to the galleys for the practice of procuring should instead have been "made general of them." He who dared to rebel so blatantly against political correctness and prevailing morals was a true madman who—not only when he spoke of the romances of chivalry—said and did things that questioned the roots of the society in which he lived.

Don Quixote's Homelands

What is the image of Spain that emerges from the pages of Cervantes' novel? It is one that is vast and diverse, without geographical borders, consisting of an archipelago of communities, villages, and towns, which the characters refer to as "homelands." It is an image similar to that of the empires or kingdoms of chivalric romance, the genre supposedly ridiculed in *Don Quixote de La Mancha*. Yet Cervantes pays it great homage and one of his literary feats is to modernize the romance of chivalry, recovering from it, through play and humor, all that could survive, and adjusting it to the social and artistic values of the seventeenth century, an era very different from that in which it had originated.

In the course of his three adventures, Don Quixote travels through La Mancha and part of Aragón and Catalonia, but the origin of many of the characters and the many references to places and things make Spain appear a much vaster, geographically diverse space with imprecise borders, defined not in terms of territories and administrative demarcations, but in terms of religion. Spain ends in those vague coastal areas where the dominion of the Moor, the religious enemy, begins.

At the same time, Spain is the context and the horizon of the relatively limited geography that Don Quixote and Sancho Panza traverse, and what is displayed with color and affection is the "homeland," the concrete and human space that memory can span—a landscape, people, customs, which men and women save in their memories as a personal heritage and which constitute their credentials. The characters in the novel travel the world over, one might say, carrying their towns and villages with them. They identify themselves by referring to these details, their "homeland," and remember the small communities where they have left lovers, friends, families, homes, and animals with irrepressible nostalgia. When, at the end of the third trip after many adventures, Sancho Panza sees his village in the distance, he falls on his knees and exclaims: "Open your eyes, beloved homeland, and see that Sancho Panza, your son, has returned . . ."

Since, in the course of time, this idea of homeland would begin to dematerialize, gradually approaching the idea of nation (which only emerges in the nineteenth century) until it becomes one with it, it should be noted that the homelands of *Don Quixote* have nothing to do with this abstract concept of nationhood, which is general, schematic, and essentially political, and is at the root of all nationalisms. This collectivist ideology, which claims to define individuals according to membership in a human conglomerate distinguished by certain traits (race, language, religion) which impose on it a specific personality, is radically different from the exalted individualism that Don Quixote and others display. Theirs is a world in which "patriotism" is a generous and positive sentiment, a love of one's native land and people, of shared memories and a familiar past, and not a means of separating oneself or establishing borders against others. *Don Quixote*'s Spain has no borders: it is a multicolored, pluralistic world of many homelands, open to the outside world and indistinguishable from it. It opens its doors to those who arrive from other parts, somehow avoiding the obstacle (insurmountable for the Counter-Reformation mentality of the time) of religion, that is, conversion to Catholicism.

A Modern Book

Don Quixote's modernity lies in its rebellious and avenging spirit, which permits the protagonist to assume that changing the world for the better is his responsibility, even when, while trying to put this into practice, he meets insurmountable obstacles, is throttled, ill-treated, and transformed into an object of derision. But it is also very much a novel of today, since Cervantes, in order to tell the exploits of Don Quixote, revolutionized the narrative forms of his time and created the basis of the modern novel. Although they may not know it, the contemporary novelists who play with form, distort time, shuffle and twist perspectives, and experiment with language, are all in debt to Cervantes.

This formal revolution which is *Don Quixote* has been studied and analyzed from all possible points of view and, yet, as with all paradigmatic masterpieces, it never runs dry, because, as with *Hamlet* or *The Divine Comedy* or *The Iliad* and *The Odyssey*, the work changes with the passage of time, recreating itself in terms of the aesthetics and values of each culture, revealing that it is a true Ali Baba cave whose treasures never end.

Perhaps the most innovative aspect of *Don Quixote*'s narrative form is the way Cervantes approaches the problem of the narrator, the basic problem that should resolve everything a novel encompasses. Who is going to tell the story? Cervantes' answer introduces a subtlety and complexity in the genre that continues to enrich modern novelists today and was for its era what Joyce's *Ulysses*, Proust's *Remembrance of Things Past*, or, in Latin American literature, García Márquez' *One Hundred Years of Solitude* or Cortázar's *Hopscotch* was for ours.

Who tells the story of Don Quixote and Sancho Panza? Two narrators: the mysterious Cide Hamete Benengeli, whom we never read directly as his manuscript is in Arabic, as well as an anonymous author who sometimes speaks in the first person, but most often from the last of three omniscient narrators who supposedly translate into Spanish and at the same time adapt, edit, and comment on the manuscript. This is a Chinese box structure: the story that we read is contained within another earlier and broader one at which we can only guess. The existence of these two narrators introduces ambiguity into the novel and an element of uncertainty about the "other" story, that of Cide Hamete Benengeli. Their presence fills the adventures of Don Quixote and Sancho Panza with a subtle relativism, an aura of subjectivity, and contributes autonomy, sovereignty, and original personality.

But these other narrators, and their delicate dialectic, are not the only ones who matter in this novel of storywriters and compulsive tellers of tales. Many characters substitute for them, as we have seen, referring to their own mishaps or those of others in episodes which constitute other, smaller Chinese boxes contained within the vast universe filled with private fictions that is *Don Quixote de La Mancha*. Making the most of the romances of chivalry (many of which were supposedly manuscripts found in exotic and outlandish places), Cervantes created Cide Hamete Benengeli as a device to introduce ambiguity and the game as central characteristics of the narrative structure. He also made transcendental innovations in another matter of capital importance to the novel's form: the narrative time.

Don Quixote's Time

In all novels, time, like the narrator, is an artifice, an intention, something created according to the needs of anecdote, and never merely a reproduction or reflection of real time.

In *Don Quixote* there are various times which, masterfully mixed, add to the novel that air of an independent world, that touch of self-sufficiency, that is crucial in giving it persuasive power. There is, on the one hand, the time in which the characters of the novel move, which covers a little more that half a year, since Don Quixote's three trips last, respectively, three days, a few months, and about four months. To this period we must add two intervals between trips (the second lasting a month), which Don Quixote spends in his village, and the last two days, until his death—altogether, then, around seven or eight months.

However, there are episodes in the novel, which by their nature increase the narrative time considerably, both toward the past and toward the future. Many of the events we learn about in the course of the novel have happened before it begins; we hear of them through the testimonies of witnesses or protagonists and we see many of them conclude in what would be the present of the novel.

But the most notable and surprising aspect of the narrative time is that many characters in the second part of *Don Quixote de La Mancha*, the duke and duchess, for example, have read the first part. Thus we learn that other realities, other times, different from those in fiction, exist, in which Don Quixote and Sancho Panza exist as characters in a book whose readers are either inside or outside the story, which is our situation, we contemporary readers. This small stratagem, in which one must see something far more daring than a simple game of literary illusionism, has important consequences for the structure of the novel. The time of the fiction expands and multiplies. The fiction remains enclosed within a greater universe, in which Don Quixote, Sancho, and the other characters have already lived and been converted into the heroes of the book and appeared in the hearts and memories of the readers of this other reality, which is not exactly the reality we are reading and yet contains it. This is just like a Chinese box, where the largest box contains a smaller one, and then a smaller and a smaller one, in a series that could, in theory, be infinite.

This is a game, which is both amusing and disturbing, and at the same time enriches the story with episodes like those with the duke and duchess (who are aware of Don Quixote's manias and obsessions from the book that they have read). It also has the virtue of graphically and pleasantly illustrating the complex relations between fiction and life—the way life produces fictions and these fictions, then, revert to life, brightening it, changing it, giving it color, adventure, emotion, laughter, passion, and surprises.

The relation between fiction and life, a recurrent theme of classical and modern literature, is seen in Cervantes' novel in a way that anticipates the great adventures of the twentieth century in which the explorations of narrative form—language, time, characters, points of view, and the function of the narrator—tempt the very best novelists.

* * *

For these and many other reasons, the immortality of *Don Quixote* is due to the elegance and power of its style, in which the Spanish language reached one of its highest peaks. One should speak perhaps not of one but of various styles in which the novel is written. There are two that can be clearly distinguished, and that, as novelistic material, correspond to the two sides or faces of reality through which the story unfolds: the real and the fictitious.

In the tales interspersed throughout the novel, the language is more rhetorical than in the central story in which Don Quixote, Sancho, the priest, the barber, and other villagers speak in a simpler and more natural way. In the added tales the narrator uses a more affected—more literary—language with which he achieves a distancing, almost fantastic effect. These differences are also to be seen in the words that come from the characters' mouths, according to their social position, level of education, and profession. Indeed, among the characters from the popular sector, the differences are evident: a humble villager would speak most transparently, while a slave, a city ruffian who defends himself in slang, would speak an argot at times totally incomprehensible to Don Quixote.

Don Quixote, in fact, does not have one single way of expressing himself. According to the narrator, he only exaggerates on chivalric themes, and speaks precisely and objectively when treating other issues. When focusing on the themes of chivalry, Don Quixote's speech becomes a grab bag of scholarly topics, erudite affectations, literary references, and fantastic ravings. No less variable is the language of Sancho Panza, whose manner of speaking changes over the course of the story, from a salty language, bursting with life and filled with refrains and sayings that express a wealth of popular knowledge, to a convoluted and ornamented mode of expression at the end which he has acquired from his master and which is like a smiling parody of the parody that is, in itself, the language of Don Quixote.

Cervantes then, instead of Sansón Carrasco, should be called the Knight of the Mirrors, as *Don Quixote de La Mancha* is a veritable labyrinth of mirrors, where everything—the characters, the artistic forms, the anecdotes, the styles—unfold and multiply in images which express human life in all its infinite subtlety and variety.

For all of these reasons, then, this pair is immortal, and four centuries after entering the world through Cervantes' pen, Don Quixote and Sancho Panza continue to ride without interruption or despondency. In La Mancha, Aragón, Catalonia, Europe, America, the world. They are still here, through rain, roaring thunder, burning sun or shining stars, in the great silence of the polar night, or in the desert, or in the tangled jungles, arguing, seeing, and understanding different things in all that they find and hear. Yet, despite their constant disputes, they need each other more and more, they are indissolubly joined in that strange union, which is the union of sleep and vigil, of what is real and what is ideal, of life and death, spirit and flesh, fiction and life. In literary history they are two unmistakable figures, one elongated and airy like a Gothic arch and the other short and squat like a three-legged good luck piggy, two attitudes, two ambitions, two visions. But in the distance, in our memory as readers of their novelesque epic, Don Quixote and Sancho Panza are joined as "one sole shadow" like the couple in José Asunción Silva's poem, which portrays the human condition in all its contradictory and fascinating truth.

ROBERTO GONZÁLEZ ECHEVARRÍA

The Knight as Fugitive from Justice: *The* Quijote, *Part I*

No sooner does Don Quijote set out from his village in search of chivalric adventures than he runs into a picaresque world at the first inn. The second inn, Juan Palomeque's, is the one most readers remember, and rightly so, because of the crucial episodes that take place within it. It is the building that defines Part I, in contrast to the duke's palatial home in Part II. But this first inn is also important because it is first and because it sets the tone or better, the dissonance, of the novel—the din of competing discourses of which it is composed (chivalric and picaresque in this case). Here, at the very threshold of his quest, Don Quijote will encounter, in the prostitutes and the innkeeper, the earliest representatives of the two themes that I am developing here—love and the law—in a picaresque setting replete with other transient characters of a similar ilk. The prostitutes represent love at its lowest level and the innkeeper the law, of which he has been a favorite object and whose representative he becomes mockingly when he knights Don Quijote. The novel's plot will circle back to an inn, Juan Palomeque's this time, in which Don Quijote will be subdued, caged, and returned home—a complete reversal of his accession to knighthood in the first inn.

This first innkeeper is a retired pícaro, or rogue, who tells his own story to boast about a misspent but adventuresome youth. As with the prisoner of sex, here we have Cervantes drawing a round character with a

---

From *Love and the Law in Cervantes*, pp. 54–74, 259–60. © 2005 by Roberto González Echevarría.

few pen strokes. Readers of his time would recognize the innkeeper's life as an itinerary of notorious picaresque emporia—gathering places where these rogues convened in large numbers to rejoice in each other's company and in their collective rejection of society's norms and the state's laws. The population of rogues formed, in fact, a "countersociety"—a society in reverse—with colonies in all the Spanish prisons, which were virtually run by the inmates, as we learn from Cristobal de Chaves's *Relación de la cárcel de Sevilla*.[1] The first innkeeper's story is a map of picaresque life of six-teenth-century Spain, as Diego de Clemencín called it in his massive nine-teenth-century edition.[2] His mock confession (relayed by the narrator) is a conceited chronicle in which he translates with great ironic flair his life as a criminal into a chivalric romance. It is the language of literature in the process of being contaminated by that of the jailhouse, as it is contained in the legal documents pertaining to the innkeeper, the only discourse capa-ble of inscribing—that is, of restraining—this seasoned crook. But by his rhetorical skill, comparable to that of the prisoner of sex, he can subvert it. Instead of being told in the first person, as in a conventional picaresque novel, the innkeeper's story is reported in an indirect style that underscores the ironic process by which picaresque adventures are narrated as if they were chivalric ones. The performance is very much a part of his self-defini-tion as a devious, skillful trickster—hence the narrator is needed to act it out, as it were. The innkeeper avails himself of a common rhetorical ruse among thugs—a form of jocular transposition and inversion of meanings and values. In their jargon, called *germanía*, it was customary to say one thing to mean the opposite, a poetic display as elaborate and baroque as that of contemporary Góngora-style verse. "Germanía," according to the Spanish Academy, derives from "hermano," "brother"; it is the secret lan-guage of criminal brotherhoods. It was also known in the sixteenth and seventeenth centuries as the language of the brothels.[3] The inversion of meanings is akin to the practice of "signifying" among American blacks and of *choteo* among Cubans.[4]

* * *

Before I look at the passage containing the innkeeper's biography and move on to examine Don Quijote's criminal career, I should perhaps give a thumbnail sketch of the picaresque. . . . It is important that I do so too because there seem to be gross misconceptions about the picaresque in the English-speaking world. These stem from the term *romance* as applied to narrative in the American academy, thanks mostly to Northrop Frye's influ-ential *Anatomy of Criticism*. This is a concept that does not exist in Spanish and has no currency in Spanish-language criticism. (To add to the confusion "romance" means "ballad" in Spanish.) I find "romance" useful in English to refer to chivalric narratives, which have stereotypical characters with little development and standard plot lines. But this is hardly the case with picaresque stories, which we call "novelas" in Spanish and do not adhere to anything resembling Frye's definition of "romance."[5]

The picaresque, as a literary genre, was inaugurated in 1554 with the publication of the anonymous *La vida de Lazarillo de Tormes y de sus fortunas y adversidades* (The Life of Lazarillo de Tormes, and of His Fortunes and Misfortunes).[6] The *Lazarillo* established the conventions of the genre: it is the first-person narrative of a petty criminal who tells his life from birth to the moment he writes, emphasizing his poverty and troubled childhood, his serving a series of depraved and abusive masters, and his being immersed in a world of thievery, violence, prostitution, and pervasive corruption. This is a world that had already appeared, but in a different mode, in the 1499 *La Celestina*. Some of these elements had also been featured in European narrative fiction, particularly Italian, from *Il Novellino* to Boccaccio and later Bandello, but not all together at once, and without the aura of criminality and persecution by judicial and penal authorities. This change is manifest in the very rhetoric the text of picaresque fiction assumes, which is part of its defiant irony. The picaresque narrative took the form of a legal document: the deposition, or relación, that the criminal gives to account and justify his current predicament, his caso, or case, typically an entanglement with the law. Lazarillo's plight is that he has married the mistress of an archpriest to serve as a cover for their cohabitation, which makes him a willing cuckold and an accessory to a clergyman's corruption. His is no simple fornication, it is complex—a fornicación calificada. Lazarillo's tone is one of ironic self-exculpation: how, having the life that I have had, could I have turned out otherwise? His is the first ironic novelistic voice, a truly revolutionary innovation in narrative fiction: a criminal telling his own life not to God, like Augustine, but to a judge, a lay temporal authority.

This template was followed forty-five years later by the book that came to be known as the quintessential picaresque novel, Mateo Alemán's (1547–1614) *Guzmán de Alfarache* (1599), whose second part (1605) was called *Malaya de la vida humana* (Watchtower of Human Life). Here the scope of the narrative has been greatly amplified and the pícaro, who has spent time as a galley slave, tells his life after having undergone a conversion to the good. So his confession is presumably one of repentance, offered as example of what not to do, but like all such pious literary texts, the relish with which evil is narrated belies the professed devout intentions. The novel is, nevertheless, studded with vexing sermonizing after each of the adventures. The zealotry of Counter-Reformation Spain has intervened in the years since *Lazarillo*. Still, the depiction of criminal life throughout a vast landscape that exceeds Spain to encompass Italy is so shocking and pitiless, that the *Guzmán* is, indeed, a powerful example of early realism. The picaresque mode continued in Spain with substantial variations in the works of Cervantes himself, but also in those of Francisco de Quevedo, Francisco López de Ubeda, and others. Elsewhere in Europe it had a vast and influential following in Lesage's *Gil Blas*, von Grimmelshausen's *Simplicius Simplicissimus*, Fielding's *Tom Jones* and *Joseph Andrews*, Tobias Smollett's *Roderick Random*, and so on until the present. There are quite a few modern picaresques, from *The Adventures of Huckleberry Finn* to *Felix Krull* and quite a few Spanish and Latin American ones. Spanish criticism credits the picaresque with being the origin of the modern novel. (The English, of course, claim the honor for Fielding, and the French, *parbleu*, for Madame de Lafayette.)

Rafael Salillas, a brilliant if today nearly forgotten nineteenth-century Spanish criminologist, maintains that the picaresque, particularly Alemán's *Guzmán de Alfarache*, is the genesis of criminology as a science because of its detailed and uncensored depiction of criminal life.[7] He makes a very persuasive case. From the perspective of literature and Cervantes, what is most relevant is that in presenting the life of the *hampa*, or underworld, the authors of picaresque novels were laying bare the most frightful manifestations of the human, all too human in general, bereft of the embellishments of morality and customs. If the Renaissance was interested in the study of man, the picaresque constituted a deeper probe than the analyses of princes, courtiers, ironic self-analysts, and Platonic lovers (Machiavelli, Castiglione, Ficino, Montaigne). For Salillas, as for Cervantes, criminal life inside and outside of prisons was like the negative (in all senses) yet accurate portrait of society. For Cervantes and for literature the most compelling aspect of picaresque life was the individuating detail, the originality of the deviant, his bizarre behavior, first captured in the fine net of legal writing, where his story would have first been told. In the picaresque the program of representation due to the casuistry of Spanish law . . . crosses over into literature to leave an indelible mark on the history of realism and of the novel. Cervantes found in the picaresque a poetics of the vile that he worked into the *Quijote* and some of the *Exemplary Stories*, as well as a poetics of everyday life, which elevated to literature the common things detailed in legal documents as they itemized and inventoried the real world in which the pícaro roamed.

The origin of the word "pícaro," from which the terms "picaresque" in general and "picaresque novel" in particular derived, has been the object of debate, as could be expected. I note that the *Oxford English Dictionary* has

both "pícaro" and "picaroon" as being used in English already in the seventeenth century. The most likely origin is the verb "picar," or "to cut," according to the great etymologist Joan Corominas.[8] The jobs that some of these
unsavory individuals held involved cutting: the "pinche de cocina," or kitchen
helper or porter, cuts up meats and vegetables, so he is nimble with knives.
From there to "picar faltriqueras," to snip pockets, was an easy transition, as
was to stab people in order to kill them, maim them, or leave marks on their
bodies. ("Faltriqueras" were pockets hanging outside the pants, shirts, or vests
that these characters would cut off and run away with.) There is a great deal of
aggression and physical violence in the picaresque, and the verb "picar" seems
like an appropriate emblem of it. To this origin some had added "Picard,"
the natives of Picardy—the old French province—who are said to have been
particularly rowdy and dangerous as soldiers of fortune. Others have even
claimed an Arabic origin for pícaro ("to be poor"—"fakir-figaro-figaro-
pícaro").[9] It seems to me that the most likely is "picar," although I still have
trouble with the dactyl "pícaro," which is difficult to account for following the
normal evolution of Spanish words from Latin to romance. Yet Corominas
assures us that changes of that nature do occur, and, of course, "pícaro" could
be a deliberate disfiguring of "picar" following the unconventional rules of the
language of germanía, where such things occurred not only to the meaning
of words but also to their pronunciation, because the pícaro's secret jargon, or
germanía, was given to wild troping and puns that transgressed ordinary laws
of linguistic transformation, as those who spoke it eschewed those of society.

* * *

This point brings me back to the passage in which the first innkeeper's story
is told:

> The innkeeper, who, as we have already observed, was a sort of a
> wag, and had from the beginning suspected that his lodger's brain
> was none of the soundest, having heard him to an end, no longer
> entertained any doubts about the matter, and in order to regale
> himself and the rest of his guests with a dish of mirth, resolved
> to humor him in his extravagance. With this in view, he told him,
> that nothing could be more just and reasonable than his request,
> his conceptions being extremely well suited, and natural to such a
> peerless knight as his commanding presence and gallant demeanor
> demonstrated him to be: that he himself had, in his youth, exercised
> the honorable profession of errantry, strolling from place to place,
> in quest of adventures, in the course of which he did not fail to visit

the suburbs of Malaga, the isles of Riaran, the booths of Seville, the marketplace of Segovia, the olive gardens of Valencia, the little tower of Granada, the bay of St Lucar, the spout of Cordova, the public houses of Toledo, and many other places, in which he had exercised the dexterity of his hands as well as the lightness of his heels, doing infinite mischief, courting widows without number, debauching maidens, ruining heirs, and in short, making himself known at the bar of every tribunal in Spain; that, at length, he had retired to this castle, where he lived on his own means, together with those of other people; accommodating knights-errant of every quality and degree, solely on account of the affection he bore to them, and to the coin which they parted with in return for his hospitality. (I, 3, pp. 15–16)

[El ventero, que, como está dicho, era un poco socarrón y va tenía algunos barruntos de la falta de juicio de su huésped, acabó de creerlo cuando acabó de oírle semejantes razones, y, por tener que reír aquella noche, determinó de seguirle el humor; y así, le dijo que andaba muy acertado en lo que deseaba y pedía, y que tal presupuesto era propio y natural de los caballeros tan principales como él parecía y como su gallarda presencia mostraba; y que él, ansimesmo, en los años de su mocedad, se había dado a aquel honroso ejercicio, andando por diversas partes del mundo, buscando sus aventuras, sin que hubiese dejado los Percheles cíe Málaga, Islas de Riarán, Compás de Sevilla, Azoguejo de Segovia, la Olivera de Valencia, Rondilla de Granada, playa de Sanlúcar, Potro de Córdoba y las Ventillas de Toledo y otras diversas partes, donde había ejercitado la ligereza de sus pies, sutileza de sus manos, haciendo muchos tuertos, recuestando muchas viudas, deshaciendo algunas doncellas y engañando a algunos pupilos, y, finalmente, dándose a conocer por cuantas audiencias y tribunales hay casi en toda España; y que, a lo último, se había venido a recoger a aquel su castillo, donde vivía con su hacienda y con las ajenas, recogiendo en él a todos los caballeros andantes de cualquiera calidad y condición que fuesen, sólo por la mucha afición que les tenía y porque partiesen con él de sus haberes, en pago de su buen deseo. (pp. 55–56)]

This is the life of an unrepentant thief and trickster who has been hauled before many criminal courts and lives off his ill-begotten fortune by continuing to fleece others. He has graduated from young pícaro and Don Juan type to middle-aged crook and is proud of it. There has been no conversion to the good here as in *Guzmán de Alfarache*; on the contrary, he shows a wistful regret for a criminal past now gone but hardly forgotten. However, the most interesting feature in the passage is the transformation of picaresque into chivalric adventures and the conquests of a common pimp into grand-style Don Juan-type erotic feats involving the seduction of widows and deflowering of maidens. The narrator echoes and magnifies in mock-heroic tones the innkeeper's own sense of self-worth in a bombastic, if ambivalent, eulogy. This is the flip side of Don Quijote's translation of tawdry, everyday reality into chivalric terms, as when he calls the whores at the inn "doncellas" (virgins), which astonishes and delights them because the very concept could not be further from their profession. The mockery highlights the innkeeper's chicanery, holding him up as the very exemplar of criminality, cynicism, and radical lack of values.

The narrator, echoing the innkeeper, accomplishes the transformation by a typically Cervantean twist, not just by following a germanía trope. By 1605, when Part I of the *Quijote* was published, the picaresque style of life had acquired a literary dimension, in great measure because of the success of Alemán's *Guzmán de Alfarache*. In other words, pícaro was a role one could play like that of knight; high and low literature had the same effect and followed common tropes, as did the language of germanía and Gongoristic poetry. The character that had been plucked out of the archive of criminal cases had become a novelistic type. It is conceivable, and Cervantes suggests it here and in "Rinconete and Cortadillo," one of the *Exemplary Stories*, that some of the real pícaros had chosen that path not because of need but to play the role and to revel as a group in their collective rejection of society. They are, in a sense, doing the same as Don Quijote by adopting the style of a literary character and setting out on a life of adventure according to books read, not to society's rules. This is the reason the innkeeper can transform pícaro into knight. Of course, given the mock-heroic tone and irony of the passage, it is most likely that the innkeeper is also shrouding in a literary mantle the reasons for his turning to picaresque life, which were more than likely poverty and his natural inclination to evil. The third-person indirect style allows the reader to perceive the distance between truth and its embellishment. The truth of the innkeeper's story is no doubt written and stored in the criminal records of all those courts and tribunals mentioned, the veritable source and archive of picaresque lives.

The traveling prostitutes, who are ennobled by Don Quijote's chivalric rhetoric, are on their way to Seville with some muleteers. Picaresque life is migratory, and the inns in the *Quijote* serve as gathering places for the cornucopia of rogues of both sexes. Seville was the capital of *picardía*, the gateway to the New World, and in general a center of criminal life. (Seville was the only port through which Spain had commerce with its American empire.) These prostitutes bring to mind similar ones in *La Celestina*, *Lazarillo de Tormes*, and *Guzmán de Alfarache*. But here they also stand in sharp contrast to Dulcinea and the knight's imaginings about this farm girl elevated to the exalted status of courtly love lady. In their kindness to Don Quijote the prostitutes also reveal a common Cervantean topic: the goodness of delinquents within the rules of their own world and independent of their being outside the law. And the prostitutes are outside the law merely by being on the road, away from their homes and the protective legal custody of fathers and brothers. Their wandering ways are a component of their depravity. Lust and criminality—love and the law—surround Don Quijote at the inn, a background against which he thrusts the rhetorical flights drawn from the courtly love tradition and the chivalric romances.

It is a contrast that also underscores the clash between the feats that Don Quijote thinks he is accomplishing and the criminal acts he is really committing. He sets out determined to deal with "grievances to be redressed, wrongs to be rectified, errors amended, abuses to be reformed, and debts to be settled" (I, 2, p. 9). Which in the Spanish has a more legalistic tone: "según eran los agravios que pensaba deshacer, tuertos que enderezar, sinrazones que enmendar, y abusos que mejorar, y deudas que satisfacer" (p. 45) ("Tuertos" has the same origin as the English "tort," in Latin "twisted.") The disparity between the justice he plans to dispense and the series of injuries, torts, and damages that he causes is crucial to understanding Part I of the *Quijote* because the knight's criminal record contributes to the novel's shape—a record that could be written by setting specific instances of misbehavior under each of the categories of offense that he plans to correct. It is a record that is the reverse of his intentions. The pursuit and capture of the hidalgo, and the restitution made for some of the injuries and damages that he causes, organize the book. The picaresque backdrop at the inn also defines Don Quijote, which is part of the reason he "officially" assumes his new identity there. It is the exact opposite, the mirror image, of the innkeeper's turning his life as a pícaro into that of a knight. From now on Don Quijote's criminal record, his wandering along roads and through wilderness and his catastrophic sojourns at Juan Palomeque's inn make him into a pícaro instead of a knight.

Don Quijote is the first hero in the Western tradition to be a fugitive from justice, one whose life is defined by flight from the authorities of an organized state. The wily Ulysses returns from war shrouded in glory, and his trek home is staked out by a series of obstacles that put his courage and mettle to the test. Aeneas's journey takes him to the solemn task of founding Rome. The pilgrim in Dante's *Divine Comedy* seeks transcendence in the sublime quest for Beatrice. The pícaros, Lázaro, Guzmán, and Pablos, lack the heroic grandeur to which Don Quijote aspires, but they do provide a close model and similar ambience, a world of criminals and representatives of justice within which the mad hidalgo will attempt to revive chivalric adventures. Don Quijote's flight and capture are cast within the discourse of the law because he is now the citizen of a body politic whose morals and mores are at odds with his heroic aspirations and his outdated concept of justice.

The pervasive presence of the law as context to Don Quijote's actions is a sharp reminder of the knight's real status—of the gap between what he thinks he is entitled to and that to which the changing social and political conditions have reduced him. As an hidalgo, or petty nobleman, he considered himself, if not completely beyond the reach of the law, at least due certain exemptions and privileges, which he elevates through the language of chivalry to the level of a *caballero* entitled to use the *don*—he was not as a mere hidalgo. Knights are above the law. But the law—that is, justice—does catch up with him, signaling the change in Spanish society, and the stark fact that he is not only heir to his deeds, as he says, but responsible for his actions—he is a subject, subject to criminal justice like any other. Hidalgos were gradually losing their privileges. The devastating humiliation of punishment is partly staved off by his madness, which protects him through Part I from the reality of his social condition and allows him to rationalize not only his defeats but his arrest and caging at the end. The mere fact that Don Quijote can be served with an arrest warrant reveals the erosion of the nobility's exemptions—he is released to the priest and barber not because of his social status but because of his insanity. The convolution of the plot through punishment and reparation at the end make the whole story meaningful: it frames, as it were, the hero (pun intended).

There are many unanswered questions about the structure of the *Quijote*'s plot, which seems to be merely episodic with no anticipated end in sight—there is one adventure after another, with characters who reappear and situations that are repeated, creating some patterns but with hardly a guiding line of development. No foreseeable end to his quest looms in the future, as in the case of Dante's pilgrim. There is no sequence of actions linked by necessity to build an Aristotelian chain of events, either, though we know from chapters 47 and 48 of Part I that Cervantes was highly conversant with the *Poetics* and its Spanish and Italian commentators. Nor is there the overall shape that would be provided by the pícaro's life, a plot structure already known and even parodied by Cervantes in the figure of Ginés de Pasamonte. This is the kind of plot that carries the rogue from birth to the moment he tells the story, proceeding through a series of events and masters that lead to his corruption and, in some instances, his conversion. There is no such pattern in the novel, in spite of Cervantes's reference to the story of Don Quijote as a caso, clearly suggesting that what he found in the archives of La Mancha was a criminal case, the record of Don Quijote's weird behavior and misdeeds. There is not even the story of a fabulous birth, like that of Amadís de Gaula, Don Quijote's model, whose youth and training as a knight are narrated in loving detail in the best-known chivalric romance.

We learn, in fact, hardly anything about Don Quijote's family and youth, as if a determining beginning had been purposely avoided. (The use of "lugar" in the first sentence of the novel is also a way of withdrawing any kind of determinism from Don Quijote's origin in the most concrete fashion, as is the narrator's refusal to reveal the name of the village.) In the first sentence of the book there is a clash between a beginning dictated by tradition, "In such and such a place there dwelt," and a Renaissance author's will to create an original work of literature: "whose name I do not care to remember." There is also an echo of a legal document in which place and time are specified, as in a relación. Don Quijote's only relevant life is the one he invents for himself as a literary character within the fiction. That life, however, is only good as a setup for the mounting yet disconnected number of episodes that occur in roads and inns. It is, in fact, the legal cast of the story, the knight's criminal acts, persecution, and capture, that gives recognizable form to the plot, along with the partial reparations for the damages and injuries that he inflicts along the way. Don Quijote's capture and submission at the end loops the plot, giving it a kind of closure. He is returned home caged, on a cart like the ones that were used to display criminals in order to hold them up to shame or carry them to the gallows. I will concentrate on this larger story here. . . .

* * *

. . . [A]fter the galley slaves episode both Don Quijote and Sancho become fugitives of the law, although that was not their first misdeed by far. We discover in the final episodes in Juan Palomeque's inn that the Holy Brotherhood had issued a warrant of arrest for the knight. Freeing the prisoners and injuring their wardens are Don Quijote's most serious crimes, for they are committed directly against the crown, and in addition were offenses perpetrated in despoblado, on the open road, in an unpopulated area. As I explained, crimes in such places were singled out by Spanish law as particularly damnable because the victims had no chance of being helped by others—"despoblado" means a barren place, a place without "pueblo," without people, outside the town, a kind of wilderness, the uncivilized— literally, that which is not within the political because it is not in the polis or city. Despoblado is a place outside the scope of the law and of justice,

the "unsheltered." In other works by Cervantes the most hideous crimes
are committed in such areas, as in "The Call of the Blood." . . . In fact,
most of Don Quijote's crimes take place in despoblado; hence toward the
end of the novel he and Sancho are called by one of the troopers of the
Holy Brotherhood "salteadores de caminos" and the knight a "salteador de
sendas y carreras" (p. 528): that is to say, highway robbers or a highway-
man, individuals known for assaulting people on the open roads. This kind
of criminal was accorded special attention and punishment in Spanish law
because it was the crown's charge to keep roads safe; therefore, offenses
committed on them were considered against the crown, not against local
or regional authorities. The laws were enacted and toughened in response
to *bandolerismo*, or brigandage, a common scourge at the time that threatened the stability of the kingdom, represented in Part II by the figure of
Roque Ginart. . . . [T]here was a special police force organized to deal
with such criminal activities in fields and roads: the Santa Hermandad, or
the Holy Brotherhood.

The Holy Brotherhood, which I have mentioned as an example of an
institution created by the Catholic kings in their effort to achieve central-
ization, was sanctioned at the Cortes de Madrigal in 1476. The seat of the
Holy Brotherhood was Toledo. It was essentially a revamping and consolida-
tion of brotherhoods, independent vigilante forces scattered through Spain
and dating back to the Middle Ages. The Holy Brotherhood's duty was to
patrol the despoblado, to pursue criminals who escaped from one jurisdiction
to another, and to punish crimes deemed as rebellious against public order,
including rape. It was more than just a rural police. It also acted as a court
of justice whose sentences were notorious for their summary expediency and
the severity and swiftness of the punishments meted out. Its *cuadrilleros*, or
troopers, were feared and hated, and the institution declined as the towns
that supported it through special taxes protested and eventually withdrew
their financing. The troopers were like members of an official posse. By Cervantes's time the strength of the Holy Brotherhood had been reduced and
it was charged mostly with the control of brigandage, but consciousness of
its presence and fear of its penchant to pass judgment and execute its harsh
sentences without delay were still very vivid, as we can gather from Sancho's
apprehensions. He says that he can hear the troopers' arrows buzzing around
his ears because the Holy Brotherhood liked to execute criminals by tying
them to a post and shooting them with their bows: "I give you notice, that all
your errantry will stand you in little stead against the' Holy Brotherhood, who
don't value all the knights-errant in the universe three farthings; and, in faith,
this minute I think I hear their arrows buzzing about my ears" (I, 23, p. 163)

[porque le hago saber que con la Santa Hermandad no hay usar de caballerías; que no se le da a ella por cuantos caballeros andantes hay dos maravedís; y sepa que ya me parece que sus saetas me zumban por los oídos (p. 248)]. The Holy Brotherhood is a constant and menacing presence in Part I. Juan Palomeque, the innkeeper, belongs to it, which leads one to believe that troopers and criminals were cut from the same cloth.

But releasing the galley slaves and injuring the guards, while being the gravest offenses, are not the only punishable crimes the knight and (sometimes) his squire commit. Had Don Quijote been brought to trial at the end of Part I, the following list of offenses could have been produced against him. All of them are covered by contemporary Spanish law, and in some of the episodes there is direct allusion to the potential application of specific statutes.

At that first inn, Don Quijote brains with his lance two carriers or muleteers who touched his arms while he is on their vigil. These are serious violent acts. When the first carrier touched Don Quijote's arms, "[He] raising his lance with both hands, bestowed it with such good will upon the carrier's head, that he fell prostrate on the ground, so effectually mauled, that, had the blow been repeated, there would have been no occasion to call a surgeon" (I, 3, p. 18) [alzó la lanza a dos manos y dio con ella tan gran golpe al arriero en la cabeza, que le derribó en el suelo tan maltrecho, que si segundara con otro, no tuviera necesidad de maestro que le curara (p. 58)]. And to the second: "[He] lifting up his lance, failed to break it into pieces on the carrier's head, but not the head itself, which split into four" (I, 3, pp. 18–29) [alzó otra vez la lanza, y, sin hacerla pedazos, hizo más de tres la cabeza del segundo arriero, porque se la abrió por cuatro (pp. 58–59)]. These are, of course, two cases of assault and battery resulting in serious injury.

The episode in which Don Quijote forces Juan Haldudo to stop flogging Andrés is shrouded in legalisms and is one of several in which the issue of justice is at the forefront. Haldudo is not breaking the law by punishing Andrés, though he may be using excessive force. As in the galley slaves episode, Don Quijote acts as judge, but in doing so he has usurped Haldudo's right to deal with his servant and threatened him with physical injury. We will learn later that Don Quijote's actions have had the opposite effect of what he intended, and that in fact Andrés is a kind of pícaro on his way to visit places like those on the first innkeeper's itinerary. In other words, he may very well have been guilty and Haldudo justified in punishing him. Don Quijote's ad hoc seigneurial justice is out of step with current conditions and, in fact, leads to crime. We may remember here the lines from Richard L. Kagan's superb *Lawsuits and Litigants in Castile: 1500–1700* . . . , which seem inspired by this very episode: "By the time Cervantes wrote about a pathetic knight setting out to preserve justice by means of chivalric valor and courageous derring-do, most of his readers would have equaled justice with the world of lawyers, judges, and other 'men of the law.' In this legalistic world, the figure of Don Quixote was not so much a joke as an anachronism. He represented a mythical age in which justice was possible without the help of lawyers and a bevy of legal briefs, but there was no room for an ageing knight errant in the labyrinth of Castile's courts."[10] The irony is not just how ineffectual Don Quijote is, but how his actions to bring about justice are themselves criminal and punishable by law.

The episode with the merchants from Toledo could have led to injury had Rocinante not stumbled, but Don Quijote did attack one of them in a fashion that, in spite of the chivalric models for the adventure, befitted a highway robber. Don Quijote has perpetrated here his first assault in despoblado against innocent and peaceful subjects availing themselves of the king's highway. One of their servants beats him to a pulp in legitimate self-defense, settling the issue without recourse to official justice.

After a brief stay at home and the acquisition of Sancho as squire, Don Quijote attacks the Benedictine friar in the episode that winds up with the battle against the Basque. This is another unprovoked assault: "and without waiting for any other reply, he put spurs to Rocinante, and couching his lance, attacked the first friar with such fury and resolution that, if he had not thrown himself from his mule, he would have come to the ground severely mauled, not without some desperate wound, nay, perhaps stone dead" (I, 8, p. 48) [Y sin esperar más respuesta, picó a Rocinante y, la lanza baja, arremetió contra el primero fraile, con tanta furia y denuedo, que si el fraile no se dejara caer de la mula, él le hiciera venir al suelo mal de su grado, y aun mal ferido, si no cayera muerto (p. 200)].

The fight with the Basque is also punishable by law, as fighting in the open fields and roads—again, despoblado—was a serious offense, and the man sustains severe wounds: "he began to spout blood from his nostrils, mouth and ears" (I, 9, p. 55) [comenzó a echar sangre por las narices y por la boca, y por los oídos (p. 111)]. Sancho knows the gravity of the crime and is quick to suggest seeking sanctuary in a church, the only place safe from the reach of the law: "Sir, said he, I think it would be the wisest course for us to retreat to some church; for, as he with whom you fought remains in a sorry condition, 'tis odd but they inform the Holy Brotherhood of the affair, and have us apprehended: and verily, if they do, before we get out of prison, we may have a chance to sweat for it" (I, 10, pp. 57–58) [—Paréceme, señor, que sería acertado irnos a retraer a alguna iglesia; que, según quedó maltrecho aquel con quien os combatistes, no será mucho que den noticia del caso a la Santa Hermandad y nos prendan; y a fe que si to hacen, que primero que salgamos de la cárcel que nos han de sudar el hopo (p. 113)]. Sancho is referring to being tortured, to which he, but not his noble master, was liable.[11] Sancho's alarm is such that he insists: "I do know that the Holy Brotherhood commonly looks after those who quarrel and fight up and down the country" (I, 10, p. 58) [sólo sé que la Santa Hermandad tiene que ver con los que pelean en el campo (p. 113)].

In the episode with the men from Yanguas and their mares (who are so seductive to Rocinante), which is in parodic contrast with the Marcela and Grisóstomo story and a heavy satire of the courtly love tradition, Don Quijote injures another man: "the knight lent the first he met with such a hearty stroke with his sword, as laid open a leather jacket he wore, together with a large portion of his shoulder" (I, 15, p. 93) [dio don Quijote una cuchillada a uno, que le abrió un sayo de cuero de que venía vestido, con gran parte de la espalda (p. 160)]. The men then proceed to thoroughly beat him, Sancho, and Rocinante and to flee for fear that they too can be hunted down by the Holy Brotherhood. More mayhem follows. Don Quijote kills more than seven sheep in the episode in which he takes the herds for armies of knights. This opens the list of property damage that he causes throughout Part I. The shepherds, in return, rain stones on Don Quijote and leave him for dead, fleeing in a hurry because they, like the men from Yanguas, also fear the Holy Brotherhood.

There follows the adventure of the corpse, in which Don Quijote attacks the men in mourning who are transporting it, knocking one down and breaking his leg. The man claims that by injuring him Don Quijote has committed a great sacrilege and crime because he had already taken orders, alluding to specific statutes of the period. The man accuses Don Quijote of "having laid violent hands on consecrated things" (I, 19, p, 128) [ha puesto mano violenta en cosa sagrada (p. 206)], to which Don Quijote replies with a bit of pettifoggery that reveals his familiarity with the law, "I touched him not with my hands, but with my lance" (p. 152) [no puse las manos sino este lanzón (p. 206)]. To add insult to injury, Sancho plunders the supply ass that the men had with them. Breaking this man's leg is the worst bodily injury that the knight causes in Part I, and whether the victim had actually taken first orders or not, Don Quijote would still be liable for a violent act committed in the open road and at night. Sancho would be prosecuted as a thief.

Next comes the famous episode of the barber's basin, in which the poor fellow is not injured because he jumps off his mount in the nick of time. But Don Quijote steals the basin, which Sancho assesses to be worth a handsome amount. Together with the provisions that they stole from the men with the corpse, Don Quijote and Sancho carry with them booty obtained by violent means on the open road. As with the merchants from Toledo, the Benedictine friars, and the men with the corpse, he has assaulted an innocent subject on the king's highway.

We have already looked closely at the episode in which Don Quijote frees the galley slaves and attacks their keepers, and here we are looking at how it structures the plot of the novel because Don Quijote is pursued and captured as a result. The whole chapter is packed with legalisms and with a very detailed depiction of the functioning of Spain's criminal justice system, which clearly Cervantes knew well firsthand. The episode is not just about the law but about its enforcement, including, of course, deviations from it and institutionalized corruption.

Sancho is the one most keenly aware of the danger they are in because of the seriousness of their offense, which has been against the crown, and not only because it was committed in the open road but because the condemned men were directly under the purview of royal authorities, as were all those assigned to the galleys. (Here domestic and foreign policy coalesced, as the prisoners provided the motive force for ships that enforced the latter.) Sancho provides the legal theory behind the potential sanctions against them. He says that the prisoners are "gente forzada del rey" (p. 236), translated by Smollett as a "chain of slaves compelled by the King to work in the galleys" (I, 22, p. 153), which reflects the legalistic precision of Sancho's words. The squire further explains, like an expert jurist, that "la justicia, que es el mismo rey, no hace fuerza ni agravio a semejante gente, sino que los castiga en pena de sus delitos" (p. 236), rendered thus by Smollett: "justice, which is the king himself, never uses violence nor severity to such people, except as punishment for their crimes" (I, 22, p. 153). Sancho means that the king, in whom natural law is invested, or who incarnates it, is discharging his duties, not acting violently. When the priest catches up with them later and, to vex Don Quijote, tells a tall tale about having been assaulted by the freed prisoners, he corroborates Sancho's legal interpretation. The perpetrator of the crime, he says, "was rebelling against his King and rightful sovereign, by acting contrary to his just commands, in depriving the galleys of their hands, and arousing the Holy Brotherhood, which hath continued so many years in undisturbed repose" (I, 29, p. 241) [quiso defraudar la justicia, ir contra su rey y señor natural, pues fue contra sus justos mandamientos. Quiso, digo, quitar a las galeras sus pies, poner en alboroto a la Santa Hermandad, que había muchos años que reposaba" (p. 344)]. "Rey y señor natural" means exactly that: his power to command issues from natural law. Don Quijote and Sancho, in fact, will from now until the end of Part I become fugitives from justice. They are being pursued both by the priest and barber and by the Holy Brotherhood, with the posses converging at the end to nab the knight.

Don Quijote as fugitive from justice is a major ironic incongruity because of his perceived exemption from the law as an hidalgo and his deranged belief that he is a knight. But at this particular point—the episodes in the Sierra

Morena—his being a fugitive is ironic in three particular ways that engage the overarching presence of penal law in the novel as applied to him. First, Don Quijote flees into the Sierra Morena to do penance for Dulcinea in the manner of chivalric heroes; but it is a penance, as Sancho reminds him, without a motive or reason because Dulcinea was not guilty of the sort of infidelity that Angelica committed in Ariosto's *Orlando furioso*, one of his master's models. Don Quijote also has to make up his own delinquency to justify the penance: his only imaginable fault would be insufficient service to his lady, an infinite debt that is by definition impossible to repay. His is a punishment without a crime—his or his lady's. Second, Don Quijote has, indeed, a genuine and pressing reason to become a fugitive because the Holy Brotherhood is surely after him for actual offenses. The lack of a real motive for penance is ironically counterbalanced by the genuine motive for flight, of which he is oblivious, but that more than justifies it. Don Quijote is a fugitive without a cause, but with a pending cause. Third, he is going to find in the Sierra Morena a mirror image of himself, Cardenio, who has a real reason to do penance because he has been betrayed by Luscinda and also because he has committed various assaults and thefts. He is remorseful too because his cowardice also led to his predicament. When Don Quijote and Cardenio meet they embrace like brothers. The ironic interplay between existent and nonexistent motives or causes is augmented by the Sierra Morena itself as a setting, as a place to expiate real and imaginary guilt—a site for literal rustication.

The Sierra Morena is a true despoblado, in the juridical sense . . . and also a wilderness like the *selva selvaggia* of the *Divine Comedy* and of literary tradition. It is a labyrinth, too, as Javier Herrero has suggested.[12] Solitude and the starkest absence of civilization are its main characteristics, not to mention an inhospitable nature. Cardenio, the quintessential inhabitant of this landscape, is a wild man, with sporadically violent contacts with other human beings. Dorotea, his counterpart in the Sierra Morena, who completes this primal and alienated couple, is dressed as a man, as if to highlight the disorder prevalent in these woods; it is chaos prior to civilization and the separation of the sexes. She has been sexually assaulted by her employer and by the servant who helped her to escape, whom she hurls down a cliff when defending herself. We do not know if he survives. These are dangerous woods. Because of all this lawlessness, the Sierra Morena threatens to become allegorical—abstract in the purity of its lacks and absences and chartable by recourse to systems of thought and belief. But this tendency is counterbalanced by the juridical nature of the despoblado, which gives it a contemporaneous air, a factuality, that withdraws it from the literary and the ideological—it is a space named and classified by the legal codes in all their casuistry and contingency. Outlaws running away from the Holy Brotherhood hide here, not lost pilgrims in search of sublime salvation. Cardenio's and Dorotea's counterparts are the galley slaves, who must be hiding in the very bowels of the earth (as Ginés de Pasamonte put it), in parts not too dissimilar to the Sierra Morena. They must be in despoblados of their own, committing the kind of crime that the priest mentions in his made-up story about them. Like Don Quijote, they are true fugitives from justice, dwelling—confined, rusticated—in some hostile region. Will they be redeemed by this punishment? When Ginés reappears it is to steal Sancho's donkey, but in Part II he has transformed himself into Maese Pedro, master puppeteer, a kind of redemption by art. Don Quijote emerges from the hills ready to take on the hideous giant Pandafilando de la Fosca Vista (Panphilanderer of the Menacing Gaze).

After serving time in the Sierra Morena the conflicts in Part I are resolved, once the characters repair to Juan Palomeque's inn. It is as if their season in the woods had purified them, as if the rustication had led to their conversion to the lawful. At the inn Don Quijote will add to the list of damages that he causes by slashing the wineskins and spilling their contents. But in so doing he slays the ghastly giant Pandafilando de la Fosca Vista and prepares the way for the scene in which justice will be served and order restored by the various marriage vows made or observed. Again, this may contain an allegorical suggestion, except for the grotesqueness of it all and the fact that the giant and the whole story of Princess Micomicona is a hoax. More importantly, the court-like scene at which settlements are reached is, after all, Palomeque's inn, the kind of picaresque abode that opened Part I. The criminal site becomes an improvised courtroom. There is an ironic appropriateness to this, for the inn and picaresque life are the true realms in which Don Quijote has moved and in which he himself will be recognized by the Holy Brotherhood troopers, one of whom

> recollected that among other warrants for apprehending delinquents, he had one against Don Quixote, issued by the Holy Brotherhood, on account of his having set the galley-slaves at liberty, as Sancho had very justly feared. This coming into his head, he was resolved to assure himself, whether or not the knight's person agreed with the description, and pulling out of his bosom a bundle of parchment, he soon found what he sought, and beginning to spell with great deliberation (for he was by no means an expert reader) between every word he fixed his eyes upon the knight, whose visage he compared with the marks specified in the warrant, and discovered beyond all doubt, that he was the very person described. (I, 45, p. 393)

[le vino a la memoria que entre algunos mandamientos que traía
para prender a algunos delincuentes, traía uno contra don Quijote,
a quien la Santa Hermandad había mandado prender por la libertad
que dio a los galeotes, y como Sancho con mucha razón había
temido. Imaginando, pues, esto, quiso certificarse si las señas que
de don Quijote traía venían bien, y sacando del seno un pergamino,
topó con el que buscaba, y poniéndosele a leer de espacio, porque
no era buen lector, a cada palabra que leía ponía los ojos en don
Quijote, y iba cotejando las señas del mandamiento con el rostro de
don Quijote, y halló que sin duda alguna era el que el mandamiento
rezaba. (pp. 527–28)]

The plot's loop is closed—Sancho's prophecy fulfilled—when the document with Don Quijote's arrest warrant is read. (The warrant, by the way, like
the sentences of the galley slaves, is another text mentioned but not reproduced in the novel—we do not get to read it.) The knight's case is closed, as it
were, as his body and the description yield a match. Here we have an instance
where casuistry's program of representation has been successful. It is now up
to the priest to plead, as had the first innkeeper, that because of Don Quijote's
mental condition he will never be convicted, and to ask that the prisoner be
released to him and the barber to return him to his village. Justice is prevailing, not just in the lofty realm in which abstract ideas, theories, and religious
doctrines can be shuffled like cards, but in the real world of warrants, arrests,
and the confinement of bodies. Because it is bodies, not souls, that are at issue
in this fallen world ruled by the law, the priest acts as a lawyer, not in his
capacity as minister of God.

The priest's argument about Don Quijote's immunity by reason of his
insanity is grounded in Spanish law going back to (at least) the *Siete partidas*
in the thirteenth century. For instance: "The same thing that we stated about
minors applies to madmen or those who are devoid of memory, who cannot be
charged for actions committed while they were suffering their derangement";
"We also state that if a man who is mad or devoid of memory, or a minor
of less than ten and a half years of age, killed another man, that he does not
commit any crime because he does not know, nor understand, the fault that
he commits"; "Furthermore, the man who is insane and does not act properly
cannot be charged because he does not know or understand right from wrong"
(Esso mismo [of what is stated about minors], dezimos, que seria del loco, o
del furioso, o del desmemoriado, que lo non pueden acusar de cosa que fiziesse
mientras que le durare la locura; Otrosi dezimos, que si algund ome que fuesse
loco, o desmemoriado, o moço que non fuesse de edad de diez años e medio,
matasse a otro, que no cae porende en pena ninguna: porque non sabe, nin

entiende, el yerro que faze); Otrosi, el ome que es fuera de su seso, non faze nin-
gun fecho endereçadamente: porende non se puede obligar, porque non sabe,
nin entiende, pro ni daño).[13] Closure, in the case of Don Quijote, is brought
about within the limits prescribed by the law. These texts, these *Partidas*, are the
foundation of those in force at the time and are effective in invalidating the one
read by the officer of the Holy Brotherhood. Both function within the system.

It is at the inn too where the barber whose basin was stolen is paid and
the innkeeper recites a list of the expenses incurred by Don Quijote, Sancho, and their mounts, in addition to the substantial damages that they have
caused in their two calamitous visits. The beginning of chapter 46 has the
tone of a court settlement, with the representatives of the Holy Brotherhood
exercising their judicial duties and the various parties' damages paid and, in
the case of the barber, with a document issued to prove it:

> the curate talked so effectually, and the knight himself acted such
> extravagances, that the troopers must have been more mad than he
> if they had not plainly perceived his defect; therefore they thought
> proper to be satisfied, and even performed the office of mediators
> betwixt the barber and Sancho Panza, who still maintained the fray
> with great animosity; for, the troopers, as limbs of justice, brought
> the case to an arbitration, and decided it in such a manner, as left
> both parties, if not fully satisfied, at least in some sort content with
> the determination, which was, that the pack-saddles should be
> exchanged, but the girths and halters remain as they were. With
> regard to Mambrino's helmet, the curate, unperceived by Don
> Quixote, took the barber aside, and paid him eight reals for the
> basin, taking a receipt in full, that cleared the knight from any
> suspicion of fraud, from thence forward, for ever, amen.... The
> innkeeper, who took particular notice of the full satisfaction which
> the barber had received from the curate, demanded payment of
> Don Quixote for the damage he had done to the bags, and the
> loss of his wine, swearing that neither Rocinante nor Sancho's ass
> should stir from the stable until he should be satisfied to the last
> farthing. The curate pacified the landlord, and Don Fernando paid
> the bill, although the judge very sincerely offered to take that upon
> himself. In this manner, universal concord was restored, so that the
> inn no longer represented the disorder in King Agramante's camp,
> but rather the peace and quiet that reigned in the time of Octavius
> Caesar: and this blessing was generally ascribed to the laudable
> intention and great eloquence of the priest, together with the
> incomparable generosity of Don Fernando. (I, 46, pp. 395–96)

[En efecto, tanto les supo el cura decir, y tantas locuras supo don
Quijote hacer, que más locos fueran que no él los cuadrilleros si
no conocieran la falta de don Quijote; y así, tuvieron por bien
apaciguarse, y aun de ser medianeros de hacer las paces entre el
barbero y Sancho Panza, que todavía asistían con gran rancor a su
pendencia. Finalmente, ellos, como miembros de justicia, mediaron
la causa y fueron árbitros della, de tal modo, que ambas partes
quedaron, si no del todo contentas, a lo menos en algo satisfechas,
porque se trocaron las albardas, y no las cinchas y jáquimas; y en
lo que tocaba a lo del yelmo de Mambrino, el cura, a socapa y sin
que don Quijote lo entendiese, le dio por la bacía ocho reales, y el
barbero le hizo una cédula de recibo y de no llamarse a engaño por
entonces, no por siempre jamás amén. . . . El ventero, a quien no se
le pasó por alto la dádiva y recompensa que el cura había hecho al
barbero, pidió el escote de don Quijote, con el menoscabo de sus
cueros y falta de vino jurando que no saldría de la venta Rocinante,
ni el jumento de Sancho, sin que se le pagase primero hasta el
último ardite. Todo lo apaciguó el cura, y lo pagó don Fernando,
puesto que el oidor, de muy buena voluntad, había también ofrecido
la paga; y de tal manera quedaron todos en paz y sosiego, que ya no
parecía la venta la discordia del campo de Agramante, como don
Quijote había dicho, sino la misma paz y quietud del tiempo de
Octaviano; de todo lo cual fue común opinión que se debían dar las
gracias a la buena intención y mucha elocuencia del señor cura y la
incomparable liberalidad de don Fernando. (pp. 530–31)]

The priest has argued his case well and has taken care of the proper
compensations. Restitution is a form of resolution, an ending of sorts, a kind
of closure provided by the legal cast of the plot rather than by a literary device
drawn from narrative tradition. The innkeeper and his wife are "made whole,"
as it were, as was the second barber. But there are others, like the shepherds
and the man whose leg was broken, who are not compensated for their losses
or injuries.

Part II of the novel, which is among various other things a profound
commentary of Part I, with episodes sometimes matching ones from the first
part as direct rewritings, has what I take to be a hilarious and complicated
gloss on this scene of reparations at the inn. I am referring to the aftermath
of Don Quijote's destruction of Maese Pedro's puppet show (II, 26), when
the knight is made to pay for every figurine smashed, with the award being
established according to the rank of the character each represents in the story
and the amount of damage inflicted to the object itself. This is a brilliant

passage in which literary characters acquire concrete existence, but only as figures in a puppet show, and while their injuries are reduced to the material damage done to their images, their status in the fiction also determines their worth. There are faint traces here of contemporary debates about religious images, but more to the point the fiction in Part I, shrouded in a legal mantle and resolved in a trial-like scene, is brought down to a miniaturized but real drama involving restitution in a manner that involves both fiction and the most trivial reality. It is as if Cervantes were saying that, indeed, the conflicts in Part I were of a judicial nature but transformed into literature to such a degree that they can be represented by this blatantly fictitious puppet theater. In short, this episode is a parody of Part I that underlines the literary role that reparations play. Cervantes, as is often the case, preempts critical commentary, such as mine here.

After the reparations the charade to cage Don Quijote for the return home is organized. This is another masterstroke, by which the knight will be punished but on his own terms, at the level of fiction. Don Quijote will still engage in two more violent acts: his fight with the goatherd and the attack on those carrying an image of the Virgin. But the overall pattern of injury, damage, judgment, and restitution is closed at the inn.

Two patterns have emerged from the foregoing. One is the overall story of crime, pursuit, capture, and confinement of Don Quijote, with the attendant plot of damages and restitution. The other is the one of rustication and redemption, or correction and reform, involving Don Quijote and the characters in the Sierra Morena. Both intersect at the inn, which is transformed from picaresque emporium into court of justice, with priests, policemen, judges, assessments of damages, negotiated settlements, and conscription. What gives shape to the *Quijote*, Part I are these underlying legal stories and the gradual merging of pícaro and knight to create a protagonist that will endure in the history of the novel: one caught in the net of the law, which confines him as it defines him and gives him social and ontological substance.

Notes

1. Chaves, *Relación de la cárcel de Sevilla*.
2. As quoted in *Volumen complementario*, p. 275.
3. See John M. Hill, *Voces germanescas, recogidas y ordenadas* (Bloomington: Indiana University Press Publications in the Humanities, 1949).
4. See Henry Louis Gates, Jr. *The Signifying Monkey: A Theory of Afro-American Literary Criticism* (New York: Oxford University Press, 1988), and Jorge Mañach, *Indagción del choteo*, 2nd. ed. (Havana: La Verónica, 1940 [1928]).
5. Northrop Frye, *Anatomy of Criticism: Four Essays* (New York: Atheneum, 1966 [1957]).

6. Though there are debates about the exact date of composition of the book, it can be safely said that the story had circulated in manuscript in the decades prior to its publication. The bibliography on this topic is endless. The best studies are to my mind Claudio Guillén, "Toward a Definition of the Picaresque" and "Genre and Countergenre: The Discovery of the Picaresque," in his *Literature as System* (Princeton: Princeton University Press, 1971), pp. 71–106 and 135–58; Fernando Lázaro Carreter, *Lazarillo de Tormes en la novela picaresca* (Barcelona: Ariel, 1972); Parker, *Literature and the Delinquent*; and my own "The Life and Adventures of Cipión: Cervantes and the Picaresque," in *Celestina's Brood*, pp. 45–65.

7. Salillas, "La criminalidad y la penalidad en el *Quijote*."

8. Ibid. See "Pícaro," in Joan Corominas's *Diccionario crítico etimológico castellano e hispánico*, cuarta reimpresión (Madrid: Gredos, 1997), 4, pp. 520–23.

9. A. R. Nykl, "Pícaro," *Revue hispanique* 77 (192–9), pp. 171–86. Nykl refutes this theory, which had been advanced by De Haan.

10. Kagan, *Lawsuits and Litigants*, p. 127.

11. Martínez Díez, "La tortura judicial en la legislación histórica española."

12. Javier Herrero, "Sierra Morena as Labyrinth: From Wildness to Christian Knighthood," *Forum for Modern Language Studies* 27, no. 1 (1981), pp. 55–67.

13. The quotes are from *Las siete partidas*, Serena partida, título I, ley 9; Setena partida, título VIII, ley 3; Setena partida, título XXXIV, ley 4.

MANUEL DURÁN and FAY R. ROGG

Constructing Don Quixote

Because there were few ancient Greek and Roman models to imitate in the field of fiction, Renaissance writers were forced to be original. In his effort to conceive the modern novel, Cervantes showed ambition, imagination, and tenacity. His novel is one of the longest produced in his generation, and it is the most audacious in terms of its structure and its characters, which seem so spontaneous that we do not think of them as an author's creation as the novel unfolds before us. No wonder, then, that *Don Quixote* has influenced profoundly so many other works in the following centuries.

Who Is the Author?
In the preface of *Don Quixote*, Cervantes beckons us to enter the enchanted world of his novel. There in the novel we find him, the author, with a "friend," or rather an acquaintance, or perhaps a stranger: Cide Hamete Benengeli, a mysterious Moorish historian. Hamete has written the "true" history of Don Quixote and Sancho, and Cervantes has helped by finding his manuscript, which becomes the story that is told to us. Thus, from the beginning, we receive mixed signals and contradictory instructions. "Some assembly required" could be the slogan for the novel. Cervantes appears again later in his novel. By writing himself into the story, he has created the first "self-aware" novel, with important consequences for novels that

From *Fighting Windmills: Encounters with Don Quixote*, pp. 57–81. © 2006 by Yale University.

91

followed, as the critic Robert Alter has observed. Cervantes breaks new ground when his novel calls attention to itself, that is, becomes a self-referential work of art. Who wrote it? Who translated it? Where and how was the text we are reading really written? Certainly Cervantes is jesting and toying with his reader, but we are given to understand that the text was written in Arabic by Cide Hamete, and we are told that Moorish historians lie or at least exaggerate most of the time. What about the person who trans-lated Hamete's work? Did he really know Arabic? Did anyone look over his translation? And where is the rest of the text of the novel? Abruptly, in the middle of an adventure, in part 1, chapter 9, we have to pause, the action is frozen and the two rivals of that adventure are paralyzed, their swords still in the air, because we have run out of text.

This device, of pausing the narrative while searching for the lost manu-script, is an example of how Cervantes distances himself in order to provide perspective to full advantage and with dramatic impact. The technique of opening up the scope of the novel may remind us of the reason why medieval cathedrals—as opposed to the Romanesque cathedrals—have high vaults. The windows are now two stories high so that more light comes through. Similarly, Cervantes, by creating a second author, opens up the novel to a larger perspective and also to some confusion. Further, in doing so, he creates suspense. In other words, the technique has two aims: perspective and dra-matic effect. We are familiar with it in many examples offered by popular lit-erature, even in such early Hollywood movies as *The Perils of Pauline*. Perhaps a character whom we have come to like or admire finds himself or herself in a dangerous predicament. Suddenly the movie reel ends with Pauline tied to the railroad tracks; the train is about to arrive at great speed, and she is in mortal danger. We are left in suspense and will have to wait a while, perchance a whole week, until a young savior arrives and frees Pauline in the nick of time. This is what happens in chapters 8 and 9 of part 1, where Don Quixote and a Basque opponent are about to do battle. Swords are unsheathed and raised, blows are about to fall. But ... the manuscript that tells our story ends here, and we will have to wait until Cervantes, by chance, finds the rest of it, in the shop of a Toledo merchant who is using it as wrapping paper.

Why should we believe an Arab historian when he casts doubt about a chapter of the novel? To complicate things further, where did Cide Hamete Benengeli obtain the information included in that chapter? Is the whole chapter a lie? Is the initial statement a lie? Who can tell us where to find the truth? Cide Hamete is troubling because he introduces a germ of doubt in the process of creating the novel: "he is both the untruthful author from whom Cervantes distances himself in order to judge the work that he himself is in the process of writing, and at the same time the scrupulous historian who reveals to the reader his effort to capture his hero in all their fullness, thus making the reader enter into the very act of literary creation."[1]

We see the superimposed and almost invisible threads by which Cervantes moves his characters—and when we begin to suspect that the threads lead to Cervantes, we find the author has momentarily eluded us and we are facing the Arab historian, Hamete Benengeli, who is, as an Arab historian, totally unreliable. At moments like these we realize Cervantes's novel has become self-conscious and includes in many mysterious ways powerful allusions to itself, to its author, and to the art of writing novels, including criticism of literature in general.

We search in vain for anything as complex in the other novels of that time. We must wait until much later to find anything resembling Cervantes's games, for his labyrinth of mirrors is almost impossible to duplicate. At the beginning of the second part of the novel, Don Quixote learns about a just-published book describing his recent adventures. He worries: how accurate is this book? Is he being portrayed in a false or indecent light?

Don Quixote is about to become a reader of the first part of *Don Quixote*. The self-referential novel is a conspicuous topic of contemporary literature. Cervantes pioneered it three centuries earlier.

Historical Versus Poetic "Truth"

One of the goals pursued by Cervantes in his novel is to separate, in the mind of his readers, history from poetry (including in this category the romances of chivalry, legends, and popular versions of the past). History is an honest and objective account of the past. Poetry, interpreted as encompassing not only poems but also fiction that mixes romance, legends, and supernatural, fantastic, irrational beings and situations, may be extremely popular but is essentially a beautiful lie and in most cases, a serious distortion of reality, an adulteration or negation of everyday experience. Common sense, plain, careful observation, and in a few cases the controlled observation and analysis of the beginnings of modern science refute the distortions and fantastic depictions of both legends and romances of chivalry. A knight who has been cut in two by the mighty sword of his adversary cannot be put back together by such a magic concoction as the Balm of Fierabras. A man is not made of cardboard; it is impossible to glue together his broken halves.

Enchanters, wizards, even one of the greatest of all wizards, Merlin, appear in the pages of the novel. They are there to explain, from Don Quixote's viewpoint, why his adventures do not turn into victories the way they should. Merlin is, surely, a ruse to entrap Don Quixote into new, frantic efforts to disenchant Dulcinea; as a deus ex machina Merlin is not totally convincing, yet Don Quixote seems to take to heart the wizard's instructions. The very absence of magic as such, magic as accepted by the author and the characters in a novel full of adventures, indicates a new turn of mind, favorable to science and common sense, unfavorable to magic and superstition.

Thus Cervantes bewilders us. He tells us that history is an effort to find out the truth. On one hand, fiction has its own rules. This praise of history, this avowed superiority of history over fiction, is given to us in a work of fiction—which, on the other hand, claims to be the narrative of true historical facts. Before we decide what is the precise message Cervantes wants to convey, we should perhaps assume Cervantes is toying with his readers and disregard his convoluted message altogether. We bear in mind that Cervantes was acquainted, directly or indirectly, with Plato's ideas about poetry (that is, in this context, fiction, novels) and scientific and philosophical truth. In *The Republic* Plato proposes to exile the poets because they embellish reality to the point of lying and thus cannot be accepted as intellectual leaders of the community. Much has been written about Aristotle's influence on Cervantes's ideas about literature, yet Plato may have had the last word: the search for truth is to be preferred to a poetic embellishment of human lives and human experience. "History is like a sacred thing; it must be truthful" (Gr., 479).

After such enthusiastic praise of history and historians, we come suddenly to a contradictory and defiant remark. History is our guide to truth and historians are truth's faithful servants, but the author of the present historical narrative may be less than perfect; even more, he may be seriously at fault; he may have left out some of the most glorious deeds of the tale's hero: "In this account I know there will be found everything that could be rightly desired in the most pleasant history, and if something of value is missing from it, in my opinion the fault lies with the dog who was its author rather than with any defect in its subject" (Gr., 68–69). Almost at the same time, Cervantes praises history and historians but makes us suspicious of the historian whose work we are now reading, and there is no doubt that, having spent five sad years as a slave in Muslim Algiers, he is fully aware that the word "dog" applied to our Arab historian is one of the worst insults available in the Muslim culture.

We are beginning to suspect Cervantes is giving his readers contradictory and ambiguous messages. Distrusting text written by a historian could ultimately result in casting doubt upon the historian's sources, viewpoints, and techniques in establishing the truth. If historical truth cannot be firmly established, what are the consequences?

Language and Its Implications

According to Michel Foucault, Cervantes should be recognized as opening new vistas and creating a new way of looking at the world that teaches us to look into the meaning of words as they relate to things. As Carroll B.

Johnson notes, Foucault, in *The Order of Things*, reminds us that modern linguistic science has shown conclusively that "there is no inherent, organic similarity between the word and whatever it stands for . . . but in Cervantes's time the arbitrary nature of the linguistic sign had not been discovered. In fact, the professional linguists of the sixteenth century assumed an organic relation. Michel Foucault considers that Cervantes had in effect discovered the arbitrary relation of word to thing, that language is related not so much to things as to mental processes, and by so doing ushered in the modern age."[2] If we assume, as many scholars did in medieval and Renaissance times, that a word designating a thing was a spiritual emanation or projection of that thing, words could become so closely intertwined with the object they designated that no personal interpretation would be possible.

Don Quixote and Sancho disagree almost all the time about the world around them because each one of them interprets what he sees according to a code. This code is based on the individual, his culture, his experience, a worldview that can be very special, and many other factors: thus the multiplicity of viewpoints and interpretations.

Don Quixote has internalized all the messages of the romances of chivalry; he sees the whole world through them. He is bound to disagree with Sancho, who sees things through a different lens, using a different code. Linguistic relativism, as discussed by Leo Spitzer, is related to a deeper phenomenon: people react to language according to cultural patterns that have been etched in their minds and are still being etched and developed during their life experiences. A sound reading of Cervantes's novel will validate the interpretation of everyday life by the characters in the novel, who in turn represent all of us, in our interpretation of the words, signs, and symbols around them. No longer will language be anchored in a solid, unbreakable relation with "things," with the world outside us. Privileged by this newfound freedom, we can defend individual interpretations and freedoms, and instead of a rigid definition of our duties and our place in the world, a new space is created where dialogue will replace the dictatorial powers of the past.

Human beings are not passive vessels waiting to be filled with words that link them to things. They are active decoders of language, signs, and symbols. Emotions may compel one person to interpret a word or a sign in a subjective way. Words like "freedom," "happiness," "privacy," and "honor" have different meanings in different cultures. Languages are not the only example of codes or signifying systems. Sancho and Don Quixote both speak Spanish, but often they use words in a different way. Don Quixote's vocabulary is much larger than Sancho's, and it also contains many words that were old-fashioned and hard for the average Spaniard of that time to understand. Moreover, Don Quixote often reacts to stimuli in a peculiar way because he associates what he sees or hears with events he has read about in his beloved romances of chivalry. Today we continue to use natural languages to communicate with each other, but we have added other systems of signs and symbols. As Carroll B. Johnson observes, "we use artificial languages such as Morse code, musical notation, shorthand, and BASIC. We are surrounded by myriad visual signs whose meaning is established by reference to agreed-upon codes. The red light means 'stop,' the green means 'go.' But at sea the same red and green lights mean 'left' and 'right,' respectively. Back in port, the red light means something else. . . . The entire world presents itself as a giant text to be read, by Don Quixote and by all the rest of us."[3]

Who Is Don Quixote?

"I know who I am," Don Quixote states early in the novel. Here he manages to define himself, his mind, his quest, his ambitions, and his love; he will be faithful to himself until the end. We seem to hear an echo of Polonius's famous advice, "This above all: To thine own self be true." The readers also get to know Don Quixote and Sancho as one would know old friends from high school. Cervantes does not make any of his main or secondary characters betray themselves. We know what to expect, and this is why we can notice important changes in the psychology of both Sancho and Don Quixote toward the end of the novel. Their adventures and misadventures mature them. They slowly evolve, visibly aging, and Sancho becomes surer of himself. All the while we witness the crisscrossing of viewpoints and opinions, a constant readjusting of perspectives with each character striving to have his view prevail yet at the same time being subtly influenced by the attitudes of other characters. No man is an island in Cervantes's novel; each character changes slowly and is enriched by the presence and influence of other characters. In other words, he creates characters who strive to seek freedom and a better knowledge of themselves, not—as in many medieval works—to illustrate certain moral norms. Cervantes's novel can be placed historically between two great waves of didactic-moralizing literature, the first in medieval times anchored in Christian morality and the second during the Counter-Reformation as a reaction against Renaissance uncertainty or skepticism. Briefly, a didactic work presents a problematic situation that will be solved by one or more characters in a right or wrong way, and the result will be underlined in an explicit statement of the moral of the story (as in many fables) or else will be implicit because it is crystal clear. Literature is thus placed at the service of a given ideology. The closest we come to didacticism in *Don Quixote* is the tale of "The Man Who Was Recklessly Curious," but the atmosphere of this tale is very different from the rest of the novel. Anselmo, driven by an unhealthy curiosity, with no goals or clear purpose, totally differs from Don Quixote and his quest. In a heroic and sustained effort, our knight wants to prove that human life can be as beautiful and fulfilling as a literary work or, to be precise, as beautiful and fulfilling as a romance of chivalry. Every one of his thoughts and actions brings him closer to his ideal: to live like a new hero of a literary work and to resemble, for instance, Amadís of Gaul, the greatest hero of chivalry romances.

Foucault caught a glimpse of that important aspect of our knight's personality, although the identification with the romances of chivalry does not take into account the times when Don Quixote acts like everybody else. His folly is intermittent and flares up only at certain moments, while the impressions of the external world can be equated, by an effort of the will, with the characters, situations, and objects found in the romances of chivalry. Don Quixote's adventures are the highlights of the novel, but if we count the intervals between one adventure and those that follow, we come to realize that many hours pass during which Don Quixote's mind approaches normalcy. Still, we must agree with Foucault: "His adventures will be a deciphering of the world: a diligent search over the entire surface of the earth for the forms that will prove that what the books say is true. Each exploit must be a proof: it consists, not in a real triumph—which is why history is not really important—but in an attempt to transform reality into a sign. Don Quixote reads the world in order to prove his books."[4]

The books in Don Quixote's library are mainly about heroes whom he wishes to emulate. He finds, however, that he stumbles, and his imperfect acts point to a flawed hero. A flawed hero is easier to approach, easier to understand, and above all easier to identify with. Perhaps more important, a flawed hero is believable, as we are all aware that flawless heroes are either nonexistent or very rare. Even such traditional epic heroes as Achilles were provided by their creators with at least one weak spot: for Achilles it was his heel, and also, psychologically, his hubris. The Teutonic hero Sigfried had a vulnerable spot in his back where a leaf prevented the dragon's blood from bathing his skin with its protective magic powers.

Our knight embodies many traits characteristic of famous heroes. He is above all brave; he defies giants or what he thinks are giants, whether windmills or wine skins; he does not hesitate to enter the lions' cage; he does battle with the Knight of the Mirrors and wins, and with the Knight of the White Moon and is defeated. He is also praiseworthy for his efforts to fight for justice. What we like most about him is his effort to reach out to others, establishing links of solidarity with other people, whether they are weak ones he wants to protect or the one and only perfect, exquisite beauty, paradigm of grace, harmony, and intelligence, Dulcinea, the idealized, sublime woman who continues in his mind the illustrious family of idealized women like Dante's Beatrice and Petrarch's Laura. Don Quixote believes in pure, essential, Platonic, Romantic (*avant la lettre*) love, and this belief lifts him far above all other characters in the novel. It is so deep and sustaining that he accepts death when he cannot proclaim it, having lost his final battle. His world is not only a world of love and beauty, it is also a perfectible world, since the courage of knights errant can win all the battles against injustice and ugly aggression from giants and monsters.

It is true that our admiration for him is tempered by our laughter at his ridiculous efforts, which end always or almost always in defeat, his lack of acceptance of his limited strength, and his constant mistakes and misunderstandings. Any reader who has enjoyed the films of Stan Laurel and Oliver Hardy recognizes in Cervantes's novel many of the essential characteristics of basic slapstick. Pride, they say, comes before a fall; we can surmise that frustration follows, which is what happens to Don Quixote and Sancho throughout the novel. Whether it is a helmet, or windmills, or wine skins, Don Quixote's efforts are frustrated. His will and his imagination are powerless against the resistance of real life represented by the objects, and the knight is ignominiously defeated by things, or rather by his miscalculation about things, their real being, their resistance and stubborn opposition to his will. Living beings are also stubborn. Sheep and pigs frustrate him, refuse to behave like enemy armies, confound and humiliate him by simply being flocks of sheep and herds of pigs. How can we respect and admire a hero when we laugh at his mistakes, his clumsy powerlessness when facing familiar objects and situations?

The heroic and flawed heroic characteristics of Don Quixote make for the paradox that may explain why the readers' opinions about our knight have varied so much from one century to another, and from one critical school to the next. Janus-like, he offers admirable traits followed immediately by serious errors of judgment. His resolve and his courage are undeniable. If we want to understand the scope of his efforts, we should not forget that he has lived for years, in his imagination, in the enchanted realm of the romances of chivalry, books where men and women are endowed with nobility, valor, grace, elegance, devotion, and heroism.

Like a butterfly from a chrysalis, Don Quixote emerges from his mediocre past with bright colors and a strange costume, ready to leave his friends and neighbors behind, ready to fly away. One day he looks around in his own backyard in his village and finds nothing that can compare with his readings. Surely the real world has sunk very low; certainly something must be done to lift it to a higher level. Don Quixote mounts his horse and goes forth. We know, as his readers, that he will fail time and again in his quest for justice. But should he not have tried? Should no one have tried to bring a little justice, a little beauty, a little love to a sad world? If we want to understand him, let us imagine spending several days or weeks in a great museum in Athens or Cairo soaking up the majesty of Greek statues, the elegance of Egyptian reliefs, and then going out to look at the people walking in the streets of Athens or Cairo. A strange feeling of melancholy or depression may torment us. We would like the passers-by to be perfect, as elegant as their idealization inside the museum. If we could do something to change reality, that would be our quest.

Because we admire his courage and his good will but laugh at his repeated failures and his lack of contact with the real world, he is for us a flawed hero and as such creates mixed and ambiguous feelings. Instead of placing his main character on a pedestal, as the writers of chivalry romances did, Cervantes paints a Don Quixote with obvious weaknesses, yet at the same time endowed with courage, high ideals, a vast knowledge in many fields of learning, and unrivalled eloquence. It is up to the reader to decide which side of the knight to emphasize in his or her mind.

A Psychological Approach

Cervantes's characters unfold and develop through both action and thought. We can almost guess what they are thinking. They react incessantly either to what they see and hear or to their inner thoughts, intent upon reaching goals that act like a beacon or perhaps like a red cape, exciting the wild bull inside each one of us. Even their long dialogues, their ceaseless conversations, are full of excitement and help us understand their inner thoughts, their dreams, and their secrets. We are constantly in and out of the characters' minds. It can be said that Cervantes is the true creator of the psychological novel, in spite of the fact that superficially what we read resembles a novel of action, an endless adventure unfolding through travels in space, that is, a "western-and-travelogue" novel. The most intriguing hints learned from this novel are that the most fulfilling adventures take place in the human heart, imagination, and consciousness. In the second part of the novel when Cervantes allows us to take a look at Don Quixote's dream world and uncovers the knight's subconscious, thus anticipating Freud by several centuries, we feel that a new layer of knowledge, and of doubts, has been added to the previous ones, making his world and ours more dramatic and more problematic.

This significant and highly original aspect of Cervantes's novel further defines and explains the personality of the main characters, in this instance that of Don Quixote as revealed in his dream during his descent to the Cave of Montesinos. Dreams have fascinated people for centuries and are present in some of the world's oldest texts, for example, the pharaoh's dream interpreted by Joseph in the Old Testament. Latin literature has contributed

Scipio's dream, complete with a trip to the moon and a vision of the future of the Roman Empire. Yet the difference between these dreams and Don Quixote's dream is essential. Most dreams coming to us from ancient times are either revelations about the future or premonitions of future disasters or coming successes. Not so with Don Quixote's dream; in it our hero is deeply troubled by his role in life and in history and especially worried about Dulcinea, who asks him for money, offering as security her undershirt. We inhabit for a few hours an underworld where the characters are distortions of their previous heroic selves. This degraded vision shows us how the subconscious mind of Don Quixote is much less sure of his role in the world and of the moral qualities of the woman he loves. Nothing similar can be found in Renaissance literature. Many years will pass before literature and, let us add, psychology will be able to exploit dreams as one of the most important tools for revealing humankind's deep secrets. The great Spanish nineteenth-century novelist Benito Pérez Galdós, who admired Cervantes, was one of the first to make extensive use of dreams in his novels, not as portents of future events but as windows into the deep areas of his characters. In contemporary letters we find dreamlike short stories by Jorge Luis Borges and Julio Cortázar in the Hispanic world, as well as similar texts in the many literatures inspired by surrealism.

We find especially remarkable the chapters where a character shifts his viewpoint and proceeds to interpret the outside world in an unexpected way. We find an important example of such changes in part 1, chapter 35, the wineskins fiasco, and in the chapters about the Cave of Montesinos, part 1, chapters 22–23. Sancho and other secondary characters are specifically affected by the happenings in these scenes, while the visions of Don Quixote during his descent into the Cave of Montesinos reveal significant changes in the subconscious mind of our hero. It is not in vain that most modern critics find part 2 more intense and more pathetic than part 1. Cervantes is slowly leading us to the climax of his novel in the last chapters of part 2. Jean Cassou, Leo Spitzer, and José Ortega y Gasset underline the importance of perspectivism in Cervantes's novels as a whole and relate it to the ambiguity and proliferation of viewpoints during Renaissance times. In drawing and painting, the laws of perspective, ignored during classical and medieval times, gained a firm foothold in Italian and Flemish art in the early Renaissance and spread to other European countries. These laws clearly underline that the vision of a landscape or a palace interior will change if the artist or the spectator is displaced right or left, up or down. Much depends on the point of view of whoever is describing a place or an event. Knowledge increases, almost exponentially, and at the same time certitude seems to elude even the most competent observers. Rigid medieval principles are vanishing, "but reason is specific, and experience limited. By a curious *boomerang* trick, reality becomes less certain the better it is known. Man has discovered Nature, but he is also discovering his own mental powers. And God, who used to establish a fixed bond between the two, has retired from the scene."[5] Reality changes according to the viewpoint of each spectator. Must we believe Don Quixote or Sancho? Must we believe the duke and the duchess or Sansón Carrasco? Thus the problem of appearance versus reality is placed at the core of everyday life.

Cervantes's Vibrant Dialogue

We are soon aware that the conversations between Don Quixote and Sancho constitute the almost impossible contact and mutual influence of two different kinds of culture. Sancho cannot read. His culture is totally oral; it has come to him by oral transmission from older generations. Sancho and Don Quixote frequently disagree, and their disagreement is often funny since it reveals a weakness on either side, most often on Sancho's, because he is revealed as an ignoramus. Yet, as Harry Levin points out, "Now, on the comic stage, Sancho would have the final word. In the pictorial vision of Daumier, the pair coexist within the same frame of reference as the bourgeoisie and the caricatured intellectuals. Yet in a book, where words are the only medium, Don Quixote enjoys a decided advantage; the very weakness of his position in life lends strength, as it were, to his position in literature; in the field of action he may encounter discomfiture, but in the verbal sphere he soon resumes his imaginary career."[6]

Sancho is cunning, and moreover he is backed by common sense and an oral tradition that is centuries old. His point of view is restated many times, yet Don Quixote ignores it or argues successfully against it. He is aware that Sancho is an uneducated peasant and has had no contact with the beautiful texts of epic poems and chivalry romances.

It is hard to find reliable statistics about literacy in Spain during the sixteenth and seventeenth centuries. Probably in some parts of rural Spain the percentage of illiterate adults could have been as high as 80 percent. "Nevertheless, at times it begins to look as though all mankind were composed of two overlapping classes: readers and writers. It seems as if from behind every roadside bush and every wooded hill another author is waiting to spring out, clutching a sheaf of verses; even a dangerous convict is busy planning the second part of his autobiography as he marches off to the galleys; and the unlooked-for pleasures a traveler may find in the attic of his inn are as likely to be a trunk full of books as the embraces of a hospitable serving girl."[7]

It would not be difficult to describe many pages of Cervantes's novel as a duel between two types of culture, the learned culture of books versus the traditional oral culture. Sancho misunderstands many statements made by his master because he does not understand key words, a result of his restricted vocabulary. Don Quixote usually has the last word, but the reader often has the impression that oral, traditional culture is closer to common sense and worthy of respect.

Cervantes knew that ordinary life is complex and subject to change from one second to the next; it is made up of intricate exchanges and highly complex relationships. It involves the subjective judgment of people who face each other, who interact with each other, and the outcome of such face-to-face relationships is always in doubt. Other writers before him may have intuited this basic psychological truth, but only Cervantes gave it full play in his novel. We all need codes for deciphering the world. Don Quixote stubbornly rejects any code except the one he has found in the romances of chivalry. Thus result the misunderstandings that will make him clash with other characters in the novel. Each character has to interpret the outside world through a vast series of filters and connections that refer back to personal previous experiences, memories, and cultural data.

The importance of dialogue in Cervantes must be underlined because it is at the core of the novel, and also because dialogue in itself assumes the need to communicate with our fellow humans and the possibility that this need will bring harmony to our relationships. In essence, dialogue is the antithesis of authoritarian control, of tyranny, in which the orders flow from above to those below, who must listen and obey and above all must not speak back or object. Throughout the novel Sancho objects to most of his master's renderings of facts and actions that follow such interpretations. What makes this dialogue possible is that although Don Quixote possesses a great deal of authority—he is the master, the senior figure, the wealthy one, and a man endowed with a vast culture in comparison to the very poor, almost destitute Sancho—the facts and common sense are usually on Sancho's side. Therefore, the contenders are, in a way, well matched, and the dialogue is not stifled by having one of the parties silence and crush the other party. On the contrary, the match can last a long time and yield moments of lucid merriment. Gerald Brenan comments that Cervantes "is a master—and what a great one!—of the art of dialogue. It was only to be expected that he should have done this well, because one of the particular pleasures to be derived from his book comes from the continual victories we witness of words over facts."[8] As the narrative unfolds, some new situation arises that we know or guess Don Quixote will manage to interpret in accordance with his peculiar fantasy and his general view of the world, "and we wait to see how he will do it. Then, no sooner has his interpretation been given than the inevitable insurmountable objection is made by Sancho or some other person, and at once the question is how he will get round it. That he always does so, and far better than one could have hoped, and in quite unsuspected ways, is due not only to his ingenuity in argument, supported by the wide range of his mind and reading, but to his remarkable rhetorical powers. The knight, who loses every time he takes to the sword, wins a battle whenever he opens his mouth."[9]

A dialogue always assumes a certain degree of equality between the speakers. The opposite of a dialogue is the sermon, the harangue, the official speech. We should not forget that Plato, presumably inspired by Socrates, in Athens invented dialogue as a literary genre during a period when democracy flourished and diverse opinions were being discussed in public. A parliamentary democracy is based on dialogue. Cervantes's Spain was strictly divided into classes, and this sociological rigidity made dialogue across class lines extremely difficult. Cervantes created a situation in his novel that required a constant crossing of class lines in the continuing dialogue between Don Quixote and Sancho. It would be hard or perhaps impossible to find a similar situation in prose writings, in Spain or elsewhere, during most of the seventeenth century. It is true that the Spanish plays of that period made a place for dialogues in which a servant, usually a "funny man," the *gracioso*, would criticize the behavior of the young nobles or members of the middle class. This group of plays, under the umbrella name of "comedia," was a genre favored by Lope de Vega and other playwrights of that time. The *gracioso*'s criticism was on the whole disregarded by the play's main characters; he could not possibly understand the motivations and values of the members of the upper classes, and therefore what the Spanish plays offered was a "dialogue of the deaf" since real contact between social classes was deemed impossible by both playwrights and the public at large.

A Philosophical Approach

There is still another way in which Cervantes's novel has made inroads in literature. The main characters, and also the secondary ones, are often transfixed by a sense of wonder. What do they see? Is it real or a fiction of their imagination? How can they agree about what is real and what is not? How can they tell the difference between what seems to be real and what is totally, positively real? For Don Quixote it is exasperating that strange transformations change dramatically what he sees, or thinks he sees, into something totally different. Who is masking reality? How can we reach to the bottom of what exists? These are questions that have fascinated philosophers and thinkers of all ages. The birth of modern science and modern philosophy has made them more urgent. Both Descartes and Kant respond to similar questions. Descartes thinks that even if an "evil geni" like the ones Don Quixote feels are tormenting him could change what we see through our senses, there is a God who guarantees the reality of the world in which we live. For Kant the situation has become more precarious; we are no longer sure to penetrate deeply into things, into the "real reality" of things.

Both Cervantes and Descartes take part in a new approach to our interpretation of the world that we see. In both cases we discern a presence, often ambiguous, of two opposed attitudes: the supernatural versus the common-sense approach. Common sense is the common denominator of Sancho Panza, as well as the curate, the barber, and all the characters that represent the average inhabitant of Spain during the development of the novel. Descartes praises common sense—although he doubts it is as common as its name implies. The supernatural, in the shape of evil enchanters and perverse magicians, plays a prominent role in Don Quixote's mind. These evil enchanters seem to find great pleasure in confusing everything so as to rob Don Quixote of his victories. The reader wonders how it is possible for him to go on after so many disappointments.

Descartes's hero—that is to say, Descartes himself—fights a great battle, which we might call "the Battle of Systematic Doubt," in which an evil enchanter or geni, *un malin génie* in French, plays an important role. Descartes doubts everything that he has learned or thinks he knows, including all of the ideas that have come to his mind. He even suspects that an evil enchanter has changed the world around him in such a way that it is impossible to find any truth. After such an acceptance of uncertainty and doubt, we wonder how Descartes comes out of the deep pit he has dug for himself. His immediate solution is to withdraw into himself. He has been thinking. He thinks. Thinking belongs to a being who thinks. He thinks, therefore he is; he exists. This immediate emergency solution is followed by a long-range one; he thinks about a perfect Being, God, who being perfect must exist and moreover does not lie. God is therefore the guarantor of the real existence of the world, and the evil geni is thus cast into the shadows where he belongs.

Let us remember that in his struggle against the irrational, Don Quixote preceded Descartes. How does our knight cope with the evil presence of enchanters, hovering all the time over his journey, robbing him of the glory that his quest and adventures should have given him?

Our memory plays a crucial role. In his Meditation III, René Descartes deals with the problem of interpretation of sensory perceptions: How do we recognize what we see? Can we be sure of our interpretations? "I remember that, when looking from a window and saying I see men who pass in the street, I really do not see them, but infer that what I see is men. . . . And yet what do I see from the window but hats and coats which may cover automatic machines? Yet I judge these to be men. And similarly solely by the faculty of judgment which rests in my mind, I comprehend that which I believed I saw with my eyes."[10]

Descartes was incorporating the old problem of appearance versus reality into the philosophical world, giving to it a new rigorous strength. Cervantes had already dealt with this problem in his novel. Descartes's philosophical writings are musings of a single man, a long soliloquy begun in a small cabin surrounded by winter snow during a war in Germany while the French troops were hibernating; yet they are so influential that many textbooks trace the beginning of modern philosophy to them. Although emblematic of the clarity and rigor of modern science, they represent one single thought, a unique viewpoint. What Cervantes offered was a multiplicity of viewpoints, often in conflict with each other. For instance, we may believe instinctively that Don Quixote is wrong in his interpretations of the everyday world that surrounds him, but we should not overlook the fact that many other characters in the novel deceive, lie, or are deceived and lied to. It is out of this complex point-counterpoint of voices and opinions in conflict that the novel is born, not only Cervantes's but also most of the novels that will follow.

Our wits are constantly put to the test by encounters with men or women whose view of the world differs from ours, and they are also challenged by the material world, the world of objects that resist us. Don Quixote experiments with the hardness or softness of material objects as he makes a valiant effort to equip himself with the armor and weapons a knight-errant needs. His helmet is a main source of trouble. "The Ingenious *Hidalgo*, when necessary, can be chary of anything that threatens to interfere with his fantasies. Because he wanted to test the sturdiness of the helmet that he had made from pasteboard, he destroyed a week's work with one swipe of his sword. The lesson is sufficient: he repairs the damage, and he also refrains from any new trials, in order not to spoil 'a helmet of the most perfect construction.'"[11]

Indeed, interpreting what our senses communicate to us is what keeps us busy all day long. We have to judge the moods of people talking to us, especially if we expect them to grant us a favor, and we also have to estimate the hardness or softness of a material object that we plan to use.

Both Don Quixote and Sancho embark on their travels, or should we say, their quest, following two lines of reasoning, two sources of knowledge and guidance: their memory and their senses. Their senses give them information that we may suspect to be the same. But how can this be true since their experiences and lives have been worlds apart, molding two different personalities? Our interpretation of the world and our immediate surroundings may vary from that of our friends and neighbors, perhaps even more from what a stranger might see and understand. This is made explicit during Cervantes's novel every time Don Quixote's interpretation clashes with what Sancho sees.

Cervantes knows that the senses give us raw material that develops differently in each individual. Is there some basic knowledge hardwired in our brain that induces us to interpret what we see and hear in a certain way? The idea of this fundamental knowledge goes back to Greek philosophy, to the "innate ideas" of classical tradition; moreover, modern science has validated this concept when analyzing the behavior of insects and birds. Humans were supposed to be guided by innate ideas combined with knowledge supplied by trial and error and by the thousand experiences of everyday life. By choosing two characters who are at opposite poles, a valiant knight who is above all an idealist and is guided by "innate ideas," in his case the ideas of chivalry romances that have been internalized and become wired to his brain, and a matter-of-fact, cowardly rustic, guided by common sense and traditional values and folk wisdom contained in proverbs and folk sayings, Cervantes creates a study in contrast. Yet, if we let this impression guide us, we may misread the novel or at least we may miss a substantial part of its meaning.

A Simple Not So Simple Read

It is possible to read Cervantes's novel as a straightforward narrative. These are the adventures and misadventures of Don Quixote and his squire, Sancho Panza. Why complicate them? They are enjoyable in and by themselves. And yet if the majority of readers follow this path, and there is little doubt that they do, there is much that they will miss. The very structure of the novel is highly complex and teems with hidden messages. As Jean Canavaggio puts it, "The more the reader familiarizes himself with this multiple universe, the more he discovers overlapping planes, stories within stories, mirrors that reflect each other to infinity. . . . The Chinese-box effect is also a result of the skill with which the novelist hides behind the pseudo-narrators to whom he lends his voice and delegates his powers."[12] Who is speaking? Can we trust the speaker? At a certain moment Cide Hamete Benengeli, the Arab historian, casts doubt about the authenticity and veracity of a chapter he is about to write. How are we to interpret such a statement? It may remind us of an old conundrum that has come to us from ancient Greece: "All the people from Crete are liars, without exception: they lie all the time. I can assure you this is true, for I am a Cretan."

Words, language, and identity baffle us. How can we absorb the vast possibilities that Cervantes presents on so many levels? Certainly we are caught off guard as the barrage of adventures, encounters, speeches, and general display of humanity bombards us. Are we reading the truth about these fictional characters? Further, Cervantes forces us to explore the inner mind and hearts of these individuals and finally foists upon us the question of what is real and what is not real. Just a simple read? Not quite.

It is now opportune to come to a preliminary conclusion: Cervantes's novel offers many new approaches to the art of storytelling and the craft of narrative prose. It is outstanding today and was probably more so when it appeared because it is so original in so many ways. Its originality was confounding and misunderstood. We are still unraveling its many messages. The next generation's interpretations may supersede our own.

NOTES

1. Canavaggio, *Cervantes*, 214.

2. Carroll B. Johnson, *Don Quixote: The Quest for Modern Fiction* (Boston: G. K. Hall, 1990), 91.

3. Ibid., 91–92.

4. Michel Foucault, *The Order of Things: An Archaeology of the Human Sciences* (New York: Vintage Books, 1973), 47.

5. Jean Cassou, "An Introduction to Cervantes," in *Cervantes across the Centuries*, ed. A. Flores and M. J. Bernadete (New York: Dryden Press, 1947), 8.

6. Harry Levin, "The Example of Cervantes," in *Cervantes: A Collection of Critical Essays*, ed. Lowry Nelson, Jr. (Englewood Cliffs, NJ.: Prentice-Hall, 1969), 37.

7. Alter, *Partial Magic*, 5.

8. Gerald Brenan, "Cervantes," in *Cervantes: A Collection of Critical Essays*, ed. Lowry Nelson, Jr. (Englewood Cliffs, NJ.: Prentice-Hall, 1969), 28–29.

9. Ibid., 29.

10. René Descartes, Meditation III, in *Great Books of the Western World* (Chicago: Great Books, University of Chicago, pub. by *Encylopaedia Britannica*, 1952), vol. 28, p. 81.

11. Canavaggio, *Cervantes*, 212.

12. Ibid., 213–14.

BRYANT CREEL

Palace of the Apes: The Ducal Chateau and Cervantes's Repudiation of Satiric Malice

In DQ 2.30, Don Quijote sees the Duke and Duchess for the first time. They are at a distance, and he sends Sancho to explain who Don Quijote is. When Sancho returns, Don Quijote tries to dismount to go meet the Duke, but Sancho's nervousness and Don Quijote's own ineptness cause them both to fall in a ridiculous way that completely shatters the dignified impression that Don Quijote had hoped to make on these important people. Don Quijote then approaches the Duke and tries to kneel before him, but the Duke stops him and embraces him as an equal. Thus begins the central episode of the second half of the novel, with what on the surface appears to be an attitude of gracious acceptance of Don Quijote and Sancho during their prolonged stay at the ducal chateau. When Don Quijote arrives at the chateau, the hospitality he is shown makes him feel for the first time that he is being treated like famous knights in literature. But the narrator makes it known from the beginning that the Duke and Duchess already know who Don Quijote is and that they plan to lead him on by fueling his delusions. Almost immediately the reader sees the courteous treatment of Don Quijote and Sancho begin to combine with a playful attitude that turns more and more aggressive during the twenty-nine chapters that are devoted to events at the ducal estate.

At first, the ambiguous attitude that the Duke and Duchess have toward Don Quijote seems harmless enough; but as the hoaxes become more bizarre

From Don Quijote *Across Four Centuries: Papers from the Seventeenth Southern California Cervantes Symposium, UCLA, 7–9 April 2005*, edited by Carroll B. Johnson, pp. 87–105. © 2006 by Juan de la Cuesta—Hispanic Monographs.

and extravagant, the reader begins to wonder exactly what motivates the Duke and Duchess to go to such lengths.[1] When one considers that Altisidora's cynical and even cruel pranks had to be carried out with the complicity of the Duke and Duchess, the fundamental good will of the ducal pair becomes more and more questionable. By 2.57, when Don Quijote and Sancho leave the ducal chateau, and especially toward the end of the novel, when in 2.69–70 the Duke and Duchess briefly intercept Don Quijote and Sancho with elaborate and mysterious histrionics as they return to their village, what initially began as Don Quijote's treatment as an honored guest has degenerated into crass insults and scapegoating. The ducal country house reveals itself to be the home of malicious ridicule, base frivolity, and aggressive ill-will. As such, it can be regarded as a metaphor for the domain of malicious satire. That type of satire and the spirit that underlies it stand in conspicuous contrast to both the childlike goodness of Don Quijote and the delicately reproving attitude with which Cervantes himself subtly and implicitly places the Duke and Duchess in an unfavorable light. My main purpose in the present comments is to explore further some of the broader implications of the pranks organized by the Duke and Duchess at Don Quijote's expense and the relation of those events to Cervantes's aesthetic ideas. I wish also to address some metaphorical dimensions of certain paradoxical motifs in the second part of the novel, such as Dulcinea's "enchantment" and Sancho's role in her "disenchantment."

In portraying the ducal household, Cervantes seems to have represented a typical phenomenon of the period. Werner Sombart, in *Luxury and Capitalism*, discusses the Spanish-Dutch era of the seventeenth century as a stage in the development of modern luxury (82). He notes that an important factor contributing to the impoverishment of the nobility in that period was that, as plebeian elements in the society became enriched, the old families tried to equal the parvenus in ostentatious display (82–83). We know that the Duke in *Don Quijote* had incurred debt because he borrowed money from the wealthy land owner whose son seduced Doña Rodriguez's daughter before escaping to Flanders, a betrayal that the Duke abetted out of self-interest. According to Sombart, the forms of domestic luxury that typically caused the nobility of the period to experience economic decline were spectacular events such as tournaments, pageants, processions, and public banquets (95). During Don Quijote's visit with the Duke and Duchess, there is a tournament (in which Tosilos is supposed to combat Don Quijote); but in depicting the spectacles organized at the ducal estate, Cervantes seems to have intended above all to draw attention to their insolent frivolity. They include—in addition to the tournament already mentioned—the occasion of the lavish announcement of the formula for disenchanting Dulcinea, that of the extravagant presentation of the story of the *dueña* Dolorida (or Countess Trifaldi), the Clavileño episode, the elaborate reception of Sancho at Barataria, and Altisidora's mock funeral and revival in 2.69. From the point of view of the Duke and Duchess, the sole purpose of these events is to provide entertainment by inciting Don Quijote's fantasies and taking advantage of Sancho's simplicity while the two are guests at their estate.

The novel presents specific instances of crass insensitivity to values on the part of the Duke, such as his high-handed treatment of Doña Rodriguez and her daughter and his accusing Don Quijote of stealing from the maidservant Altisidora while Don Quijote was a guest in his house (2.57); but the most damning symptom of his degeneracy is his attitude of false sincerity towards the people to whom he extends his hospitality, Don Quijote and Sancho. Certainly the expected norm of behavior in an aristocratic country retreat (a "casa de placer" or "casa de recreo") would be one of high courtesy and affable socializing. Georg Simmel, in his analysis of the valuable sociological art form known as "sociability" (*The Sociology of Georg Simmel* 40–57), explains that its first condition is "tact" based on a superficial avoidance of attentions to reality and on an avoidance of ego-stresses and personal and even individual attitudes in deference to a collective, common consciousness. Simmel holds that the symbolic ritual of sociability is ultimately grounded in a tacit recognition of social realities such as the interdependence of the individual and the collectivity. I would suggest as well that "sociability" reinforces certain types of moral awareness, such as the principle of universal human solidarity.[2] In any case, Simmel also notes that sociability is of a democratic nature and thus requires that one treat others not only as equals but as being more valuable or even superior. The *eclesiástico* (chaplain) at the home of the Duke and Duchess is the first to violate the requirements of tact when he inveighs against Alonso Quijano on a personal level (he does not acknowledge the persona Don Quijote); but the Duke and Duchess follow suit in their general behavior toward Don Quijote, both by being insincerely courteous toward him and by amusing themselves at Don Quijote's expense. They transgress the democratic spirit of sociability by treating Don Quijote as an inferior, with the result that, in Simmel's words, the sociological art form of sociability is made to "degenerate into a sociological naturalism" (Simmel 47) in which the naive formalism of an elevating histrionics is displaced by crude factuality (lavish enactments of a farcical theatricality—the hoaxes—notwithstanding).

My emphasis on the issue of propriety may seem to trivialize the broader ethical implications of the subject under discussion. However, as Nicolai Hartmann points out in his observations on the values of social intercourse, the existing forms of social intercourse are profoundly necessary to life; and all human relationships, even those that are external and seemingly unimportant, are based on trust and the power of good faith. Hence, "all propriety in social encounter with others calls for a like propriety in them," and one who violates the forms of social intercourse "refuses to others what he claims from them for himself" (*Ethics*, 2:304–305). Such a transgressor in little things, by offending against social forms, offends against the inner ethos, which reappears in those forms in a way that is diminished but unmistakable. So it is that—to cite examples that could be applied to the Duke—an inconsiderate man shows himself to be immodest: like a real criminal, such person is rightly "subject to condemnation and punishment, to boycott and ostracism" (Hartmann, 2: 304–305). In an observation that is reminiscent of Simmel's mention of "degeneration into a sociological naturalism," Hartmann notes that "without established social custom mankind sinks into formlessness and savagery" (2: 302).

Specifically relevant to the Duke's and Duchess's behavior toward Don Quijote and to possible sources drawn on by Cervantes for the ethical perspective presented in the episode with the Duke and Duchess is a passage in Aristotle's *Nicomachean Ethics* mentioned by Hartmann as concerning the virtue of social deportment that consists in "the rightly balanced, tactful relation to jesting, which is dignified and yet is appreciative of humor" (Hartmann, *Ethics*, 2: 308). One of the two deficient extremes of that attitude fits the Duke. In Aristotle's words, "Those who go to excess in raising laughs seem to be vulgar buffoons. They stop at nothing to raise a laugh, and care more about that than about saying what is seemly and avoiding pain to the victims of the joke" (*Nicomachean Ethics*, 1128a 5–8) (trans. Irwin, 112). Such a tactless intrusion of personal motives contrasts with the genial tact implied both in Alonso Quijano's masking (as in a costume party) of his own real personality with the identity of Don Quijote and with the respectful hospitality that Don Quijote had been shown shortly before by Diego de Miranda. Stanislav Zimic has observed that for perceptive readers the impression of insensitivity on the part of the Duke and Duchess is heightened by what seems to be a subtly implied attitude of indulgence on the part of Don Quijote, and he notes that several critics have pointed out that at the home of the Duke and Duchess Don Quijote sometimes seems to be conscious of the attempts to deceive him.[3]

More important for the present comments, however, is—I repeat—the fact that the malicious spirit in which the Duke and Duchess satirize Don Quijote is conspicuously opposed to the spirit and attitude with which Cervantes satirizes the Duke and Duchess. In fact, Cervantes even manages to endow the Duke and Duchess with certain exemplary qualities: for example, in 2.57, before Don Quijote and Sancho go to Barcelona, the Duke gives Sancho two hundred gold *escudos*. If one surveys passages in *Don Quijote* that can be interpreted as subtle clues to Cervantes' aesthetic ideas, one repeatedly encounters references that take implicit exception to such attributes of malicious satire as crude naturalism and a disposition of vengeful ill will. I will limit myself to a few representative examples. When Don Quijote discusses the greatness of Homer's and Virgil's portraits of Ulysses and Aeneas, he says that those poets painted their heroes "no como ellos fueron, sino como habían de ser, para quedar ejemplo a los venideros hombres de sus virtudes" (1.25: 237)[4]. In Don Quijote's advice to Sancho before Sancho's governorship, he tells him, "Cuando te sucediere juzgar algún pleito de algún tu enemigo, aparta las mientes de tu injuria y ponlas en is verdad del caso.... Al culpado ..., muéstratele piadoso y clemente; porque aunque los atributos de Dios son todos iguales, más resplandece y campea a nuestro ver el de la misericordia que el de la justicia" (2.43: 842). In a conversation with Don Diego de Miranda, Don Quijote takes issue with satiric malice partly because of its tendency to be personal:

> Riña vuesa merced a su hijo si hiciere sátiras que perjudiquen las honras ajenas, y castíguele y rómpaselas ... ; porque lícito es al poeta escribir contra la invidia y decir mal de los invidiosos ... con que no señale persona alguna; pero hay poetas que a trueco de decir una malicia se pondrán a peligro que los destierren a las islas del Ponto. (2.26: 650–51)[5]

(We have already noted that an analogous assertion of personal attitudes has been seen as being incompatible with sociability). The narrator refers to the lion that Don Quijote challenges as "más comedido que arrogante" (2.17: 657). The following observation, which the narrator applies to the *eclesiástico* at the home of the Duke and Duchess could also be applied—partly because of the ambiguous meaning of the word "sus"—as an apt description of the Duke and Duchess, and their disparagement of Don Quijote: "destos que quieren que la grandeza de los grandes se mida con la estrecheza de sus ánimos" (2.31: 765). The foregoing passages, in addition to having specific relevance to the contexts in which they appear, create a critical perspective for viewing the behavior of the Duke and Duchess, as well as generally what Cervantes terms "maliciosa sátira": both that of such minor poets as Vicente Espinel[6] and of great mockers and iconoclasts of heroism like Góngora and Quevedo. Ramón Menéndez Pidal has observed of such mocking of the heroic that, unlike Góngora and Quevedo, "Cervantes nunca hizo esto" ("Cervantes y el ideal caballeresco" 226).

The malicious ridicule of Don Quijote extends to Sancho as well, such as that which occurs in relation to the bizarre events surrounding the "disenchantment of Dulcinea." When that motif is interpreted metaphorically, it becomes less enigmatic. Dulcinea represents the suprasensible ideal. In ugly peasant form,[7] she is "enchanted" in the sense that her "true" (in the sense of "ideal") form is distorted by empirical accident—specifically, I would propose, by the degrading effects of poverty. One argument in support of this interpretation is that it finds its logical basis in the circumstance that peasants are usually of low social status and hence poor. Yet this reading of the enchantment motif is also supported by clues in the text. When Don Quijote speaks to the young peasant woman who Sancho says is Dulcinea appearing to Don Quijote in enchanted form, Don Quijote says to her, " ... el maligno encantador ... ha puesto nubes y cataratas en mis ojos ... y ha transformado tu sin igual hermosura y rostro en el de una labradora pobre ..." (2.10: 607). Also, in the Cave of Montesinos the "enchanted" Dulcinea has a companion borrow money from Don Quijote on her behalf. It is interesting also that when Don Quijote gives her his last four reales (Dulcinea had asked for six), he tells her, "Decid ... a vuestra señora que ... me pesa en el alma de sus trabajos, y que quisiera ser un Fúcar para remediarlos ..." (2.23: 711). The reference, of course, is to the Fuggers, the great German banking family that was the chief supporter of Charles V. In his *Outline of History*, H. G. Wells writes, "Charles V was not so much a Habsburg emperor as a Fugger emperor" and that Charles's election was secured by a vast amount of bribery (737). It is understandable that these references would be made in this novel in the context of attention to the issue of poverty among the common people. J. H. Elliott (*Imperial Spain* 199–200) explains that Charles V's dangerous credit transactions had incalculably disastrous consequences for sixteenth- and seventeenth-century Spain. Those actions led to the mortgaging of Spain's resources and establishing the domination of foreign bankers over the nation's sources of wealth. The *servicios* that the Crown compelled the *Cortes* to impose to pay for those loans ultimately had to be paid by the common people, who, as a consequence, were unable to pay their rents and were reduced to utter misery, many wandering naked or filling the prisons. In any case, Dulcinea's "enchantment" is the displacement of her ideal essence, including its physical manifestations, by non-essential qualities that arose from the accidental, extrinsic causes of social circumstances. From this point of view, the "enchantment of Dulcinea" motif has the broader metaphorical implication that just as wealth has the power to turn an ordinary reality into an ideal image, poverty can turn an ideal image into an ordinary reality.[8]

Metaphorical interpretation also helps to clarify Sancho's role in the "disenchantment of Dulcinea." In general, insofar as Sancho corresponds to an aspect of the character Don Quijote (his attachment to practical reality), his privation while in Don Quijote's service represents Don Quijote's own repudiation of the practical demands of everyday life that nevertheless accompany him wherever he goes. The afflictions that Sancho experiences while he is governor dramatize the idea that people in government posts must conform to the whims of the powerful. Since Sancho represents, among other things, the principle of surrender to the material, natural order, his being whipped or whipping himself can be seen to be logical as a way to disenchant Dulcinea when it is interpreted as a repudiation of subjection to natural .necessity, such as that which entraps the "enchanted Dulcinea." Because the Duke and Duchess seek to amuse themselves by aggravating Don Quijote's madness, it is also logical that they would impose a solution to Dulcinea's enchantment that would not be practicable because of the strain it places on relations between Don Quijote and Sancho.[9] Don Quijote is determined axiologically, and so he defines Dulcinea in ideal terms. She thus becomes a projection of Don Quijote's freedom of will. One could argue that the efforts of the Duke and Duchess to make Don Quijote a puppet in charades that entail the "enchanted Dulcinea" (in a manner reminiscent of the way Ginés de Pasamonte exploits the naiveté of others and manipulates them by aping their fantasies) is motivated not just by a malicious desire to compromise the source of Don Quijote's freedom of will but also by an aggressive wish to discredit his idealism by mocking and debunking the values that inspire it.[10] One has to be careful not to infer too much about the Duke and Duchess on the basis of what we know from seeing them at their country estate, but it seems accurate to assert that they have little serious regard for the kind of idealism that drives Don Quijote, given both their willingness to make sport of it and their own neglect of it. Their interest in idealism seems to be limited to a desire to disparage it for the sake of entertainment. The Duke and Duchess seem to want to make Don Quijote look ridiculous because they want to justify their repudiation of the old, high conception of noblesse. While it would be incorrect to refer to "quixotic" tendencies on the part of the Duke and Duchess that are similar to those of Don Quijote, in this confrontation between two instances of megalomania it would be hard to determine which is the more pathological. Perhaps one could say that the monomania of Don Quijote is more psychopathic, while the smug irreverence of the Duke and Duchess is more sociopathic, especially by the standards of high courtesy.

The lack of a genuine idealism on the part of the Duke and Duchess is, then, the key to understanding the thematic import of their game of obstructing the "disenchantment of Dulcinea," of preventing Don Quijote from restoring Dulcinea to mythopoeic form so that he can resume his former relationship with her. With that obstruction the Duke and Duchess increase Don Quijote's feelings of impotence and drive a wedge between him and Sancho, whom Don Quijote depends upon to maintain his practical links to the real world. Since the "enchanted" Dulcinea is trapped in the empirical order and Don Quijote is unable to renounce his devotion to her, the actions of the Duke and Duchess have the effect of confining Don Quijote's emotional center in the empirical order as well, a situation that ultimately leads to his demise.

In general, Don Quijote's preoccupations remain impervious to the trivializing finiteness of everyday reality, yet he maintains a deep and loyal relation to that reality. In contrast, the Duke and Duchess, with their wealth and their cajoling elitism, hover "above" the real world; but they are "imprisoned" by that world in the same way that the master can be said to be enslaved by the bondman. By shedding their idealism, they have become reduced to the same paltriness that they seek to rise above. Alonso Quijano's physical death prevents Don Quijote from succumbing spiritually, and he remains "in a higher place"; yet the Duke and Duchess remain confined in a lower one, in the sphere of "ambición soberbia" (2.32: 770, referred to in similar terms by Sancho in 2.53: 926 and by Don Quijote in 2.42: 840 as a "golfo profundo de confusiones") that was repudiated by Sancho when he left his governorship.[11] The narrow-mindedness of the Duke and Duchess explains their puerility and their efforts to compensate for their own pettiness by mocking a social inferior who in the arena of subjective culture is actually their superior (as Don Quijote observes, "la sangre se hereda y la virtud se aquista, y la virtud vale por sí sola lo que la sangre no vale": 2.42: 841). The Duke's and Duchess's malicious urge to debunk the naive high-mindedness or innocence of social "outsiders" culminates in the final episode involving Altisidora, where she pretends to have died of unrequited passion for Don Quijote and appears lying on a bier at her own mock funeral. When the prank is over, she tells Don Quijote (I will translate her words, since the translations I have seen by Putnam, Cohen, and Rutherford seem to me to be inadequate),

> Good God alive, Don Codfish, mind of mortar, like a date stone, more stubborn and hard than a peasant with a one-track mind when he's got his sights set on something—if I come at you I'll scratch your eyes out. Do you in any way think, Don Vanquished and Don Beat-to-a-Pulp, that I died because of you? Everything you've seen tonight has been staged—I'm not a woman who for a hunched-over old camel like you would let myself feel pain in the dirt under one of my fingernails, let alone die for you. (2.70: 1044)[12]

One could suspect that what Altisidora says is true, that since Don Quijote is old, gaunt, and poor he is not desirable to women, which is why his mistress has to be a fantasy. Is Altisidora completely blind to Don Quijote's extraordinary spiritual stature? Perhaps she is not.[13] She may recognize that quality enough to find Don Quijote even less desirable, and her tirade may have the subtly ironic implication that, unlike in literature, in the world of reality ethical idealists are not prized as mates because their reluctance to rely on cunning to advance themselves in life makes them less reliable as providers. As Don Quijote himself observes, "el mundo [es] enemigo siempre de premiar los floridos ingenios ni los loables trabajos" (2.62: 998).

The novel *Don Quijote* as a whole can be seen as an elaborate tribute to the feeling of ethical idealism, as a value of the self that is opposed to values of means. For Don Quijote, knight errantry is spirituality. However, ethical idealism is also profoundly practical. It addresses the crucial human concerns of what is valuable in life and what can be done to attain it.[14] The negative opposite of Don Quijote's orientation is represented in the ethical inertia of the Duke and Duchess, their stagnation in a luxurious world of sensuous pleasure, histrionics, and indifference to values and ends. These are characteristics that the Duke and Duchess share with Don Diego de Miranda, whose preening manner of dress compares to that of the Duchess and contrasts so comically with Don Quijote's greasy leather jerkin and student's shirt that are described when he disrobes at Don Diego's house (in 2.18).[15] Whereas Don Quijote represents an ideal of self-abnegation and self-transcendence, Don Diego and especially the Duke and Duchess represent the urge to exalt themselves by what Thorstein Veblen refers to as a display of invidious pecuniary emulation. In this way they represent, respectively, earlier and later stages in the rise and decline of aristocratic culture. As Sombart notes,

> ... old aristocratic principles [of probity, candor, and disinterestedness] declined rapidly in all countries during the seventeenth and eighteenth centuries.... [T]he changed outlook of the nobility was bound to swell the great stream of luxury....
> (*Luxury and Capitalism* 85)

It is not the case, however, that—for all his nobility of soul and his attainments here of subjective culture—Don Quijote represents the good and the Duke and Duchess the bad in black and white terms. Just as the Duke and Duchess know how to act like genteel hosts if they choose to do so, Don Quijote knows how to act violent and barbaric. Apart from the many instances of his gratuitous attacks on unsuspecting travelers, he joins the Duke in the predatory ritual of killing a wild boar; and, like the Duke, he turns a deaf ear to Sancho's objections. Also, Don Quijote is not without his elitist tendencies, even if they are limited to occasional comically defensive

reflexes in relation to such matters as Sancho's loquacity or engaging plebe-
ians in combat. In their way, the Duke and Duchess are direct descendants
of Don Quijote's culturally atavistic tendencies. As Veblen notes, "In the
later barbarian culture society attained settled methods of acquisition and
possession under the quasi-peaceable regime of status. Simple aggression
and unrestrained violence in great measure gave place to shrewd practice
and chicanery. . . ." (*The Theory of the Leisure Class* 236). In the new order,
good-nature, equity, and indiscriminate sympathy become hindrances to
self-advancement, success now being the reward for a freedom from scruple,
sympathy, honesty, and regard for life (Veblen 223). "Strategy or cunning
is an element invariably present in games, as also in warlike pursuits and in
the chase" (Veblen 273). It is no accident that one finds in the context of the
stay at the ducal chateau, when Sancho makes the rounds of his "insula" in
2.49, that gambling and the deceit that accompanies it are met with earnest,
civic-minded disapproval and penalized accordingly.

In the eyes of the Duke and Duchess, Don Quijote's arrival at their
chateau is an opportunity for them to exercise their cunning in a series of
farces in which Don Quijote is the leading dupe. In his essence, Don Quijote represents the Renaissance affirmation of an inspired civic and religious
morality based on a striving for the realization of higher values. Yet in spite
of his amazing erudition and high character, he is impulsive and emotionally
determined. This characteristic makes him easy for the Duke and Duchess to
manipulate and exploit for the purposes of their entertainment. Even when
he is about to depart from their country house in 2.57, Don Quijote seems
to remain oblivious to having been made the butt of irony. In answer to the
Duke's accusation that he stole three nightcaps and two garters from Altisidora, his first words are, "No quiera Dios . . . que yo desenvaine mi espada
contra vuestra ilustrisima persona, de quien tantas mercedes he recibido . . ."
(2.70:951). Don Quijote seems, again, restrained by a scruple of manners
of which the decadent Duke is incapable. Is a broader implication of Don
Quijote's discourse on the difference between an offense and an affront (in
2.32, after his rebuttal to the *eclesiástico*) that the ridicule he and Sancho are
subjected to at the ducal chateau actually constitutes an affront? He says that
unlike when one is merely offended, a man is affronted when the person
who injured him "sustentó lo que había hecho, sin volver las espaldas y a pie
quedo" (2.32: 772). Perhaps one can see in such contrasting characteristics a
series of stages and variants in the pattern of the aristocracy's cultural evolution, and perhaps these stages are represented in a series of characters in this
novel. There would seem to be a movement from Don Quijote (the pristine,
tonic, old heroic stage, revived in the high morality of the great figures of the
Renaissance); to Diego de Miranda (noble turned prosperous private citizen

given to self-centered and trivial Epicurean pursuits[16]); to Ricote (a merchant representing the economic force of wealth, the basis of a new aristocracy and a condition for the erosion of old aristocratic ideals: Sancho encounters Ricote while he and Don Quijote are still guests at the home of the Duke and Duchess); to the Duke and Duchess (the stage of lavish waste, self-trivialization, and hollow elitism, which the image of Don Quijote occasionally parodies and makes appear ridiculous).

Yet in order to avoid stereotyping the high nobility, Cervantes has Don Quijote and Sancho, soon after they leave the ducal estate, encounter in 2.58 a group of young nobles engaged in the culturally healthy activity of dressing as shepherds and reciting the eclogues of Garcilaso and Camões. The incompatibility of this situation with the decadence at the ducal chateau is suggested chapters later, when Don Quijote refers to verses of Garcilaso that were being sung when he and Sancho arrived at Altisidora's mock funeral in 2.69. He says, "¿qué tienen que ver las estancias de Garcilaso con la muerte desta señora?" (2.70:1045). Also, the motifs in 2.58 of becoming entangled in invisible nets (deceit) in a "feigned Arcadia" (false paradise) and trampled by bulls (subjected to vile abuse) hearken back metaphorically to the recent visit with the Duke and Duchess. In the *societas leonina* (or "sociation with a lion") of the relationship between the Duke and Duchess on the one hand and Don Quijote and Sancho on the other, the Duke and Duchess assume that all the advantage is on their side. In contrast, in the earlier "Adventure of the Lions," the lion that was confronted by Don Quijote acted like a gracious host and displayed his superiority precisely by deferring to his unexpected visitor. In contrast, the inferiority of the Duke and Duchess makes itself evident precisely in the disadvantage at which they place their unsuspecting guests. A broad and quite bitter, though subtle, satirical implication of the entire episode involving the ducal chateau is that the only way frivolous people like the Duke and Duchess could have respect for heroic idealism is as a practical joke; and the only way a heroic figure like Don Quijote could be highly regarded in the real world of cunning manipulation is, also, as a practical joke. Can the lack of virility of character at the Duke's estate be seen to be figuratively suggested in the baroquely flamboyant effeminacy of the bearded *dueñas*? Perhaps the Clavileño episode was intended to imply the degree to which the malicious pranks of the Duke and Duchess are earthbound and unconvincing, except for simpletons like Sancho, who believe that it is in their interest to pretend to be convinced when they see themselves being manipulated.

In sum, the general purpose of the episode involving the stay of Don Quijote and Sancho at the ducal chateau is to contrast two opposed attitudes: Don Quijote's scrupulously ceremonious high-mindedness and self-effacement are contrasted with a world in which the standard is smug contempt and idle malice—a world where naively sincere good faith is countered by mocking duplicity, where kind earnestness is met by ridicule and smugness, and a noble indifference to worldly possessions is contrasted to frivolous luxury and waste. On another level, the contrast is between differing degrees of sensitivity to the ethical implications of form, insofar as form is determined by spiritual essence. A low degree of such sensitivity is represented by the Duke and Duchess, and a high degree is represented by Don Quijote. Northrop Frye notes that satire is both an attitude and a form (*Anatomy of Criticism* 310). The degeneration of comic gaiety is represented by the *eclesiástico's* personal attack against Don Quijote that clashes with a festive occasion, but especially by the grotesque and malicious farces enacted by Altisidora. Frye, again, defines decorum in literature as "the suiting of style to ... a subject." It is "the poet's *ethical* voice, the modification of his own voice ... to the vocal tone demanded by a subject or mood" (*Anatomy* 269). The requirements of tone can be determined by the genre of a work, and comedy requires a prevailing comic mood (*Anatomy* 171–72, 269). *Don Quijote* is a comic epic, and Cervantes observes the requirements of comic tone and avoids pathos by never evoking either the laughter that Don Quijote's gullibility provokes or any pain that Don Quijote might be experiencing. The principles of sociability can be seen as being similar to comic decorum in literature. Both sociability and comedy are aesthetic forms of play in which the serious problems of social interaction in the real world are on the surface largely subordinated to conventional form-laws in order to achieve an equilibrium between the purposes of the individual and those of the collectivity (Simmel, *Sociology* 53–56). Pathos is incompatible with the decorum of comedy, just as it is incompatible with the decorum of sociability. Far from confronting the Duke and Duchess because of their neglect, Don Quijote never indulges the poignancy of his personal feelings when he finds himself being maliciously ridiculed. So successfully does he resist doing so that the reader must wonder if he ever even experiences such pain. An analogous phenomenon is the difficulty in this novel of identifying the author's attitude toward the events portrayed. Simmel regards the character of an author's or narrator's personality in literature as being comparable to the way the giver or host of a party becomes completely absorbed in a group in order to defer to the cultivation of pure sociable form (Simmel, *Sociology* 53). With his dignified and healthy restraint during the hoaxes organized by the Duke and Duchess, Don Quijote actually sets a tone of congenial sociability even after the Duke and Duchess have abused and compromised that tone. So it is that Don Quijote, as a guest at the ducal chateau, can be seen as the image of Cervantes the author discreetly observing the requirements of comic decorum as he elaborates a subtle discourse of satiric irony. Like Don Quijote, Cervantes—the consummate ironist—almost never asserts his personal attitudes toward his characters, even when he is describing characters who inappropriately insist on asserting such personal attitudes themselves.

Notes

1. Javier Salazar Rincón sees the Duke and Duchess as making buffoons of Don Quijote and Sancho in order to use them as an antidote against boredom (*El mundo social dal Quixote* 66). Similarly to Pavel Novitsky, who sees the Duke and Duchess as being motivated by "dull cynicism and decadent cruelty" (*Cervantes and Don Quijote 15*), Luis Murillo regards the Duke's and Duchess's subjection of their guests to subtle, cruel humiliation as being attributable to "a refined perversity," which they conceal with exquisite courtesy (*A Critical Introduction to "Don Quixote"* 178). Ruth El Saffar regards the Duke and Duchess as being motivated by "a disinterested desire to be entertained" (*Distance and Control* 97). Anthony Close views the Duke and Duchess as cultivating the art of the *burla* as a sort of masque and as doing so with the innocent intention of paying homage to *Don Quijote* and participating communally in the comic merriment afforded by the novel ("Seemly Pranks" 71–73, 87). Close argues that any malicious mischief that characterizes the pranks organized by the Duke and Duchess is inherent in the spirit of the devilry that is a conventional element of the *burla* and the civilized good fun that it provides (70, 72). Part of the basis of his argument is his claim that Cervantes saw the *burlas* at the ducal estate in a positive light (70). However, he arrives at that view by incurring the fallacy of identifying Cide Hamete Benengeli with Cervantes (70) and overlooking the fact that the fictional Arab historiographer can be perceived as being motivated by an intention to ironically ridicule an "exemplary" Christian hero. It is interesting that Azorín expresses impatience toward the circumstance that, in spite of the fact that since the end of the eighteenth century the "stupid cruelty" of the Duke and Duchess had been recognized by critics (he cites the example of Vicente de los Rios's *Análisis del Quijote*), "hoy existen todavía comentadores qua encarecen la afabalidad y generosidad y cortesía de los duques" (*Obras completas* 2: 944). Those words were originally published in 1914. The fact that almost one hundred years later critics still admire the Duke and Duchess can be seen as a tribute to Cervantes's subtlety. To continue reviewing critical opinion as to the motives of the Duke and Duchess, Stainislav Zimic takes the same view of those motives as Salazar Rincón and, in addition, sees their obsessive need for jokes and laughter as a symptom of the lack of worthy pursuits in their lives (*Los cuentos y gas novelas dal "Quixote"* 277). Henry Sullivan refers to the "jocose cruelty" to which Don Quijote is subjected at the ducal estate as a "theater of sadism" (*Grotesque Purgatory* xi, 57,147). Francisco Márquez Villanueva regards the Duke and Duchess as seeking the pleasure of humiliating Don Quijote and of enlisting Altisidora's assistance for that purpose. Above all, he notes, they want to prove that love would be defeated by sensuality. Márquez Villanueva's perspective is similar to the view I will present here, that the Duke and Duchess want to mock higher values that they themselves do not cultivate.

2. For Scheler's views on what he terms "the principle of universal human moral solidarity," see his *Formalism in Ethics* 279, 368, 496, 527–38.

3. *Los cuentos y las novelas del "Quijote"* 272. See also 270 and 270 n.3 for
Zimic's own emphasis on the ambiguity with which the degree of Don Quijote's
awareness is presented and for references to overstatements as to evidence of Don
Quijote's lucidity at the ducal estate on the part of G. Torrente Ballester and M.
Van Doren. I would suggest that Torrente Ballester and Van Doren might have
been influenced by Miguel de Unamuno's view (presented in his "Vida de Don
Quijote y Sancho," 84) that Don Quijote's "madness" is of the imagination but not
of the understanding, or by Francisco Maldonado de Guevara's "Del *Ingenium* de
Cervantes al de Gracián," in which it is asserted that Don Quijote consciously and
creatively imitates his own madness. In general, Cervantes makes the issue of Don
Quijote's awareness of the malice of the Duke and Duchess ambiguous. A good
example of that ambiguity is Don Quijote's response to Altisidora's tirade. Don
Quijote tells the Duchess,

> ... todo el mal desta doncella nace de ociosidad, cuyo remedio es la
> ocupación honesta y continua. Ella me ha dicho aquí que se usan randas
> en el infierno; y pues ella las debe de saber hacer, no las deje de la mano;
> que ocupada en menear los palillos, no se menearán en su imaginación
> la imagen o imágenes de lo que bien quiere, y ésta es la verdad, éste mi
> parecer y éste es mi consejo. (2:70: 1045. See note 6 below)

These words would fit a situation in which Don Quijote believed that Altisidora did mean her insults (because she was just pretending to love him) as much as
one in which he believed she did not mean them (because she was embarrassed by
his not having reciprocated her advance). Incidentally, the mention of "el infierno"
in Don Quijote's words cited above can be interpreted as an oblique reference to the
ducal estate, in spite of the fact that on the surface it refers to elements of Altisidora's
description of a scene in hell in which a dozen devils were playfully kicking Avell-
laneda's second part of Don Quijote as though it were a ball because it was so bad
(2.70: 1043). In any case, it would seem that ultimately Cervantes wants the reader
to see Don Quijote's belief that he has been well treated by the Duke and Duchess
partly as being a result of his capitulating to his own megalomania, and not merely
to hold him up as a model of good will and of presenting oneself as appreciative
toward one's host as a matter of principle. When Don Quijote and Sancho, on their
way back to their village, experience anxiety as they are escorted to the ducal chateau
under duress, Don Quijote recognizes the place and says with surprise, "sí en esta
casa todo es cortesía y buen comedimiento; pero para los vencidos el bien se vuelve en
mal y el mal en peor" (2.69: 1034). His memory of his previous stay with the Duke
and Duchess is thus represented as being positive.

4. Passages quoted from *Don Quijote* are from the 1969 edition by Martin de
Riquer; any translations are mine.

5. The specific reference is to Ovid's exile to the coasts of the Black Sea, but
the general sense could also be a reference to Lope de Vega, who in 1588 was exiled
from Madrid and the Kingdom of Castile for writing libelous verses against Elena
Osorio.

6. See 2.8: 592 and 592 n.9.

7. At the home of the Duke and Duchess, Don Quijote describes the
enchanted Dulcinea as follows: " ... halléla encantada y convertida de princesa en
labradora, de hermosa en fea, de ángel en diablo, de olorosa en pestifera, de bien

hablada en rústica, de reposada en brincadora, de luz en tinieblas, y finalmente, de Dulcinea del Toboso en una villana de Sayago" (2.32: 776).

8. As Karl Marx observed in relation to the power of money, "*money* transforms the *real essential powers of man and nature* into what are merely abstract conceits and therefore *imperfections*—into tormenting chimeras—just as it transforms *real imperfections and chimeras* . . . into *real powers* and *faculties*" (*Economic and Philosophic Manuscripts* 168–69; emphasis in original). In the former case, one thinks of the transformation of Aldonza Lorenzo into a princess, an event that makes an actual relationship with her as unrealizable for Don Quijote as if she were an ugly and ordinary rustic. In the latter case, one thinks of how the ordinary behavior of the Duke and Duchess is disguised in a veneer of prosperity and elegance.

9. For a discussion of the antagonism between Don Quijote and Sancho that develops in relation to the disenchantment of Dulcinea, see Carroll Johnson, *Cervantes and the Material World* 32–36.

10. Joaquin Casalduero comes close to this view with his observation that in Part II of *Don Quijote*, "toda confirmación del espíritu [del hombre de acción] es siempre paródica" (*Sentido y forma del "Quijote"* 294).

11. It is in this sense only that Ruth El Saffar's view that the Duke and Duchess "often find themselves trapped in their own illusions" *(Beyond Fiction 120)* would seem to me to be accurate. In the book in which that observation appears, El Saffar does not explain her meaning; but in *Distance and Control* she observes that the Duke and Duchess are trapped in the sense that they "are controlled to some extent from within their play by the very characters whom they intend to manipulate" (93). Such developments (described by El Saffar on 93–98) occur to such a small extent that to say that the Duke and Duchess are "trapped" by them seems to me to be an exaggeration. Trapped they are, but in a different way—in an ethical bind. The main value of El Saffar's observations is that they record the fact that the Duke and Duchess are susceptible to their own insecurities at betraying the social norms by which they are supposed to live.

12. "Vive el Señor, don bacallao, alma de almirez, cuesco de dátil, más terco y duro que villano rogado cuando tiene la suya sobre el hito, que si arremeto a vos, que os tengo de sacar los ojos! ¿Pensáis, porventura, don vencido y don molido a palos, que yo me he muerto por vos? Todo lo que habéis visto esta noche ha sido fingido; que no soy yo mujer que por semejantes camellos había de dejar que me doliese un negro de la uña, cuanto más morirme." (2.70: 1044)

13. Carroll Johnson observes that Altisidora "appears actually to fall in love with . . . [Don Quijote]. At the very least, she is truly offended and hurt when he announces he would rather be true to Dulcinea than to have a fling with her" (*Don Quixote: The Quest for Modern Fiction 66*). F. Márquez Villanueva would seem to agree with Johnson's observation concerning Altisidora's injured vanity, but not with the view that Altisidora might have fallen in love with Don Quijote: "Claro que ni ella ni nadie iba a morirse por amores de Don Quijote, pero sí que su perversa comedia descarrila irremisiblemente ante la entereza sin mella ni doblez del caballero." (*Trabajos y días* 331)

14. See Nicolai Hartmann 1:1–46 on the practical character of philosophical ethics.

15. See my *Don Quijote, Symbol of a Culture in Crisis* 53–62 for a discussion of Diego de Miranda and a survey of how criticism has interpreted him.

16. For a discussion of the critical tradition of interpreting Diego de Miranda as a Christian Epicurean (in the works of authors such as Vicente Llorens, Marcel Bataillon, and Francisco Márquez Villanueva), see my *Don Quijote, Symbol of a Culture in Crisis* 56–57.

WORKS CITED

Aristotle. *Nicomachean Ethics*. Trans. Terence Irwin. Indianapolis: Hackett, 1985.

Azorín, (Martínez Ruiz, José). "Sobre el *Quijote*." In *Obras completas*, II. Madrid: Aguilar, 1959, 941–46.

Casalduero, Joaquín. *Sentido y forma del "Quijote."* Madrid: ínsula, 1949.

Cervantes de Saavedra, Miguel. *El ingenioso hidalgo don Quijote de la Mancha*. 1605, 1615. Ed. Martín de Riquer. Barcelona: Editorial juventud, 1968.

Creel, Bryant L. *Don Quijote, Symbol of a Culture in Crisis*. Valencia: Albatros Hispan6fila, 1988.

Close, Anthony. "Seemly Pranks: The Palace Episodes in *Don Quixote* Part II." In *Art and Literature in Spain, 1600–1800: Studies in Honor of Nigel Glendenning*. London: Tamesis, 1993.

Elliott, J. H. *Imperial Spain, 1469–1716*. New York: St. Martin's Press, 1964.

El Saffar, Ruth. *Beyond Fiction: The Recovery of the Feminine in the Novels of Cervantes*. Berkeley: U of California P, 1984.

———. *Distance and Control in "Don Quijote": A Study in Narrative Technique*. Studies in the Romance Languages and Literatures 147. Chapel Hill, NC: U of North Carolina Department of Romance Languages, 1975.

Frye, Northrop. *Anatomy of Criticism: Four Essays*. Princeton: Princeton UP, 1957.

Hartmann, Nicolai. *Ethics*. 1926. Trans. Stanton Coit. 3 vols. London: Unwin, 1932.

Johnson, Carroll. *Don Quixote: The Quest for Modern Fiction*. Boston: Twayne, 1990.

———. *Cervantes and the Material World*. Urbana, IL: U of Illinois P, 2000.

Maldonado de Guevara, Francisco. "Del *Ingenium* de Cervantes al de Gracián." *Anales Cervantinos* 6 (1957): 97–111.

Márquez Villanueva, Francisco. *Trabajos y días cervantinos*. Alcald de Henares: Centro de Estudios Hispánicos, 1995.

Marx, Karl. *The Economic and Philosophic Manuscripts of 1844*. Trans. Martin Milligan. New York: International Publishers, 1964.

Menéndez Pidal, Ramón. 1948. "Cervantes y el ideal caballeresco." In *España y su Historia*. 2 vols. Madrid: Ediciones Montauro, 1957. 2: 213–34.

Murillo, Luis. *A Critical Introduction to "Don Quijote."* New York: Peter Lang, 1990.

Novitsky, Pavel I. *Cervantes and Don Quixote: A Socio-historical Interpretation*. Trans. Sonia Volochova. New York: The Critics' Group, 1936.

Salazar Rincón, Javier. *El mundo social del Quijote*. Madrid: Gredos, 1986.

Scheler, Max. *Formalism in Ethics and Non-Formal Ethics of Values*, (1913–1916). Trans. Manfred S. Frings and Roger L. Funk. Evanston, IL: Northwestern UP, 1973.

Simmel, Georg. *The Sociology of Georg Simmel*. Trans. and ed. Kurt H. Wolff. Glencoe, IL: The Free Press, 1950.

Sombart, Werner. *Luxury and Capitalism*. 1913. Trans. W. R. Dittmar. Ann Arbor: The U of Michigan P, 1967.

Sullivan, Henry W. *Grotesque Purgatory: A Study of Cervantes' "Don Quijote," Part II*. University Park, PA: Penn State UP, 1996.

Unamuno, Miguel de. "Vida de Don Quijote y Sancho, según Miguel de Cervantes Saavedra explicada y comentada." 1905. In idem, *Ensayos*, ed. Bernardo G. de Candamo. 2:66–361. Madrid: Espasa-Calpe, 1958.

Veblen, Thorstein. *The Theory of the Leisure Class: An Economic Study of Institutions*. New York: The Modern Library, 1934.

Wells, H. G. *The Outline of History, Being a Plain History of Life and Mankind*. New York, Macmillan, 1921.

Zimic, Stanislav. *Los cuentos y las novelas del "Quijote."* Madrid: Iberoamericana, 1998.

MYRIAM YVONNE JEHENSON
and PETER N. DUNN

Discursive Hybridity:
Don Quixote's and Sancho Panza's Utopias

It is a given of social theory that no discursive field is homogeneous. It produces different meanings and subjectivities, exposes conflicts and contradictions, and thereby enables new forms of knowledge and practice to emerge. Nowhere does this truism become more apparent than in the sixteenth century, when new realities exposed ancient discourses that were once held to be indisputable and not open to contradiction. Nicolaus Copernicus seemed literally to turn the Ptolemaic world upside down by moving the sun to the center of the universe: "In the middle of all sits the sun enthroned" (quoted in Boas 81); and Andreas Vesalius's dissection of human bodies revealed systemic inaccuracies in Galen, the most respected of medical authorities. Already in the fourteenth and fifteenth centuries the views of ancient writers had begun to be challenged, but by the middle of the sixteenth century Vesalius could write, in 1542, that "those who are now dedicated to the ancient study of medicine, almost restored to its pristine splendour in many schools, are beginning to learn to their satisfaction how little and how feebly men have laboured in the field of Anatomy from the time of Galen to the present day" (quoted in Boas 129). The Jesuit José de Acosta, on passing the Torrid Zone and finding it cold and not, as Aristotle had said, scorching, would exclaim, "[w]hat could I do then but laugh at Aristotle's *Meteorology* and his philosophy?" (quoted in Grafton 1).

From *The Utopian Nexus in* Don Quixote, pp. 1–20. © 2006 by Vanderbilt University Press.

127

The Reformation had already shaken the roots of the Church's certainties. And no less unsettling was the fact that many of these new realities had been discovered not by traditional Scholastics, nor by the hermeneutical tools of the Humanists, but often through empirical evidence. The invention of the printing press, which had furthered the acquisition of ancient knowledge, now became crucial in promulgating awareness of the contradictions between the old and the new. It also made available to a wider audience the early modern age's challenges to ancient theories in mathematical geography and astronomical methods. The authority of revered books, then, seemed to be sharply challenged everywhere. And it is from this world of change that Don Quixote emerges still holding on to the same—the absolute truth of his treasured books.

It would be incorrect to say, however, that the century's "new" learning wholly supplanted the "old." In fact, as Anthony Grafton points out, these scientific thinkers were "no intellectual radicals." They "used classical precedents as well as modern evidence to support their iconoclastic enterprises" (Grafton 115). The same can be said of legists and reformists of the century. As we shall see below, Spanish theologians, philosophers, and lawyers will blend Biblical narratives, the tradition of the Church Fathers, pagan myths, and historical precedent in dealing with questions of legal theory, ethics, and history in the century.

One of the issues that would be heavily impacted in this heady intellectual age was the ongoing question of the originary condition of humankind, which the discoveries of the Indies (as the Americas were then referred to) had intensified. Since the "barbari" were not civilized, how was their condition to be categorized? Were "barbari" natural slaves, as Aristotle had maintained, or were they "educable?" As such, could they be Christianized? This question spawned others. Since the "barbari" had never been exposed to civilization, could they be said to be living in a state analogous to the original condition of our first parents? Could the lost Eden itself, which scholars, theologians, and folklore never affirmed to have disappeared altogether, be found in this New World, as Columbus believed? Traces of these contemporary conflicts will be discernible in Don Quixote. The fact that they are often refracted and distorted in the discourse of a madman does not make them less relevant to our study.

Don Quixote, then, is a product of an age of hybridity,[1] in which the experience of practical men enlarged and challenged knowledge once restricted to scholars. It was an age in which feudalism yielded to capitalism, in which the wealth of merchants created possibilities of acquiring titles once reserved to aristocrats, a period in which the views of the ancients were both challenged and employed in explaining the new and the experimental. This cultural polyphony resonates throughout Cervantes's novel.

* * *

When Don Quixote loses his wits (I:1), he decides to "become a knight errant and travel the world with his armor and his horse to seek adventures and engage in everything he had read that knights errant engaged in . . ." (I:1, 21) ["hacerse caballero andante y irse por todo el mundo con sus armas y caballo a buscar las aventuras y a ejercitarse en todo aquello que él había leído que los caballeros se ejercitaban" (40–41)]. But what does this notion of *adventure*, so inclusive for Don Quixote and for Sancho Panza, convey?

In *Ideology of Adventure*, Michael Nerlich has sketched a history of the transformations of the idea of adventure as a program for living. Following Mikhail Bakhtin, Nerlich points out that in the literature of classical antiquity, the hero's adventures are ordeals prescribed by the gods (4). In the middle ages, on the other hand, a new conception arises. The "essential hallmark" is that "adventures are undertaken on a *voluntary* basis . . . (*la quête de l'aventure*, '*the quest for adventure*') thereby glorifying both the quest and the adventurer himself (5: emphasis his). Nerlich marks the contrast between the classical and the medieval heroic adventure thus: "*Aventure*, which in its literary occurrences before the courtly romance means fate, chance, has become, in the knightly-courtly system of relations, an event that the knight must seek out and endure, although this event does continue to be unpredictable, a surprise of fate" (5).

The knight, then, *seeks* adventure. He is not a pawn in the hands of a god, nor merely instrumental in fulfilling the god's plan. The element of obligation nevertheless remains, now internalized as part of the whole system of courtly values, of what it means to be a knight. Hence the medieval knight is obliged by his courtly code to seek, like Parzifal, the Holy Grail, or to fight, like Gawain, the Green Knight. In the case of Don Quixote, however, adventure consists of two phases. One is the personal, freely chosen, adventure in which Quijada, Quesada, or Quijana transforms himself, creates a new persona, leaves his village, and embarks on a new life. The other is the knight-errantry which he adopts. The latter carries with it the duty to seek the kinds of adventure that from time to time he enumerates: to rescue damsels in distress, to humble proud giants, and so forth.

We are particularly interested in the first phase in which the country hidalgo transforms himself and leaves home. To embark freely on an adventure, as Don Quixote does, is to create a new and ideal space, a compatible setting within which desire and fantasy can take shape. In exceeding the commonly accepted and limited notion of what constitutes an adventure, that is, by transforming his entire life into an adventure, Don Quixote extends an ideal space into a world lived without temporal or spatial horizons. In the relevant words of Georg Simmel's elegant phenomenological essay, "The Adventure," "the most general form of adventure is its dropping out of the continuity of life" (243). While it forms a part of our whole existence, adventure "occurs outside the usual continuity of this life" (243).

The structural relation of adventure to life, then, is homologous with that of a dream sequence because adventure is "bound to the unified, consistent life-process by fewer threads than are ordinary experiences" (Simmel 244), and when recalled later it seems dreamlike. The "more fully [the adventure] realizes its idea, the more dreamlike it becomes in our memory" (244). Unlike the ordinary incidents in our everyday lives, an adventure is independent of "before" and "after." It is literally *out of* the ordinary, and so is the adventurer. Analogues of the adventurer for Simmel include the artist and the gambler. The former because his work of art "cuts out a piece of the endlessly continuous sequences of perceived experience" (245), the latter because, in the process of gambling, he has "abandoned himself to the meaninglessness of chance" (246).

Like Bakhtin's chivalric hero, Don Quixote "can live only in this world of miraculous chance, for only it preserves his identity. And the very code by which he measures his identity is calibrated precisely to this world of miraculous chance" (Bakhtin, *Dialogic* 152). Like Simmel's gambler, Don Quixote needs "to draw chance into his teleological system by means of omens and magical aids, thus removing it from its inaccessible isolation and searching in it for a lawful order, no matter how fantastic the laws of such an order may be" (246). In *Don Quixote*, both knight and squire are made to function within such a teleological system regulated by omens and magical aids.

In a geographically imprecise setting ("in a village of La Mancha whose name I am not about to tell you" [our translation] (I:1, 13) ["un lugar de la Mancha de cuyo nombre no quiero acordarme" (35)], an hidalgo emulates his chivalric heroes in creating for himself "*a miraculous world in adventure-time* (Bakhtin, *Dialogic* 154: emphasis his). His actions are allowed to unfold largely among roads and inns that provide insular settings in which he can transform reality by means of "magical aids" into the feudal chivalric past he wishes to resurrect. In his self-created world an illiterate laborer can not only become a knight's squire, but be promised a governorship. Even in the urban setting of Part II, disillusionments can still be subjected, though less successfully, to the knight's teleological system of omens and magic: the "enchantment" of Dulcinea, the unfulfilled "adventure" of the Enchanted Boat (II:29), the humiliating *burlas* to which Don Quixote and Sancho are subjected in the ducal palace, to name three salient examples.

In Part I, traces of the social and material problems of the time in which the book is written, though present, are more nuanced and stylized since they do not occasion serious self doubt for Don Quixote the adventurer. Part I, especially in the mind of the knight (but certainly not in the world he traverses), is suggestive of the subtext that Henry Ettinghausen finds to be active throughout the novel. Ettinghausen has characterized it as the "nostalgic praise of a utopian communistic mythic past" ["la alabanza nostálgica de un mítico pasado utópico-comunista"], of which "the most outstanding characteristic is ... precisely the absence of the idea and the sense of private prosperity in the power of money" ["la característica más distintiva ... es precisamente la ausencia del concepto y sentimiento de la prosperidad privada en el poder del dinero" (27)]. Thus, Don Quixote's nostalgic evocation of a golden age before the notions of "mine" and "thine" prevailed is wholly discordant with the real economic extremes between the haves and the have-nots that are subtly alluded to and which ... are insistently repeated in theological and *arbitrista* treatises of the time. In Part II, on the other hand, the protagonists on the road to Barcelona, and in Barcelona itself, will be exposed to armed bandits, to corpses of hanged men, and to brutal realities of power and corruption over which they have no control.

Nostalgias for utopia are of course always indicative of crises in the contemporary context from which such nostalgias emerge. To cite Carlo Ginsburg: "Only in periods of acute social change does an image emerge, generally a mythical one, of a different and better past; a model of perfection in the light of which the present appears to be a deterioration, a degeneration ... The struggle to transform the social order then becomes a conscious attempt to return to this mythical past" (77–78). But for most of Part I such crises are either under erasure or palliated by comic decorum. References to the natural catastrophes at the end of the sixteenth century, for example, are passed over throughout the novel: the famine, the floods of the period 1596–1602 whose aftermath augmented the century's already-dismal economic and social tensions, and the plagues that entered northern Spain in 1596 and spread southward reaching Andalucía in 1599. In Seville alone, the bubonic plague claimed 8,000 victims, and its total casualties may have reached a half million out of a Castilian population of about six million. Unmentioned are the consequent increase in the depopulation of the land, the unrest in the towns, the "[l]ittle Ice Age which resulted in years of cold and wet summers" (Geoffrey Parker 17–28), and the hardships which continued through the next decade (Lynch, *Hispanic World* 6–11; Domínguez Ortiz 68–70).

In the mind of the chivalric knight of Part I, a skinny old nag can become a knight's noble stallion through naming; forgotten rusty armor and shield knightly accoutrements through the application of cardboard and paste; and a humble village girl the lofty Princess Dulcinea through the transformed hidalgo's wishing it so.[2] In the still chivalric setting fabricated by the Duke, and Duchess in the palace of Part II, a setting equally unbounded by specific temporal or spatial horizons, the aged hidalgo, in poor health (II:18, 568; Rico 772), can nevertheless see himself recognized as an energetic knight-errant, and so alluring that "girls only have to look at me and love sweeps them away!" (II:44, 745) ["no ha de haber doncella que me mire que de mí no se enamore!" (990)]. And an illiterate peasant can aspire to being a count (II:65, 890; Rico 1163), and can eventually become a wise governor, leaving constitutions named after him (II:51, 797; Rico 1053).

The transformation of Aldonza Lorenzo into Dulcinea is of course not random but necessary once the hidalgo, now Don Quixote, chooses to seek adventure. In the chivalric *vita nuova* that Don Quixote has created for himself, love must have its place. And it must be love of the courtly kind. Through it, he will perfect himself as a knight in service to his lady. Love becomes a spiritual ordeal: adventure and love "seem . . . to stand in a symbiotic relation, [with] love inspiring the adventures that make a knight worthy of love" (Bloch 141). Both adventure and love, then, serve to isolate the individual from the particular community to which he belongs, for "[l]ove conceived as an obsession with another serves to sever the individual's bond with society" (Bloch 141). By embracing adventure as a way of life, and its necessary corollary in idealised courtly love, Don Quixote has transformed himself in accordance with his fictional models. He has also separated himself from his former life in order to create a new existential space in which his utopian desires and fantasies can be played out.

As Elizabeth Eisenstein has pointed out, it is not that Don Quixote reads books of chivalry because his life is boring, but the other way around. It is the adventures he reads about in his books of chivalry that make his routinized lifestyle impossible to maintain (Iffland 25–26). The flesh and blood person remains identical with itself, and in his memory retains the links with the past—his family, his property, and his ancestry—but Quixote the adventurer now becomes discontinuous with Quijada, Quesada, or Quexana, the country hidalgo. Once he has freed himself from the trammels of the everyday, the new persona emerges and, like Simmel's adventurer, "treats the incalculable element in life in the way we ordinarily think is by definition calculable . . . The obscurities of fate are certainly no more transparent to him than to others, but he proceeds as if they were." While "to the sober person, adventurous conduct often seems insanity . . . for . . . it appears to presuppose that the unknowable is known," for Don Quixote, as for Simmel's adventurer, "the unlikely is likely;" and what for the ordinary individual "is likely easily becomes unlikely" (Simmel 249–50). Hence, the escape of the aging and intelligent country hidalgo from his cramped and tedious domestic routine is as much an adventure as it is madness.

Such fantasies fill a need, as Julio Caro Baroja confirms when he cites the indignant response of a woman who opened one of the novels, *La busca*, by his uncle, Pío Baroja. "Why would I read books about poor people and suffering? I have enough poverty at home! I want books that tell about princesses, lords, salons, and things I've never seen!" ["¿Para qué—decía—voy a leer libros en que se habla de pobres y de miserias? ¡Ya tengo bastante pobreza en casa! Lo que yo quiero son libros en que se hable de princesas, de títulos, de salones y cosas que no he visto nunca!" (318)]. Here we have, in the twentieth century, a testimonial of how satisfying Don Quixote's timeless world of romance must have been. It also allows us to correct a time-honored assertion that *Don Quixote* killed the romances of chivalry and that Cervantes wrote the last *novela de caballerías*. In eighteenth-century England, Samuel Johnson read *Don Felixmarte de Hircania*. In Spain, as late as 1900, the Imprenta Universal's "Biblioteca Moderna" was still selling abbreviated editions, in twenty or thirty pages, of such works as *Carlo Magno, o los doce pares de Francia, El caballo de madera, Pierres y Magalona, Oliveros de Castilla, Tablante de Ricamonte,* among others (Caro Baroja, *Literatura de cordel* 319–20). "What would Cervantes have said," Caro Baroja asks rhetorically, "had he known that around the year 1900 the novels of chivalry continued to be read in the inns and the fields of La Mancha and Andalucía, as they had been around 1600 or earlier?" ["¿Qué hubiera dicho Cervantes de comprobar que, allá por los años 1900, los libros de caballerías se seguían leyendo en las ventas y campos de La Mancha y Andalucía, como por los de 1600 o antes?" (*Literatura de cordel* 318)].

If Cervantes's project had really been to discredit the romances of chivalry, it would have been a vain pursuit. Referring to the romances that incited Don Quixote to madness, for example, Caro Baroja observes the "plain fact that a great many level-headed people enjoyed them without ill effect, just as nothing happened to the readers of the serials in newspapers and magazines, with [even the nineteenth century] General O'Donnell, who was regarded by his contemporaries as icy cool, being the greatest reader of all" ["la realidad es que gustaron de ellos cantidad de gentes sesudas, sin que les pasara nada, como tampoco les pasó más tarde a los lectores de folletines, con el general O'Donnell a la cabeza, hombre gélido según sus contemporáneos . . ." (*Literatura de cordel* 317)].

Simmel touches our argument most closely in the observation that the adventurer "is also the extreme example of the ahistorical individual, of the man who lives in the present" (245). The adventures of our Manchegan knight have an additional and more complicated twist in that the present in which he chooses to live is a virtual past. His present is a no-time, an *uchronia* in which he will install his utopian project, as well as a no-place, a *utopia*. For Don Quixote, it is not the everyday temporal dimension, but adventure, that fills his life with meaning. Fernando Savater's perspective on the function of adventure in the life of the traditional hero is certainly applicable here to Don Quixote's project. "Adventure," Savater explains, "is a *time that is full* in contrast with the empty and interchangeable time of routine" ["La aventura es un *tiempo lleno* frente al tiempo vacío e intercambiable de la rutina" (170: his emphasis)]. Adventure, then, is the essential category within which the deeds of any knight—his trials, submission to ordeals, encounters with the marvellous, with monsters and with sorcerers—is to be evaluated. If he succeeds in his adventures, it is because of his virtue and the nobility of his aims. If he fails, the opposite is true. To alter Don Quixote's celebrated phrase somewhat, in his chivalric *vita nuova*, the Knight is the architect, the sum total, of his adventures: "each man is the architect of his own fortune" (II:66, 893) ["cada uno es artífice de su [a]ventura" (1168)].

The notion of adventure as the creation of an ideal space within which desire and fantasy can take shape opens up another perspective in Cervantes's novel. By focusing on an hidalgo and a poor laborer as its adventurers, the text directs our attention to the desires emanating from two different cultures and two different value systems. The confrontation of these diverse cultures, while distilled through the medium of humor, also discloses two important elements: how the fantasies of a representative of the underclass differ from those of the dominant culture and how social positionality determines the shape of the adventures each representative plays out in the ideal space.

For Don Quixote, desire is manifested in his chivalric project to restore the traditional values that were lost in the times following the prehistoric Age of Gold, and thereby to win glory and renown. For the laborer Sancho, desire is projected onto a promised *ínsula* which will make him wealthy, titled, and free from toil. The shape their desire takes makes the protagonists' fantasies different. Constructed by his class in society, Don Quixote, the petty country gentleman and hidalgo, is conservative in the utopia he tries to revive. He turns to the hierarchized golden world of classical antiquity and to the frugality lauded in the Hesiodic and Ovidian Arcadias in which he can afford to indulge. Sancho Panza, on the other hand, knows only too well how far removed is the real world of restraint, toil, and poverty that has constructed him from Don Quixote's romanticized image of austerity. Being an illiterate laborer, he does not have access to his master's literary capital. He does have access, however, to another "golden world," one that is equally ideal and mythical, and one that had also pervaded the European imaginary for centuries and had been fashioned, unlike the classical Hesiodic myth, by the collective memory of the *pueblo*. Called by A. L. Morton "the people's utopia," it is the myth of Cockaigne, reinforced by the magical tales brought back to Spain by *indianos* made wealthy in the wondrous "tierra de Xauxa" or "isla de Jauja" the Spaniards had found in Peru. The Inca Garcilaso de la Vega, son of a Spanish nobleman and an Incan princess, describes in his *Comentarios reales/ Royal Commentaries* (bk. III: ch. 24) one of the many marvels with which Peru would present the Spaniards, namely, the golden quarter Coricancha:

> That garden, which now serves to supply the monastery with vegetables, was in Inca times a garden of gold and silver such as existed in the royal palaces. It contained many herbs and flowers of various kinds, small plants, large trees, animals great and small, tame and wild, and creeping things such as snakes, lizards, and snails, butterflies and birds, each placed in an imitation of its natural surroundings.
>
> There was also a great maize field, a patch of the grain they call *quinua*, and other vegetables and fruit trees with their fruit all made of gold and silver in imitation of nature. There were also in the house billets of wood done in gold and silver, which were also to be found in the royal palace. Finally, there were figures of men, women, and children cast in gold and silver, and granaries and barns, which they call *pirua*, to the great majesty and ornamentation of the house of their god, the Sun. Each year, at the great festivals they celebrated, they presented the Sun with much gold and silver which was used to decorate his temple. New devices were continually invented for this purpose, for the silversmith assigned to the service of the Sun did nothing else but make these figures, together with an infinite quantity of plate as well as pots, jars, vases, and vats used in the temple. In short, in the whole of the house there was no implement necessary for any function that was not made of gold and silver, even the spades and hoes for weeding the gardens. Thus with good reason, they called the temple of the Sun and the whole building *coricancha*, "the golden quarter." (trans. Livermore vol. I:187–88)

[Aquella huerta que ahora sirve al convento de dar hortaliza era, en tiempo de los Incas, jardín de oro y plata; como los había en las casas reales de los Reyes, donde había muchas yerbas y flores de diversas suertes, muchas plantas menores, muchos árboles mayores, muchos animales chicos y grandes, bravos y domésticos, y sabandijas de las que van arrastrando, como culebras, lagartos y lagartijas, y caracoles, mariposas y pájaros y otras aves mayores del aire, cada cosa puesta en el lugar que más al propio contrahiciese a la natural que remedaba.

Había un gran maizal y la semilla que llaman *quinua* y otras legumbres y árboles frutales, con su fruta todo de oro y plata, contrahecha al natural. Había también en la casa rimeros de leña contrahecha de oro y plata, como los había en la casa real; también había grandes figuras de hombres y mujeres y niños, vaciados de lo mismo, y muchos graneros y trojes, que llaman *pirua*, todo para ornato y mayor majestad de la casa de su Dios el Sol. Que como cada año, a todas las fiestas principales que le hacían le presentaban tanta plata y oro, lo empleaban todo en adornar su casa inventando cada día nuevas grandezas, porque todos los plateros que había dedicados para el servicio del Sol no entendían en otra cosa sino hacer y contrahacer las cosas dichas. Hacían infinita vajilla, que el templo tenía para su servicio hasta ollas, cántaros, tinajas y tinajones. En suma, no había en aquella casa cosa alguna de que echar mano para cualquier ministerio que todo no fuese de oro y plata, hasta lo que servía de azadas y azadillas para limpiar los jardines. De donde con mucha razón y propiedad llamaron al templo del Sol y a toda la casa Coricancha, que quiere decir barrio de oro. (*Comentarios reales*, ed. Miró Quesada, vol. I:170)]

Juan Ruiz's *Libro de buen amor* (stanza 122a; stanza 3416) had evoked the "Cucaña" of those who aspired to the easy life. In its Spanish conflation with the Peruvian analogue we find it referred to in Rueda's *Paso* titled *La tierra de Xauxa* and in Mateo Alemán's *Guzmán de Alfarache* (pt. I: bk. 2, ch. 6). It is nevertheless important to keep in mind two things at this point. First, as Alexandre Cioranescu has reminded us, the myth of a golden age and that of Cockaigne are not fundamentally different. They both constitute imaginary nostalgias for utopia:

> The nostalgic side of utopia, which consists in exorcising reality by conjuring up a perfectly happy society, is simply a repetition, made conscious and orderly, of that same series of insoluble questions and imaginary solutions that led to the creation of the myth of the golden age or that of the land of Cockaigne.

[L'aspect nostalgique de l'utopie, qui consiste à exorciser la réalité par l'évocation d'une société parfaitement heureuse, n'est que la répétition, devenue consciente et méthodique, de la même série de curiosités insolubles et de solutions imaginaires, qui ont conduit à la création du mythe de l'âge d'or ou de celui du pays de Cocagne. (Cioranescu, *L'ávenir du passé* 47)]

Second, that although Sancho Panza's utopia includes the vision of a life free from toil and one in which he can stuff his belly, as the denizens of Cockaigne do, the pragmatic squire also aspires to the easily acquired noble status his master will provide him in installing him as a governor or a count.

We now focus briefly on the culture from which the figure of a Sancho Panza, and the "people's utopia," would have emerged. Early in the nineteenth century, Juan Eugenio Hartzenbusch saw this popular culture as essentially an oral one, and he located Cervantes's novel within the context of the carnivalesque (Rico p. ccxxv). Among recent critics, Augustin Redondo has also associated many of the incidents in which Sancho Panza himself participates, or is forced to participate, with the carnivalesque world of popular culture. Maurice Molho is explicit in affirming that the mechanism that underlies Cervantes's fashioning of Sancho is folkloric, and that Sancho is a popular archetype: "even if no Sancho Panza appears in folklore," states Molho, "there exists number of figures who, like Sancho, can be derived from the same original archetype" ["si no hay ningún Sancho Panza folklórico, sí existen varias figuras que, como la de Sancho, se dejan derivar de un mismo arquetipo original" (231)].

It is often remarked, and rightly so, that the knight and his squire are established "as traditional figures of fun in the popular mind" (Russell 318). But even before Cervantes transferred the folkloric figure of Sancho to the literary medium of *Don Quixote*, his name had already become a part of popular phraseology: "There goes Sancho with his nag" [*Allá va Sancho con su rocín*]; or alluding to his peasant cunning: "Whoever tries to cheat Sancho has a lot to learn" [*Quien a Sancho quiera engañar, mucho ha de estudiar*]; or to the figure's folkloric delusions of grandeur: "Sancho has hidalgo delusions" [*Rebienta Sancho de hidalgo* (Márquez Villanueva, 51; our translations)]. Sancho was a familiar carnivalesque presence at Salamanca, as Caro Baroja has shown, where students celebrated the feast of *Sancto Panza* ["the Holy Belly" (*Carnival* 111–12; our translation)].

Looking beyond Sancho Panza himself, we find a popular subculture that is part and parcel of the novel. Cervantes appropriates and makes ample use of a repertory of existent popular *refranes* in *Don Quixote*. Sancho's wife Teresa, for example, is depicted in the novel and in popular sayings as the conventional rustic housewife (II:5): "Sancho's wife—spin, pray and cook" [*la mujer de Sancho, rueca, religión, y rancho*] (Molho 251), and Aldonza as loose and flighty: "Aldonza will do as well as any other girl" [*moza por moza, buena es Aldonza* (251; our translations)]. In Aldonza's case, Joaquin Casalduero believes that the name, which conjured images of easy virtue, when paired with the "spiritual" Dulcinea, would have elicited much laughter from the contemporary reading public (Molho 289 n. 23). This may well be, but the association of Aldonza with easy virtue, was not an absolute. Sebastián de Covarrubias tells us that the name Aldonza, "many noble ladies of this kingdom have borne" ["hanle tenido señoras muy principales destos Reynos" (80a)].

There exists, then, in *Don Quixote* another culture, that of the *vulgo*—Sancho, Teresa, Juan Palomeque, the *ama*, the rustics—who speak in a different register, a lower level of discourse, that is juxtaposed to the culture of such figures as Don Quixote, Cardenio, Don Fernando, the priest, Dorotea, and others. This other culture consists of a community that shares stories, jokes, naming by reference to popular sayings, and proverbs, a linguistic register that Don Quixote, in accusing Sancho of being a "corrupter of good language" (II:19, 579) ["prevaricador del buen lenguaje" (786)], would deem "incorrect." This culture is clearly distinct from that of the novel's pseudo-rustics and performers of literary pastoral who, on one occasion, are described as "so many of them that this place, so crowded with shepherds and sheepfolds, seems to have been transformed into the pastoral Arcadia" (I:51, 437) ["tantos que parece que este sitio se ha convertido en la pastoral Arcadia" (581)]. It introduces what Homi Bhabha would call a "Third Space of enunciation, which makes the structure of meaning and reference an ambivalent process, [and which] destroys . . . [the] mirror of representation in which cultural knowledge is customarily revealed as an integrated, open, expanding code" (37). In other words, it serves as utopian discourse.

The effect is to highlight, by contrast, the fantasy performance of the novel's pseudo-rustics: that of the wealthy Eugenio, who admits to being "pure of blood, and in the flower of my youth, and [having] a rich estate" (I:51, 434) ["limpio en sangre, en la edad floreciente, en la hacienda muy rico" (577)], and who plays the role of a love-sick goatherd; of the "shepherds" Anselmo, Marcela, and Grisóstomo, who play the game with serious consequences; of the frolicking pretty "pastoral" youths in the countryside, scions of wealthy families (II:58), or of respected members of their communities (Marcela's uncle is the village priest). Such contrasts between cultures subjects the fantasy of idealized country living to doubt and can highlight the sometimes serious consequences of playing literary games with the emotions, as in the case of Grisóstomo.

When Don Quixote, for example, pictures the innocence and bucolic bliss that he and Sancho's family will enjoy in a pastoral setting, Sancho reacts. More country-wise than Quixote, and with his daughter in mind, Sancho reminds his master that the countryside harbors lusty predators: "there are shepherds more wicked than simple, and I wouldn't want her to go for wool and come back shorn; love and unchaste desires are as likely in the countryside as in the cities" (II:67, 901) ["y hay pastores más maliciosos que simples, y no querría que fuese por lana y volviese trasquilada, y tan bien suelen andar los amores y los no buenos deseos por los campos como por las ciudades" (1177)]. Eugenio the goatherd tells those who are taking Don Quixote home that "[f]armers who by nature are crafty . . . become the very embodiment of craftiness when idleness gives them the opportunity . . ." (I:51, 435) ["La gente labradora, que de suyo es maliciosa y dándole el ocio lugar es la misma malicia . . ." (578)]. And the text discloses, in the case of the wealthy farmer's daughter Dorotea, part of the peasant "upper crust" of the *labradores ricos*, a story of ambition and erotic manipulation that is negotiated with extraordinary pragmatism, though couched in the guise of modesty and victimization.

The reader's attention is consistently directed to the gratuitousness and artificiality of the country dwellers' performances. The affair of Leandra, also a *labradora rica*, and Vicente de la Rosa, for example, is figured as comically implausible; the high melodrama of Marcela, highlighted as spectacle;[3] and the exquisite fancy-dress *fête champêtre* of the "shepherdesses" in Part II, chapter 58, displayed as pure divertimento. While the poised, articulate "shepherds" and the spellbinding "shepherdesses" grace the pastoral vignettes in the novel and charm their "readers," the utopian discourse produces, in contrast, images of a contemporary reality consisting of "authentic" village neighbors. There are the rustic Lorenzo Corchuelo and his daughter Aldonza—tough, sweaty, bronzed by the sun (I:25, 155–56; Rico 283, I:31, 203–4; Rico 358–60); Sancho's daughter, barefoot and disheveled (II:50, 782; Rico 1036); and Sancho's wife Teresa, either "wearing a dun-colored skirt so short it looked as if it had been cut to shame her" (II:50, 783–84) ["con una saya parda—parecía según era corta que se la habían cortado por vergonzoso lugar—(1036)" or "disheveled and half-dressed" (II:73, 930; Rico 1212).

In the same way, language exposes to irony any romanticized view of rusticity. The laborers en route to Camacho's wedding find the archaism of Don Quixote's language wholly alien to the countryside in which he utters it, for "all of this was like speaking to them in Greek or in gibberish . . ." (II:19, 576) ["era hablarles en griego o en jerigonza" (782)]; and the anachronism of the Don's literary utopia is ironized in the reception accorded it by the bewildered goatherds in Part I, chapter 12. Side by side with Don Quixote's eloquent harangue on the romanticized askesis of the Classical golden world, the utopian discourse figures "real" goatherds eating salted goat meat, a half cheese harder than any mortar, and a heap of dried acorns.

The novel's other culture, then, is not a mere backdrop or picturesque diversion. Though filtered through the literary medium, it nevertheless introduces the world of the "folk" or *pueblo*, thereby exposing the ideological contradiction of the myth of idealized country living and the permeability of all fixed social categories. Rooted in the people's communal practices and language, it presents, in Antonio Gramsci's terms, "a reflection of the conditions of cultural life of the people" (189–90). It is not an autonomous world that is sealed off from the novel's "high" culture, but its effect is to set up an ironizing frame around the pseudo-Arcadians who would appropriate and intellectualize country living in production and circulation (II:58), as well as around those who would turn love into tragic pastoral poetry (I:11–14). The challenge that the rustic world presents in the novel becomes three-fold: it discloses, in the interstices between the disparate cultures, fissures in the smooth surface of the novel's utopic façade; it reveals the cultural capital that has been distributed unequally in *Don Quixote*; and it subjects to humor any notion "of the inherent originality or 'purity'" of hierarchical claims (Bhabha 37).

The repertoire of *refranes* provides an example of this challenge. Proverbs are, as Don Quixote admits to Sancho, wise sayings, "brief maxims derived from the experience and speculation of wise men in the past" (II:67, 902) ["sentencias breves, sacadas de la experiencia y especulación de nuestros antiguos sabios" (1178)]. Sancho's adept and "elegant" use of such experiential wisdom is highlighted by the narrator, who says in praise of Sancho that "the area in which he displayed the most elegance and the best memory was in his use of proverbs" (II:12, 528) ["en lo que él [Sancho] se mostraba más elegante y memorioso era en traer refranes" (720)]. The Duke's page also remarks on the pleasure Sancho's proverbs bring to the Duke and Duchess (II:50, 789), and even Don Quixote tries to compete with Sancho in using them: "I am speaking in this manner, Sancho, so you may understand that, like you, I too know how to pour down rainstorms of proverbs" (II:7, 499) ["Hablo de esta manera, Sancho, por daros a entender que también como vos sé yo arrojar refranes como llovidos" (682)]. But Don Quixote displays frustration at his inability to match Sancho's facility: "Tell me, where do you find them, you ignorant man, and how do you apply them, you fool, when to say only one that is really applicable, I have to perspire and labor like a ditchdigger" (II:43, 735–36) ["¿dónde los hallas, ignorante, o cómo los aplicas, mentecato? Que para decir yo uno y aplicarle bien, sudo y trabajo como si cavase?" (977)]. Though Sancho is their primary exponent in the novel, proverbs are seen to constitute an essential part of the other culture's capital. The Priest admits: "I can't help thinking, that everyone in the Panza family was born with a sack of proverbs inside" (II:50, 788) ["todos los deste linaje de los Panzas nacieron con un costal de refranes en el cuerpo" (788)]. As Sancho himself complains to Don Quixote: "Why the devil does it trouble you when I make use of my fortune, when I have no other, and no other wealth except proverbs and more proverbs?" (II:43, 736) ["¿A qué diablos se pudre de que yo me sirva de mi hacienda, que ninguna otra tengo, ni otro caudal alguno, sino refranes y más refranes" (977)]. Such cultural capital, Elias Rivers reminds us, is powerful: "Sancho's *Refranero* is his own ... Disticha Catonis. It is his oral heritage's answer to Don Quixote's written cultural dicta" (79).

Differing modes of narration in the novel also constitute examples of a cultural register and modus operandi that provide this "social articulation of difference" (Bhabha 2). The "normal" way in which the principal storytellers and the pseudo-Arcadian denizens tell their tales, that is, with a well-defined beginning, a middle, and a foreseeable end, contrasts with the subculture's form of storytelling. We remember Sancho's hilarious mode of narrating the comings and goings of La Torralba (I:20), and we can certainly identify with the ecclesiastic's impatience in the ducal palace at Sancho's similarly interminable tale of the rich hidalgo from Medina del Campo (II:31, 662–64; Rico 885–87). To the literate mind, Sancho's narrative is disjointed, fragmented, and unfamiliar. We laugh at Sancho, as we are meant to, but we are not allowed to forget that Sancho's *modus narrandi* is as "normal" as is that of the principal storytellers. It is simply one with which the literate reader and the characters from the dominant culture are less familiar. As Sancho asserts, it belongs to an "other" culture, for "[t]he way I'm telling it is how tales are told in my village" (I:20, 145) ["De la misma manera se cuentan en mi tierra todas las consejas" (213)]. His telling of the story of La Torralba is also purposeful, a brilliant tactic on Sancho's part to keep Don Quixote a captive audience and not to be abandoned within sound of the terrifying fulling hammers (I:20). The tactic works, at least until Don Quixote breaks the generic contract and interrupts the narration. We may note at this point that such a mode of storytelling is presented as characteristic of the other culture in the novel. It is parodied in the rambling narration by the mock laborer from Miguel Turra in Barataria, and governor Sancho is as irritated by it as Don Quixote and the ecclesiastic at the ducal palace had been with him.

Examples of the popular culture within the literary world of *Don Quixote* occasion some of the most humorous moments in the novel. When the pseudo-rustic Eugenio, for example, inscribes the tale of Leandra and Vicente de la Rosa's love in the generic conventions of romance, Sancho, reducing "humanity to its common nature," as Pierre Bourdieu would have said (*Language* 88), debunks so artificial a world. He shows that bliss in the peasant world has nothing to do with Eugenio's mastery of generic conventions, still less with Don Quixote's romantic askesis, but with somatic gratification whenever it may be available. Sancho ignores Eugenio and walks away in order to "stuff" himself:

> I'm going over to that brook with this meat pie, where I plan to eat enough for three days, because I've heard my master, Don Quijote, say that the squire of a knight errant has to eat whenever he can, and as much as he can . . . (I:50, 433)

> [yo a aquel arroyo me voy con esta empanada, donde pienso hartarme por tres días; porque he oído decir a mi señor don Quijote que el escudero de caballero andante ha de comer cuando se le ofreciere, hasta no poder más. (575)

The text nevertheless reveals its serious aspects even as it encourages us to laugh at Sancho's concern with food. Later, the Cura will feel obliged to invite the Duke's page to his home for supper because the resources of Sancho's wife Teresa are simply too humble, and she "has more desire than provisions for serving so worthy a guest" (II:50, 790) ["más tiene voluntad que alhajas para servir a tan buen huésped" (1044)].

Sancho shows the same skeptic indifference to any idealized view of country living that he has shown to Eugenio's perspective on country loving. Sancho hears the Cura say that he already knows "from experience that mountains breed learned men and shepherds' huts house philosophers" (432) ["de experiencia que los montes crían letrados y las cabañas de los pastores encierran filósofos" (575)]. But neither the kind of verbal performance at which his cultured "betters" play, nor the Cura's *experiencia* of the learned men and philosophers he claims inhabit the countryside, accords with Sancho's "real" experience of the rustic content and practice of country living and storytelling. Sancho simply walks away. At other times, Sancho does more than ignore his educated "betters" by showing up their vacuity, as in the case of the humanist Primo in Part II, chapter 22, who wastes people's time by collecting irrelevant trivia. As Sancho impatiently exclaims: "As for asking fool questions and giving nonsensical answers, I don't need to go around asking my neighbors for help" (II:22, 601s) ["para preguntar necedades y responder disparates no he menester yo andar buscando ayuda de vecinos" (813)]. The confrontation between these two cultures, then, elicits our laughter because of its incongruity, because we do not expect it. It defamiliarizes the givenness of the dominant culture's modus narrandi and operandi, discloses the permeability of hierarchical rank ["revela lo insustancioso de las escalas jerárquicas" (Molho 258)], and thereby "opens up the possibility of a cultural hybridity that entertains difference without an assumed or imposed hierarchy" (Bhabha 4).

The permeability of fixed categories/identifications also throws into relief the pretentious emulation of their "betters" on the part of the other culture. At Camacho's wedding, as students and countryfolk chatter away about classist differences, the text demonstrates the reciprocal influence of cultural products: we hear that "the fair Quiteria's [lineage] is superior to Camacho's" (II:19, 577) ["los linajes ... [el] de la hermosa Quiteria se aventaja al de Camacho" (783)]; and we see that Sancho's wife Teresa, in La Mancha, is hurt by the supposed airs of "the gentlewomen we have in this village who think that because they're wellborn the wind shouldn't touch them, and who go to church with all the airs of queens, and seem to think it's a dishonor to look at a peasant woman" (II:50, 785)] ["por ser hidalgas no las ha de tocar el viento, y van a la iglesia con tanta fantasía" (1039)]. But the utopian discourse subjects Teresa's "oppression" to doubt when she receives the fine necklace from the duchess and believes herself to be a governor's wife. She asks the priest if he knows of anyone who can buy her a petticoat like that of these country *hidalgas*, one that is "nice and round and just the way it should be, right in fashion and the best quality" (II:50, 788) ["un verdugado redondo, hecho y derecho, y sea al uso y de los mejores que hubiere" (1042)], and is convinced she will surpass the country *hidalgas* by becoming a countess (1042). As humorous as these incidents are, they are also purposeful. The text allows neither culture to be privileged. However widely differentiated these registers may seem to be, in the interstices we see the circularity of their cultural influences.

A similar reciprocity is true of the protagonists' utopian constructs. Don Quixote sees the Hesiodic age as "golden" because it is communal, free from toil, and devoid of greed in its simple abundance. The popular image that Sancho envisions for his *ínsula* is also "golden," but because of its sumptuous abundance and its exemption from toil which his hypothetical title and black slaves will make possible (I:19). Despite differences, both worlds betray three fundamental similarities: 1) in each, the real world (or the attempt to exorcise it through the fantasy) is present, as Emmanuel Levinas would put it, "in the image as it were between parentheses" (6–7); 2) each discloses its human centeredness; and 3) in each we discern the desire for abundance which, whether couched in simplicity or sumptuousness, is its foundational concept. As Cioranescu sums it up: "A parallel fiction, the preoccupation with human destiny, and the exclusively materialistic solution are the three basic characteristics that utopia and the land of Cockaigne have in common" ["La fiction parallèle, la préoccupation envers le destin de l'homme, et la solution strictement matérialiste sont les trois traits fondamentaux qu'ont en common l'utopie et le pays de cocagne" ("Utopie" 95)]. But, as each protagonist strives to have his fantasies actualized, he will discover the gap between aspiration and actualization.

Notes

1. We use the term "hybridity" as it is formulated by Homi K. Bhabha in *The Location of Culture*. For Bhabha, the notion of "hybridity" constitutes the process of "remaking the boundaries" of a culture, of "exposing the limits of any claim to a singular or autonomous sign of difference" (219). It is the "hybrid gap" (58), the third or "*in-between* space that carries the burden of the meaning of culture" (38: emphasis his). It is in this Third Space that "cultural differences 'contingently' and conflictually touch" (207). For a fascinating account of how contingently and conflictually the "new" discoveries touched the methods and theories of the "old," see Grafton.

2. For Murillo, repeated by Rico, the humor is enhanced by the incongruous fact that this princess lives in a *pueblo* that is far from "lofty," one in which the majority of the inhabitants are Moorish.

3. "I think it will be something worth seeing; at least, I'll be sure to go and see it, even if I knew I would not get back to the place tomorrow" (I:7; our translation) ["Y tengo para mí que ha de ser cosa muy de ver; a lo menos yo no dejaré de ir a verla si supiese no volver mañana al lugar" (129)]. "We'll all do the same, the goatherds responded" (I:7, 82) ["—Todos haremos lo mesmo—respondieron los cabreros" (129)]. "And so my advice, Señor, is that tomorrow you be sure to attend his burial, which will be something worth seeing . . ." (I:7, 85) ["Y así os aconsejo, señor, que no dejéis de hallaros mañana a su entierro, que será muy de ver . . ." (134)). "It seems to me, Señor Vivaldo, that we must consider our lingering to see this extraordinary funeral as time well spent, for it most certainly will be extraordinary" (I:8, 86–87) ["Paréceme, señor Vivaldo, que habernos de dar por bien empleada la tardanza que hiciéremos, en ver este famoso entierro, que no podrá dejar de ser famoso . . ." (135–36)]. Marcela's theatrical entrance on the scene, atop the rock, simply climaxes the spectacle all are anxious to see.

BARBARA FUCHS

Don Quijote *1 and the*
Forging of National History

Cervantes protests too much when he reiterates throughout *Don Quijote* his goal of demolishing the romances of chivalry. As critics have long noted, his exertions also seem misdirected: the foibles of the chivalric romance are hardly a worthy target for the sophisticated irony of the text.[1] Instead, *Don Quijote* presents a sustained reflection on history itself, and on the construction of historiographical knowledge, that is as radical as the novel's famous interrogation of truth versus literary fiction. This essay traces the destabilization of historical truth in the first part of *Don Quijote*, arguing that the novel shatters not the "fingidas y disparatadas historias de los libros de caballería" (false and nonsensical histories of the books of chivalry), as the end of the second part claims, but the immutable, unquestionable narrative of the nation's history. National history, national heroes, and national purpose, Cervantes suggests, are themselves subject to narrative elaboration and embroidery—to the highly mediated processes of memory. In the wake of Hayden White's *Metahistory*, we have become used to the idea that a rhetorical apparatus organizes our understanding of the past, just as it does literary narratives. By charting the general problematization of historical truth in the first part of *Don Quijote*, and the more precise interrogation of the medieval, chivalric past through the figure of that "true historian," Archbishop Turpin, I show how the text foregrounds the notion of a deliberately

From *Modern Language Quarterly* 68, no. 3 (September 2007): 395–416. © 2007 by the University of Washington.

145

constructed history, mounting an oblique challenge to the historiographical project of early modern Spain.[2]

Through constant comparisons between historical and literary texts, Cervantes problematizes the idea of a singular truth of history and reminds the reader how history is fabricated in the telling. In several episodes Don Quijote justifies his admiration for chivalric heroes by sizing them up in relation to historical figures, who obviously fall short of their imaginative counterparts. The historical exemplars have no greater purchase on him because they are historical; instead, they pale in comparison to the literary heroes. On one level, these exchanges are simply literary in jokes, through which Cervantes ably sends up both Aristotelian and Renaissance standards of verisimilitude. Yet what interests me about these episodes is not Don Quijote's comical inflation of the romance heroes but the concomitant deflation of the historical actors and the way that the very comparison casts their ostensible truth in doubt.[3] Cervantes's novel reminds us again and again that national history, like chivalric romance, is a fabulous construction. It may be more verisimilar than the fictional stories of knights and ladies, but it is on a continuum with them. Moreover, in challenging the received truths of national history, Cervantes often reveals the contradictions inherent in imagining a heroic past—one couched in Christian and chivalric terms—for a nation that often served as Christendom's other.

Cervantes wrote at the end of a century that had seen important transformations in the idea of history. The discovery of the New World, in particular, posed a crisis for received historical knowledge. New World narratives repeatedly reminded their readers that the ancients had not known of this place. The balance between the authority of first-person accounts and received traditions of knowledge changed radically. Furthermore, the truth of the New World was so unlikely—and its referents were so distant—that New World events were often considered fabulous, akin more to chivalric romance than to history. Thus in his definition of *fábula* in the 1611 *Tesoro de la lengua castellana o española*, Sebastián de Covarrubias Orozco notes how vulnerable historical exploits in the Indies are to skepticism:

> Rematemos con que algunas vezes damos nombres de fábulas a las cosas que fueron ciertas o verdaderas, pero en su discurso tienen tanta variedad que parecen cosas no acontecidas sino compuestas e inventadas de algún gallardo y locano ingenio. Los que avéys leydo las Corónicas de las Indias, cosa que passó ayer, tan cierta y tan sabida, mirad quántas cosas ay en su descubrimiento y en su conquista, que exceden a quanto han imaginado las plumas de los vanos mentirosos que han escrito libros de cavallerías, pues estas

vendrán tiempo que las llamen fábulas y aun las tengan por tales
los que fueren poco aficionados a la nación Española.

[Finally, we sometimes call fables things that were certain or
true but that in their narration are so varied that they seem not
as though they occurred but as though they were composed and
invented by some brave and youthful mind. Those of you who
have read the Chronicles of the Indies, something that occurred
yesterday, that is so certain and well known, note how many things
there are in the discovery and conquest of those lands that exceed
what the quills of the vain liars who write books of chivalry have
imagined. Yet there will come a time when those who hold Spain in
low regard will call these fables and hold them as such.]⁴

But of course, placing the Spaniards' feats under *fábula* in the first place
suggests a certain ambivalence vis-à-vis their historicity. Or perhaps, as
Covarrubias implies, it is merely a matter of time before all history seems
like a fable. A related, common topos of Spanish history in the period holds
that only writerly modesty keeps the heroic feats of Spaniards from acquiring the status of epic.⁵

The very category of history is complicated for Covarrubias. He begins
with the standard Greek etymology of the term: "Es una narración y exposición
de acontecimientos passados, y en rigor es de aquellas cosas que el autor de la
historia vio por sus propios ojos y da fee dellas, como testigo de vista" (It is a
narration and exposition of past events, and more precisely of those things that
the author of the history saw with his own eyes and swears to as an eyewitness)
(692). However, he soon moves into authorization via prior texts and, indeed,
into a much broader sense of history: "Pero basta que el historiador tenga buenos originales y autores fidedignos de aquello que narra y escrive, y que de industria no mienta o sea floxo en averiguar la verdad, antes que la assegure como tal.
Qualquiera narración que se cuente, aunque no sea con este rigor, largo modo se
llama historia, como historia de los animales, historia de las plantas, etc." (But
it is enough that the historian have good originals and reliable authors on what
he narrates and writes, and that he not lie on purpose or be lax in finding out
the truth, before he ensures that it is such. Any narration related, whether or
not with this rigor, is roughly called a history, such as a history of animals, a history of plants, etc.) (692). Intentionality makes all the difference: as long as the
historian does not set out to deceive ("de industria no mienta"), his version will
suffice. The expansion of the category of history to "qualquiera narración que se
cuente" suggests a loss of chronological referentiality, even though the examples
relocate that referentiality in the natural world.

For purposes of reading *Don Quijote*, it is perhaps most important to remember that the Spanish term *historia*, which today means both history and story, only gradually and conflictively acquired the second meaning in the early modern period (it does not fully show up in Covarrubias, for example). As Bruce Wardropper argued in a seminal essay, Cervantes's constant references to his narrative as an *historia* constitute a playful attempt to reflect on its historicity, or lack thereof.[6] The self-consciousness of a tour de force sentence early in the text exposes the paradoxical chiasmus between historicity and knowledge:

> Autores hay que dicen que la primera aventura que le avino fue la del Puerto Lápice, otros dicen que la de los molinos de viento; pero lo que yo he podido averiguar en este caso, y lo que he hallado escrito en los anales de la Mancha, es que él anduvo todo aquel día y, al anochecer, su rocín y él se hallaron cansados y muertos de hambre; y que, mirando a todas partes por ver si descubriría algún castillo o alguna majada de pastores donde recogerse y adonde pudiese remediar su mucha hambre y necesidad, vio, no lejos del camino por donde iba, una venta, que fue como si viera una estrella que, no a los portales, sino a los alcázares de su redención le encaminaba. (1.2)

> [Some authors say his first adventure was the one in Puerto Lápice; others claim it was the adventure of the windmills; but according to what I have been able to determine with regard to this matter, and what I have discovered written in the annals of La Mancha, he rode all that day, and at dusk he and his horse found themselves exhausted and half-dead with hunger; and as he looked all around to see if he could find some castle or a sheepfold with shepherds where he might take shelter and alleviate his great hunger and need, he saw an inn not far from the path he was traveling, and it was as if he had seen a star guiding him not to the portals, but to the inner towers of his salvation.] (26)[7]

Cervantes seems acutely conscious of the problems posed by historiographical claims to authority when, as in this passage, only the fictional construction of an omniscient observer provides access to interiority, motivation, or perception. The historian, by contrast, cannot furnish a fully satisfying story.

Yet there is also a specific historiographical and ideological context in which such literary games are played. Sixteenth-century Spain was caught in the double bind of constructing an official, respectable history for the new nation even as it negotiated local accounts that often replaced the Moorish past with a retroactive Christian identity. This dynamic led to many more or less explicitly fictional pseudohistories, which, broadly speaking, observed the forms of history with a deliberately falsified content or, perhaps less problematically, reproduced them for literary purposes. Cumulatively, these pseudohistories cast historiography into a crisis: going through the generic motions of history—calling one's text a history, invoking authority, following a chronological order—was not enough to ensure the reliability or factuality of a text.

Among the most famous pseudohistories were Miguel de Luna's scandalous *Historia verdadera del rey don Rodrigo*, which attempted to rewrite the Moorish invasion of Spain as a welcome reprieve from Christian sinfulness, and the fake gospels of the Sacromonte. Both appeared in the closing years of the sixteenth century, shortly before the first part of *Don Quijote*. Allusions to these controversial pseudohistories signal Cervantes's own skepticism of received historical knowledge. This is perhaps most evident at the end of the first part, where the narrator claims that further news of his historical subject, Don Quijote, may be found only in ancient Gothic "pergaminos" (parchments) in a leaden box: "Ni de su fin y acabamiento pudo [el autor] alcanzar cosa alguna, ni la alcanzara, ni supiera, si la buena suerte no le deparara un antiguo médico, que tenía en su poder una caja de plomo, que según él dijo, se había hallado en los cimientos derribados de una antigua ermita que se renovaba" (Nor could he find or learn anything about Don Quixote's final end, and never would have, if good fortune had not presented him with an ancient physician who had in his possession a leaden box that he claimed to have found in the ruined foundations of an old hermitage that was being renovated) (1.52; 445). This is a clear allusion to the famous forgeries of the *plomos* of the Sacromonte, which appeared in Granada in 1595. These syncretic writings on leaden tablets, presumably planted by persecuted Moriscos, offered a theological rapprochement between Christianity and Islam while suggesting also that Arabs had played a central role in the evangelization of Spain, in the first century AD. Their spectacular discovery had been anticipated a few years earlier, in 1588, during the demolition of what the *plomos* refer to as the Torre Turpiana (Turpin's tower), the minaret that had long served as a bell tower for Granada's cathedral. There an old leaden box full of ancient Christian "relics" had made its appearance. While these finds may seem ridiculous to modern readers, and indeed were loudly denounced by scholars in the period, the fake gospels and the relics of "Arab martyrs" were enthusiastically embraced in Granada, which was struggling to imagine for itself the Christian past to which it could not, in historical terms, lay claim.

In this intellectual context, Cervantes's ending to the first part of *Don Quijote* reads as a mockery of both the fake gospels and their fanatical reception by Granada.[8] In "The Moriscos and Don Quijote" L. P. Harvey argues that pseudohistory, in a broader sense, is the target of Cervantine satire: "The attack on the novels of chivalry operates at the level of the fiction concerning Alonso Quijano, but at the level of Cide Hamete Benengeli, the creator of Alonso Quijano, the butt of Cervantes' gibes was not the novel of chivalry so much as pseudo-history." Américo Castro similarly identifies the *plomos* as the "blanco principal del sarcasmo cervantino" (principal target of Cervantes's satire) (349).[9] Unlike Wardropper, that is, Harvey and Castro read Cervantes's interrogation of history not only for its literary productivity—that is, for how skepticism about *historia* produces the novel—but for its ideological significance. More recently, Mary Malcolm Gaylord has explored Cervantes's historical skepticism in light of the huge historiographical enterprise of writing the Spanish past, in particular the story of its New World conquests (117–47). Building on their claims, I suggest, first, that Cervantes's critique extends not just to pseudohistory but to the history of Spain more generally, and second, that this critique is so interwoven with the attack on preposterous fictions that history itself suffers a kind of fictional contagion. My argument takes me not to the New World or to the official histories but to popular versions of history and to the pressures of medieval stories on the later construction of Spain.

Romance and History

In a series of episodes, Don Quijote's beloved heroes of chivalric romance are contrasted with historical heroes from the national pantheon, figures who run the gamut from popular myth to actual historicity. The humor of these exchanges lies in Don Quijote's gullibility, his desire to believe that his heroes performed amazing feats. Yet when the fictional knights are juxtaposed with the historical figures, the overall effect is to cast doubt on the reality of the latter and on the willingness of Spanish subjects to believe in their own heroes. As the historian Pedro M. Cátedra shows, the pedagogical apparatus of early modern Spain threatened to confuse these boundaries, for children were taught to read from cheap print—popular pamphlets that covered everything from famous historical figures, such as the Cid, to short chivalric fiction. These various materials were often equalized through renderings in ballad form.[10] Might a popular culture based on the indiscriminate reading of history and romance have predisposed Cervantes or his readers, schooling them, as it were, in pseudohistory?

The juxtaposition of chivalric fiction and national history occurs over and over again in the first part, from Don Quijote's own first meditation on the matter, when his madness is described:

Y asentósele de tal modo en la imaginación que era verdad toda aquella máquina de aquellas sonadas soñadas invenciones que leía [i.e., the romances of chivalry], que para él no había otra historia más cierta en el mundo. Decía él que el Cid Ruy Díaz había sido muy buen caballero; pero que no tenía que ver con el Caballero de la Ardiente Espada, que de sólo un revés había partido por el medio dos fieros y descomunales gigantes. Mejor estaba con Bernardo del Carpio, porque en Roncesvalles había muerto a Roldán el encantado, valiéndose de la industria de Hércules, cuando ahogó a Anteo. (1.i)

[He became so convinced in his imagination of the truth of all the countless grandiloquent and false inventions he read that for him no history in the world was truer. He would say that El Cid Ruy Díaz had been a very good knight but could not compare to Amadís, the Knight of the Blazing Sword, who with a single backstroke cut two ferocious and colossal giants in half. He was fonder of Bernardo del Carpio, because at Roncesvalles he had killed the enchanted Roland by availing himself of the tactic of Hercules when he crushed Antaeus.] (21)

Don Quijote's first point of reference is the great hero of Spanish medieval history, whose feats are immediately minimized relative to those of the chivalric hero. When he instead valorizes Bernardo, slayer of the great paladin Roland, the text suggests how chivalric fiction and national history may work at cross-purposes. Bernardo is a national hero for the Spanish, but only because he vanquishes Roland, flower of all chivalry. In this version, the Spanish Bernardo stands in for Roland's Saracen enemy in a striking local departure from the *matière de France*. In the struggle against the Franks, Spain cannot align itself with Christendom but is instead uncomfortably relegated to the space of the religious and ethnic other. Both the Cid and Bernardo also complicate any simple division between Moors and Christians by forging pragmatic alliances with Moors, to great effect. From these first addled musings of its protagonist, then, the text foregrounds the complexity of constructing a national past that is both heroic and European.

But Cervantes's interrogation of national mythmaking extends much farther, as he ironizes the hyperbolic valor of both romance and historical figures. In the famous discussion of chivalric romance at the inn, Cervantes juxtaposes chivalric fiction and actual books of history to great effect, showing how they both rely on exaggeration and larger-than-life protagonists. In an old valise, the innkeeper has *Don Cirongilio de Tracia, Felixmarte de Hircania,* and the *Historia del Gran Capitán Gonzalo Hernández de Córdoba, con la vida de Diego García de Paredes* (all actual books published in the sixteenth century). The curate condescendingly criticizes the innkeeper's preference for the chivalric romances over the history:

> "Hermano mío," dijo el cura, "estos dos libros son mentirosos y están llenos de disparates y devaneos. Y este del Gran Capitán es historia verdadera y tiene los hechos de Gonzalo Hernández de Córdoba, el cual, por sus muchas y grandes hazañas mereció ser llamado de todo el mundo GRAN CAPITAN, renombre famoso y claro y dél solo merecido. Y este Diego García de Paredes fue un principal caballero, natural de la ciudad de Trujillo, en Estremadura, valentísimo soldado, y de tantas fuerzas naturales, que detenía con un dedo una rueda de molino en la mitad de su furia. Y puesto con un montante en la entrada de una puente, detuvo a todo un innumerable ejército, que no pasare por ella. Y hizo otras tales cosas, que si como él las cuenta y las escribe él, asimismo con la modestia de caballero y de coronista propio las escribiera otro, libre y desapasionado, pusieran en su olvido las de los Hétores, Aquiles y Roldanes. (1.32)

> ["Dear brother," said the priest, "these two books are false and full of foolishness and nonsense, but this one about the Great Captain is truthful history and tells the accomplishments of Gonzalo Hernández de Córdoba, who, because of his many feats, deserved to be called the Great Captain by everyone, a famous and illustrious name deserved by him alone; Diego García de Paredes was a distinguished nobleman, a native of the city of Trujillo, in Extremadura, a very courageous soldier, and so strong that with one finger he could stop a millwheel as it turned; standing with a broadsword at the entrance to a bridge, he brought an immense army to a halt and would not permit them to cross; and he did other comparable things, and he recounts them and writes about them himself, with the modesty of a gentleman writing his own chronicle, but if another were to write about those feats freely and dispassionately, they would relegate all the deeds of Hector, Achilles, and Roland to oblivion.] (269)

The curate locates García de Paredes's identity precisely in Trujillo, so that despite his reputation he represents a chorographic heroism that contrasts with the vague and exotic origins of the "Thracian" and "Hircanian" heroes of fiction that the innkeeper favors in the exchange (1.32; 269).[11] He also claims a distinction between the doing and the telling: if García de Paredes were not narrating his own story, his feats would eclipse those of epic heroes. Yet in fact the text in question is unremittingly boastful, even though many of the brawls and scrapes it relates are more characteristic of a soldierly picaresque than of an exemplary, heroic life.[12] The textual history of the narrative is so complex, moreover, that it cannot be assigned to García de Paredes in any straightforward fashion, although he probably wrote at least some kernel of it. To complicate matters further, the text does not include the legendary feats that the curate singles out. The stopping of the millwheel is, instead, simply one of the myths surrounding this character, while the story of the bridge occurs in the *Crónica del Gran Capitán* (Sánchez-Jiménez and Sánchez-Jiménez, 235).[13] Finally, given the textual history of the *Breve soma* and the intervening dissonance of the picaresque, claiming that the authenticity of the text depends on its first-person narration only ironizes its complicated relationship to historical truth.[14]

In any event, the innkeeper is not impressed by the curate's comparison. A stopped millwheel, he scoffs, pales next to five giants split at the waist or entire armies routed like sheep. (The alert reader will remember that Don Quijote, in his madness, takes sheep for armies in chapter 18, a further ironizing of this hyperbole.) More important, I would argue, the curate has already capitulated to a chivalric view of the world: instead of focusing on Gonzalo Hernández de Córdoba, widely credited as the first modern general for his transformation of Spain's army and his command of artillery, he privileges García de Paredes, an outsized, somewhat anachronistic figure of personal heroism, who is famous for such feats as the standoff at the bridge and who lives on more through legend than through the rather unsavory published account of his doings.

Despite his own unwitting penchant for the colorful and the chivalric, the dogged curate tries to impress on the innkeeper the distinction between history and fiction, swearing about the latter that "nunca tales caballeros fueron en el mundo, ni tales hazañas ni disparates acontecieron en él" (there never were knights like these in the world, and their great deeds, and all that other nonsense, never happened) (1.32; 270). The naive innkeeper, outraged, claims that state authority supports the books of chivalry, so they cannot be false: "¡Bueno es que quiera darme vuestra merced a entender que todo aquello que estos buenos libros dicen sea disparates y mentiras, estando impreso con licencia de los señores del Consejo Real, como si ellos fueran gente que había de imprimir tanta mentira junta, y tantas batallas y tanto encantamentos, que quitan el juicio!" (That's really something: your grace

wants me to think that everything these good books say is foolishness and
lies, when they've been printed with the permission of the gentlemen of the
Royal Council, as if they were the kind of people who'd allow the printing of
so many lies, and so many battles and so many enchantments it could drive
you crazy!) (1.32; 270).[15] Clearly, at one level we are meant to dismiss the
innkeeper as a Don Quijote manqué, another example of the gullible reader.
But the passage also makes us question the construction of national memory,
placing the real heroes on a continuum with the false, where the only things
that separate the two are degrees of hyperbole and external, a priori distinctions by an authoritative audience.

Cervantes underlines the point by placing the main *historical* figure at
the center of this debate in the *literary* text that the characters next encounter,
the *Novela del curioso impertinente* (*Tale of the Man Who Was Recklessly Curious*). The novella's historical setting is unspecified until the very end, when
the hero, Lotario, is killed "en una batalla que en aquel tiempo dio Monsiur
de Lautrec al Gran Capitán Gonzalo Fernández de Córdoba" (in the battle
between Monsieur de Lautrec and the Great Captain Gonzalo Fernández
de Cordoba, which had just taken place) (1.35; 312).[16] Yet the true referent cannot guarantee historicity, and the curate's first comment as the story
ends questions its verisimilitude: "'Bien,' dijo el cura, 'me parece esta novela,
pero no me puedo persuadir que esto sea verdad, y si es fingido, fingió mal el
autor, porque no se puede imaginar que haya marido tan necio'" ("This novel
seems fine," said the priest, "but I cannot persuade myself that it is true; if it is
invented, the author invented badly, because no one can imagine a husband so
foolish") (1.35; 313). Thus the historical figure cannot rescue the story from
inverisimilitude, and the sly repetition of the name from the earlier debate
contributes to the sense that the telling of the various stories differs merely
in degree of invention—millwheels versus giants, as it were. There is also, I
suspect, a subtle joke on accuracy and authenticity in the perfectly standard
variation of the name—Hernández versus Fernández—from one episode to
the next.

The most vociferous comparison of history and chivalric fiction comes
in Don Quijote's debate with the canon of Toledo toward the end of the first
part. The canon recommends reading the book of judges, or simply history, for
a healthy dose of heroism and provides a list of nation-building figures:

> Un Viriato tuvo Lusitania; un César Roma; un Aníbal Cartago;
> un Alejandro Grecia; un Conde Fernán González Castilla; un Cid
> Valencia; un Gonzalo Fernández Andalucía; un Diego García de
> Paredes Estremadura; un Garci Pérez de Vargas Jérez; un Garci
> Laso Toledo; un Don Manuel de León Sevilla, cuya lección de sus

valerosos hechos puede entretener, enseñar, deleitar y admirar a los más altos ingenios que los leyeren. Esta sí será letura digna del buen entendimiento de vuestra merced, señor Don Quijote mío, de la cual saldrá erudito en la historia. (1.49)

[Lusitania had a Viriato, Rome had a Caesar, Carthage a Hannibal, Greece an Alexander, Castile a Count Fernán González, Valencia a Cid, Andalusia a Gonzalo Fernández, Extremadura a Diego García de Paredes, Jerez a Garci Pérez de Vargas, Toledo a Garcilaso, Seville a Don Manuel de León. Reading about their valorous deeds can entertain, instruct, delight, and astonish the highest minds. This would be a study worthy of your grace's intelligence, Señor Don Quixote, and from it you would emerge learned in history.] (424)

Like Diego García de Paredes, the heroes of Spain all have specific local allegiances. Spanish history seems to require the suturing together of many stories, building blocks of an as-yet-unattainable nation as unified as "Rome." But Don Quijote refuses to be convinced by the catalog of local heroes, and his extended response to the canon effectively places literary and historical figures on a continuum of fictionality that renders them all suspect. If the giant Fierabrás did not exist, did the Twelve Peers of France? If they did not exist, what about the chivalric knights of Spanish history? Don Quijote produces another list, this one of historical figures, concluding with "otras muchas hazañas hechas por caballeros cristianos, destos y de los reinos estranjeros, tan auténticas y verdaderas, que torno a decir, que el que las negase carecería de toda razón y buen discurso" (many other deeds performed by Christian knights from these kingdoms and from foreign ones, deeds so authentic and true that I say again that whoever denies them must be lacking in all reason and good sense) (1.49; 427). The canon, forced to recognize that the issue is more complicated than it first appears, retreats into qualifications, making special dispensations for Spanish figures:

No puedo yo negar, señor Don Quijote, que no sea verdad algo de lo que vuestra merced ha dicho, especialmente en lo que toca a los caballeros andantes españoles, y asimesmo, quiero conceder que hubo Doce Pares de Francia, pero no quiero creer que hicieron todas aquellas cosas que el arzobispo Turpín dellos escribe.... En lo que hubo Cid, no hay duda, ni menos Bernardo del Carpio, pero de que hicieron las hazañas que dicen, creo que la hay muy grande. (1.49)

[I cannot deny, Señor Don Quixote, that some of what your grace
has said is true, especially with regard to Spanish knights errant;
by the same token, I also wish to concede that there were Twelve
Peers of France, though I cannot believe they did all those things
that Archbishop Turpin writes about them.... As for El Cid, there
can be no doubt that he existed, and certainly none about Bernardo
del Carpio, but I think it exceedingly doubtful that they performed
the deeds people say they did.] (427)

National history, it seems, is as prone to hyperbole as the chivalric romance.
The distinctions among these *historias* are, if anything, a matter of degree,
and presumably also of national allegiance. Moreover, in such figures as
Bernardo national history produces its own necessary fictions, to challenge
romance with romance.

The exchange between Don Quijote and the canon introduces, too, a
veiled critique of sacred history and memorialization, first, through the canon's initial recommendation that Don Quijote turn to the sacred scriptures
for tales of heroism, and second, through Don Quijote's insistence that there
is material evidence of the truth of chivalric romance: a certain peg with
which the hero of a Provençal romance steered a flying wooden horse can
be plainly seen, he claims, in the Royal Armory. When the canon laments
not having seen it, Don Quijote further embroiders his story, claiming that
the peg is sheathed in leather to prevent its becoming moldy. This artifact
sounds strikingly like a lay version of a relic: for Don Quijote, irrefutable
evidence of the truth of his creed; for others who are not already firm believ-
ers, less persuasive. The Erasmian skepticism vis-à-vis the romance relic in
this episode prefigures the knowing reference to the leaden box—remarkably
like the sacred "finds" in Granada—two chapters later, at the end of the first
part. Yet the force of Cervantes's novel goes well beyond the mockery of the
Grenadine fake gospels, to a more sustained interrogation of how the history
of the nation is crafted.

Turpinades

Beyond the general problematization of the distinction between history
and romance in *Don Quijote*, Cervantes considers specific cases that reveal
how complicated it is to enlist the medieval past in the project of national
history. A striking figure connects the episodes in which he interrogates
received historical truths, whether national or religious. The first planted
artifacts found in Granada, a few years before the *plomos* of the Sacromonte, were located in the Torre Turpiana. This detail must have been
irresistible for Cervantes: contemporary pseudohistory makes its appear-

ance in a building presumably named for the famous medieval churchman Archbishop Turpin, purported author of the story of Roland. The matter of Turpin—apocryphal historian, chivalric chronicler, dynastic prop—recalls throughout the first part of *Don Quijote* the contradictions inherent in forging a national history from a chivalric past. Tellingly, much of the Turpin material concerns precisely the construction of the nation, on the border between France and Spain.

The historical Turpin, who lived in the eighth century, was a monk at the Abbey of Saint-Denis and later archbishop of Rheims. Yet he is most interesting not for his historical existence but for the text associated with his name. Turpin was presumed to be the author of the *Historia Karoli Magni et Rotholandi*, a Latin chronicle of Charlemagne's fantastic exploits in Spain.[17] The twelfth-century chronicle explicitly foregrounds Turpin's authorship and thus its own historicity via a prologue in which the author identifies himself as Turpin. Enormously popular, the text circulated widely throughout Europe, with versions in Catalan, French, Galician, German, Irish, Old Norse, Provençal, Spanish, and Welsh.[18] More than two hundred manuscripts survive. The chronicle remained popular well into the sixteenth century, with editions of the Latin text printed in 1566 and 1583.[19] In Spain itself the text proved controversial, given its blatant attempt to co-opt local, proto-Spanish legends with a vision of French expansionism.[20] By contrast, in France the *Pseudo-Turpin Chronicle*, as it is now generally known, became an important document in the canonization of Charlemagne and in the writing of French royal history.[21] As one critic describes it, the text was an essential element in the "'historification' of Carolingian legend" (Short, 2), that is, in precisely the conflation of chivalric fiction and national history that would most intrigue Cervantes.

Although Turpin's pseudohistory is primarily associated with the matter of France, it bears directly on the Spanish national imaginary, for it begins with Charlemagne's vision of Saint James (or Santiago), patron saint of Spain. The king has subsequent visions of a path of stars leading to Galicia, where, unbeknownst to all, Saint James's body lies buried. The saint appears to Charlemagne once again in a dream, urging him to follow the path of stars and liberate his place of burial from the Saracens. The chronicle then narrates Charlemagne's battles in Spain, the taking of Santiago de Compostela from the Saracens, and the establishment of the cathedral and shrine dedicated to Saint James. Thus a French text on French matters challenges the essential Spanish myths of Saint James as patron of the Reconquista and early evangelizer, replacing them with a story of French expansionism. As it often does, the material history of the text tells us much about how it was understood by its early readers. In the mid-twelfth century Turpin's chronicle was bound with four other manuscripts on the saint's life into the *Liber Sancti Iacobi*, or *Book of Saint James*. The codex, presumably assembled to encourage pilgrims to visit the saint's shrine at Compostela, still resides in the archives of the cathedral there (Short etc.). Despite its phenomenal popularity, however, by the late fifteenth century the *Pseudo-Turpin* had been widely discredited as a historical hoax. In the 1534 *Pantagruel* Rabelais has the trickster Panurge entertain his audience with "les fables de Turpin, les exemples de Saint Nicolas, et le conte de la Ciguoigne" (the fables of Turpin, the tales of Saint Nicholas, and the story of the stork), as though to liken Turpin's fables to Mother Goose tales.[22]

The figure of Turpin materializes several times in the first part of *Don Quijote* as a dubious guarantor of historical truth. His appearance marks the spot at which historical truth intersects most problematically with chivalric romance, for his "historical" authorship of the Roland chronicle, about a battle that occurred years after Turpin's death, exposes the text as a fiction.[23] Moreover, the French story of Roland's death at Roncesvalles at the hands of the Saracens is directly challenged by the purely Spanish account of Bernardo del Carpio as a local hero fighting off the French invaders, in most versions by allying himself with the Saracens themselves. The story of Bernardo, which Ramón Menéndez Pidal describes as a "necessary nationalist response to French Carolingian epic,"[24] was recounted in several versions of the earliest chronicle histories of Spain as a central event in the construction of a Christian Iberian alternative to the Franks, and also circulated broadly in *romances* and on the early modern stage.[25] In these narratives, which project a Spanish nation back to the eighth century, Bernardo resists Charlemagne's attempted conquest of Iberia, embodying the Spanish love of liberty and *patria* even as he allies with the Saracens.[26] Thus the canon's exasperated response to Don Quijote in 1.49 is particularly telling: Turpin's account of the Twelve Peers of France and the legend of Bernardo, which the canon juxtaposes, cannot both be true, regardless of their individual historicity, because they are mutually contradictory. Through the references to Turpin, then, Cervantes obliquely signals a central problem in the construction of Spanish history: whether through its native heroes or as a land of Saracens, Spain is often the *antagonist* in the chivalric tradition and cannot easily be incorporated into an expansive myth of Christendom.[27] National history cannot be sutured to chivalric fable but must in fact construct an (equally fictive) alternative.

Despite the international popularity of the *Pseudo-Turpin*, the story of Saint James has particular consequences for early modern Spain, for the myth had prospered with the fortunes of the Reconquista. By the sixteenth century the cult of James was extremely powerful; it undergirded the very idea of a Spanish nation. The *voto de Santiago*, an annual tax levied on harvests by the church of Compostela, was expanded by the Catholic kings to encompass the whole of the newly unified nation, in what Márquez Villanueva calls the "administrative nationalization [*estatalización*] of the Jacobean myth" (282). But this nationwide levy led to great resistance, and legal challenges to the veracity of the Saint James legend ensued. The Vatican took up the issue and, after scandalously suggesting that the mission of James to Spain had never occurred, was forced to acknowledge it as a traditional belief of the Spanish church. These controversies took place during Cervantes's lifetime and were part of the historical context that led to the pseudohistories that fleshed out Spain's Christian past. To return to the place of Turpin in these historiographical controversies: in 1619, shortly after the publication of the second part of *Don Quijote*, the *Pseudo-Turpin* was finally removed from the *Liber Sancti Iacobi* at Compostela, presumably because of embarrassment at its fraudulence. In all likelihood, Turpin's text had become a liability for Compostela.

Beyond the patent inauthenticity of the text, however, lies the more complex question of the relation between a French—subsequently European—text and the Spanish versions that might contest it. Both the Bernardo del Carpio story and the Spanish versions of the discovery of Santiago's body contrast markedly with the claims of the *Pseudo-Turpin*. Recent work on the chronicle indicates that it was expanded and modified to serve the purposes of Compostela before its inclusion in the *Liber Sancti Iacobi*, a process that suggests a local investment in resolving the discrepancies.[28] The paradoxes of national identity, I submit, are equally, if not more, difficult to resolve: how can Spain champion a Frankish myth of self-determination against Saracens when the best it can offer as a local champion is Bernardo, slayer of Roland and himself an ally to the Saracens? In this light, the constant attempts by other characters to redirect Don Quijote's fascination from the chivalric heroes to the great figures of Spanish history threaten to take the would-be knight from the frying pan of fancy into the fire of national mythmaking.

In the first part of *Don Quijote*, the curate first mentions Turpin during the Inquisition of the Books. Referring to him ironically as the "verdadero historiador Turpín" (true historian Turpin) (1.6; 48), the curate spares him only because his fictions provided material for Boiardo and Ariosto. In a scene that comments obliquely on the relation between national history and knight-errantry, Don Quijote interrupts the inquisition with his delusions, so that, the narrator tells us, certain Spanish historical epics and an actual history of Charles V—"*La Carolea y León de España, con Los Hechos del Emperador*" (*The Caroleid* and *Lion of Spain*, with *The Feats of the Emperor*)—inadvertently go into the bonfire along with the "lying" books of chivalry. Once restrained,

Don Quijote addresses the curate as "señor Arzobispo Turpín" and reproaches him for favoring courtly knights over knights-errant in the tournament Don Quijote imagines. The books that both chronicle and undergird the increasing power of the monarchy in the modern state may burn, that is, but their destruction is not enough to reverse the change of fortune for the anachronistic knight-errant. On the other hand, the books' connection to royal power cannot save them from the general fate of the tales of chivalry, while the Turpin material is spared.

Finally, Turpin reappears in Don Quijote's exchange with the canon of Toledo, where his intervention mediates between an ostensible truth of history and its eventual written form.[29] The canon suggests that the *writing* of history is the problem ("I cannot believe they did all those things that Archbishop Turpin writes about them"); it introduces the space for creative exaggeration and deformation, and in the context of the actual *Pseudo-Turpin* it casts into doubt both monarchical and ecclesiastical histories. Don Quijote and the text's primary narrator are of course well aware of the problem of constructed history where it relates to Don Quijote's own feats and their recording. What will the enchanter who writes his history know about him? How can readers correct for an interested telling? But the specific problem that Don Quijote faces, in a history chronicled by an *historiador arábigo*, recalls the peculiarly Spanish version of this dilemma, as a national history viewed through the lens of chivalry threatens to collapse into a history of otherness or into a hyperbolic legend indistinguishable from fiction. The primary narrator warns us early, soon after discovering Benengeli's manuscript, that any doubt of its veracity must be due to its author's necessary antipathy for a Spanish knight, but Cervantes's own use of such a figure as his narrator complicates the supposed connection between difference and unreliability, and between Spain and Christian heroism. What is more, Archbishop Turpin, far from guaranteeing the truth of history, often marks its fraudulence.

Cervantes's inquiry into the vexed status of historiography makes perfect sense in the context of Spanish concerns over how to record the past of the new nation and how to furnish a national memory. In this light, literary anxieties about truth and verisimilitude have serious implications for historiography, which suffers from the same embroidery and hyperbole. This is what one might call the contagion of fictionality, a problem that worried many of Cervantes's early modern contemporaries, particularly Tasso: given a sufficiently sophisticated awareness of how texts construct a semblance of truth, all textual truths become suspect.[30] Sources, authorities, material remnants, and traditions all come under critical interrogation in the first part of *Don Quijote*, suggesting an *escrutinio* of history as central as, and perhaps more radically skeptical than, the critique of chivalric novels. More important, perhaps, the Spanish construction of a national past, dizzyingly elusive amid chivalric fantasies and counterfantasies, Morisco forgeries and Galician extortions, is revealed as the most fragile of tissues.

NOTES

1. Perhaps the clearest statement is by Américo Castro, who deems the critique of chivalric romance a "pretext" ("Cómo veo ahora el Quijote" [1971], in *Cervantes y los casticismos españoles y otros estudios cervantinos* [Madrid: Trotta, 2002], 336). See also L. P. Harvey, "The Moriscos and Don Quijote" (Inaugural Lecture in the Chair of Spanish, delivered at King's College, University of London, November 11, 1974).

2. In moving past the ostensible critique of chivalric romance, Mary Malcolm Gaylord reads the Maese Pedro episode (*Don Quijote*, 2.26) and its multiple frames as an interrogation of national historiography, with a particular emphasis on the epistemological crisis that the New World represents ("Pulling Strings with Master Peter's Puppets: Fiction and History in *Don Quixote*," *Cervantes* 18, no. 2 [1998]: 117–47).

3. On Don Quijote's relation to literary and historical exemplars see Timothy Hampton, *Writing from History: The Rhetoric of Exemplarity in Renaissance Literature* (Ithaca, NY: Cornell University Press, 1990), 237–96.

4. Sebastián de Covarrubias Orozco, *Tesoro de la lengua castellana o española*, ed. Martín de Riquer (Barcelona: Alta Fulla, 1998), 823. Translations are my own unless otherwise noted.

5. See, e.g., the opening of the anonymous, mid-sixteenth-century *El Abencerraje*, a tale of Spanish heroism that paradoxically involves befriending Moors.

6. Bruce Wardropper, "Don Quijote: Story or History?" *Modern Philology* 63 (1965): 1–11. Wardropper argued that Cervantes's awareness of the "ill-defined frontier between history and story" made his narrative a novel rather than a romance (5).

7. Miguel de Cervantes Saavedra, *El ingenioso hidalgo Don Quijote de la Mancha*, ed. Martín de Riquer (Barcelona: Planeta, 1997); *Don Quixote*, trans. Edith Grossman (New York: Ecco, 2003). Occasional silent emendations have been made to the translation for accuracy.

8. Harvey suggests that the lively literary pseudohistories of the period, such as Luna's *Historia verdadera del rey don Rodrigo* or Pérez de Hita's *Guerras civiles de Granada*, set the stage for the fake gospels.

9. Thomas Case traces the close connection between the *plomos* and the vexed narrative authority of the "Arabic" historian who chronicles Don Quijote's adventures and, more significantly, the problem of textual authority per se ("Cide Hamete Benengeli y los *Libros plúmbeos*," *Cervantes* 22, no. 2 [2002]: 9–24).

10. Pedro M. Cátedra, *Invención, difusión y recepción de la literatura popular impresa (siglo XVI)* (Mérida, Badajoz: Editora Regional de Extremadura, 2002), 151.

11. On the importance of chorography for sixteenth-century Spanish historiography see Richard L. Kagan, "Clio and the Crown: Writing History in Habsburg Spain," in *Spain, Europe, and the Atlantic World: Essays in Honour of John H. Elliott*,

ed. Richard L. Kagan and Geoffrey Parker (Cambridge: Cambridge University Press, 1995), 73–99.

12. The text in question is the *Breve suma de la vida y hechos de Diego García de Paredes, la cual el mismo escribió y la dejó firmada de su nombre como al fin de ella aparece,* included in the *Crónica del Gran Capitán Gonzalo Hernández de Córdoba y Aguilar* (Alcalá de Henares, 1586), rpt. in *Crónicas del Gran Capitán,* ed. Antonio Rodríguez Villa (Madrid: Bailly/Balliére, 1908), 255–59. On the authorship of the text and its relationship to Cervantes's irony see Antonio Sánchez-Jiménez and Mario Sánchez-Jiménez, "La *Suma de las cosas que acontecieron a Diego García de Paredes y de lo que hizo*: Apuntes sobre su autoría," *Revista de estudios extremeños* 60 (2004): 231–41.

13. The second episode occurs on p. 213 of Rodríguez Villa's edition and depends on García de Paredes's tricking the French into coming between their own artillery and the Spaniards.

14. Although Sánchez-Jiménez and Sánchez-Jiménez conclude that the *Breve suma* was probably based on García de Paredes's own writings, they note that its complex textual history, of which Cervantes's readers would have been aware, adumbrates any reading of the passage (239).

15. Hampton notes, "Yet, even as the romance text offers the matter of fantasy to each member of society, its authority is explicitly linked to the centralized Spanish state" (246).

16. The battle in question is that of Cerignola (1503), where the Gran Capitán defeated the French and consolidated Spanish control over Naples. Thus this seemingly offhand historical reference updates the rivalry between France and Spain that is foreshadowed in the story of Bernardo del Carpio vanquishing Roland.

17. Riquer annotates this text as "cierta mentirosísima crónica" (a certain most mendacious chronicle) (74n13). For a good summary of the complex theories on the *Pseudo-Turpin*'s authorship see the introduction to Santiago López Martínez-Morás, *Épica y camino de Santiago: En torno al Pseudo-Turpin* (Sada: Castro, 2002).

18. Stephen H. A. Shepherd, "The Middle English 'Pseudo-Turpin Chronicle,'" *Medium Aevum* 65 (1996): 21.

19. Ian Short, "The *Pseudo-Turpin Chronicle*: Some Unnoticed Versions and Their Sources," *Medium Aevum* 38 (1969): 3.

20. For the Cluniac order's influence in Spain through the myth of Santiago see Francisco Márquez Villanueva, *Santiago: Trayectoria de un mito* (Barcelona: Bellaterra, 2004).

21. The eleventh-century *Chanson de Roland,* the influential antecedent to the *Pseudo-Turpin,* has long been prized as a foundational text in the imagining of a French nation. For this tradition, and for an important reexamination of it, see Sharon Kinoshita, *Medieval Boundaries: Rethinking Difference in Old French Literature* (Philadelphia: University of Pennsylvania Press, 2006).

22. François Rabelais, *Les cinq livres: Gargantua, Pantagruel, Le tiers livre, Le quart livre, Le cinquième livre,* ed. Gérard Defaux (Paris: Librairie Générale Française, 1994), 369.

23. Cf. this mark of pseudohistory with the appearance of the Gran Capitán in the *Novela del curioso impertinente.*

24. Ramón Menéndez Pidal, *Romanceros del rey Rodrigo y de Bernardo del Carpio,* ed. R. Lapesa, D. Catalán, and A. Galmés (Madrid: Gredos, 1957), 143.

25. The story appears in the thirteenth-century Latin chronicles of Lucas de Tuy (*Chronicon mundi,* 1236) and Rodrigo Ximénez de Rada (*De rebus Hispaniae,*

1243) and is discussed also in Alfonso X's *Primera crónica general* (1270), edited and published by Florián de Ocampo as *Las quatro partes enteras de la crónica de España que mandó componer el serenissimo rey don Alonso llamado el sabio, uista y emendada mucha parte de su impresión por el maestro Florián Docampo* (Zamora, 1541). For a good summary of the versions see David G. Burton, *The Legend of Bernardo del Carpio: From Chronicle to Drama* (Potomac, MD: Scripta Humanistica, 1988). Burton's focus is Juan de la Cueva's 1579 play, *La libertad de España por Bernardo del Carpio*, which Cervantes may well have known; it was first published in Seville in 1583 and is now available in an edition by Anthony Watson (Exeter: University of Exeter, 1974). For the romances on Bernardo see Menéndez Pidal.

26. Strikingly, the Bernardo corpus values the liberty of Spain—anachronistic though those two terms may be—over feudal loyalty to Alfonso II. In some versions Alfonso offers to make Charlemagne king of Spain in return for his aid against the Saracens; this betrayal of the nation is what Bernardo sets out to correct. Thus, for example, in the famous *romance* "Por las riberas de Arlanza" ("By the Banks of Arlanza") Bernardo challenges Alfonso: "Y porque no herede yo / quieres dar tu reino a Francia. / Moriram los castellanos / antes de ver tal jornada, / montañeses e leoneses / y esa gente esturiana / y ese reino de Saragoca / me prestará su companha. / Saldrelos a recebir / y darles he la batalla, / y si buena me saliere / será el bien de toda España; / y si mala me saliere / moriré yo en la demanda" (So that I do not inherit, you wish to give France your kingdom. The Castilians shall die before seeing such a day; Cantabrians and men of León, the people of Asturias, and that kingdom of Saragossa will all lend me their company. I will come out to meet [the French] and fight them, and if it goes well, it will be well for all Spain, and if it goes ill, I will die in the attempt) (Menéndez Pidal, 185).

27. In a remarkable description, "Por las riberas de Arlanza" conflates Bernardo's martial excellence with that of the Moorish king Muza, his eventual ally at Roncesvalles, so that the two men become indistinguishable: "También lo mirava el rey, / que fuera buela una garra; / diciendo estava a los suyos: /—Esta es una buena lanca, / si no es Bernaldo del Carpio, / éste es Muça el de Granada" (The king also looked at him, while a heron flew by; he said to his men, "This is a fine lance; if it isn't Bernardo del Carpio, then it's Muça of Granada) (Menéndez Pidal, 185).

28. Klaus Herbers, "Intención y finalidad," in *El Pseudo-Turpín: Lazo entre el culto jacobeo y el culto de Carlomagno; Actas del VI Congreso internacional de estudios, Jacobeos*, ed. Klaus Herbers (Santiago de Compostela: Xunta de Galicia, 2003), 22. Herbers suggests, moreover, that the link to Charlemagne makes Compostela more European (3g). See also Fernando López Alsina, "La prerrogativa de Santiago en España según el Pseudo-Turpín: ¿Tradiciones compostelanas o tradiciones carolingias?" in Herbers, *El Pseudo-Turpín*, 113–29.

29. Turpin appears also in the second part, in another tongue-in-cheek mention, where he is described by Don Quijote as the author of a certain *Cosmografia*. According to Riquer, no text of that name was ever associated with Turpin (570–71n13).

30. Critics have long noted Tasso's anxiety about how the romance marvelous complicates the truth value of the historical poem. See Hampton, 81–133; and my *Mimesis and Empire: The New World, Islam, and European Identities* (Cambridge: Cambridge University Press, 2001), 13–34.

Chronology

1547	Miguel de Cervantes Saavedra is born in Alcalá de Henares to Rodrigo de Cervantes and Leonor de Cortinas, his wife. Baptized on October 9.
1568	Writes poems commemorating the death of Isabel de Valois, third wife of Philip II.
1569	Travels to Rome, in the service of Cardinal Giulio Acquaviva; enlists in military.
1571	Wounded in battle of Lepanto, where Turks are defeated. Loses the use of his left hand.
1575	With his brother Rodrigo, captured by Turks, brought to Algiers, enslaved, and held for ramsom.
1576–1579	Makes four attempts to escape captivity.
1576	Rodrigo, ransomed by his family, released; arranges brother's rescue, which fails.
1580	Ransomed by Trinitarian monks; returns to Spain.
1581	Attempts career as dramatist in Madrid.
1584	Daughter Isabel de Saavedra born to Ana Franca de Rojas; marries Catalina de Salazar y Palacios.
1585	Publishes first book, a pastoral romance, *La Galatea*.

1587	Becomes a commissary requisitioning provisions for the Armada.
1597	Employed as tax collector in Andalusia and jailed for irregularities in his accounts.
1605	Publishes *Don Quixote*, part 1.
1609	Joins lay confraternity of Slaves of the Most Holy Sacrament in Madrid.
1613	*Exemplary Novels* (12 stories) published. Becomes an acolyte in the Franciscan Order of the Roman Catholic priesthood.
1614	*Voyage to Parnassus*, a mock-heroic allegory in verse, published. Continuation of *Don Quixote* published by someone otherwise unknown and possibly using a pseudonym.
1615	Publishes *Don Quixote*, part 2, and *Eight Plays and Interludes, New and Never Performed*.
1616	Dies in Madrid on April 22 or 23.
1617	Posthumous publication of *The Trials of Persiles and Sigismunda*, a romance.

Contributors

HAROLD BLOOM is Sterling Professor of the Humanities at Yale University. Educated at Cornell and Yale universities, he is the author of more than 30 books, including *Shelley's Mythmaking* (1959), *The Visionary Company* (1961), *Blake's Apocalypse* (1963), *Yeats* (1970), *The Anxiety of Influence* (1973), *A Map of Misreading* (1975), *Kabbalah and Criticism* (1975), *Agon: Toward a Theory of Revisionism* (1982), *The American Religion* (1992), *The Western Canon* (1994), *Omens of Millennium: The Gnosis of Angels, Dreams, and Resurrection* (1996), *Shakespeare: The Invention of the Human* (1998), *How to Read and Why* (2000), *Genius: A Mosaic of One Hundred Exemplary Creative Minds* (2002), *Hamlet: Poem Unlimited* (2003), *Where Shall Wisdom Be Found?* (2004), and *Jesus and Yahweh: The Names Divine* (2005). In addition, he is the author of hundreds of articles, reviews, and editorial introductions. In 1999, Professor Bloom received the American Academy of Arts and Letters' Gold Medal for Criticism. He has also received the International Prize of Catalonia, the Alfonso Reyes Prize of Mexico, and the Hans Christian Andersen Bicentennial Prize of Denmark.

CAROLYN A. NADEAU is a professor in the Hispanic studies department at Illinois Wesleyan University. She also has published a critical edition of Quevedo's *El buscón* and has written on mythological female figures in the comedia and other topics.

HOWARD MANCING is a professor of Spanish at Purdue University. His work on Cervantes includes *The Cervantes Encyclopedia* and *The Chivalric World of Don Quixote: Style, Structure, and Narrative Technique.*

EDWARD H. FRIEDMAN is a professor of Spanish and comparative literature at Vanderbilt University. His many texts include *Cervantes in the Middle: Realism and Reality in the Spanish Novel from* Lazarillo de Tormes *to* Niebla and *The Unifying Concept: Approaches to Cervantes'* Comedias. He also is coeditor of *Magical Parts: Approaches to* Don Quixote and has been president of the Cervantes Society of America.

MARIO VARGAS LLOSA is a Peruvian novelist. He also has written essays, drama, short stories, and an autobiography. In 1990, he lost in a run-off election for the presidency of Peru.

ROBERTO GONZÁLEZ ECHEVARRÍA is a professor of Hispanic and comparative literature at Yale University. He is the editor of *Don Quixote: A Case Book*, a CD-ROM on Cervantes (for Primary Sources Media), and other works, and a co-editor of *The Cambridge History of Latin American Literature*. He also is the author of *Myth and Archive: A Theory of Latin American Narrative* and other titles. In addition, he has been on the editorial board of the journal *Anuario de Estudios Cervantinos*.

MANUEL DURÁN is an emeritus professor at Yale University. He has authored or coauthored 40 books and more than 150 articles on Hispanic writers, poets, and culture, including two major volumes on Cervantes. Additionally he has published volumes of poetry.

FAY R. ROGG has been chairman and professor of Spanish in the Modern Languages Department at the Borough of Manhattan Community College, The City University of New York. She coauthored *El Arte de Escribir*, a writing skills text.

BRYANT CREEL is a professor of Spanish at the University of Tennessee. Among other works, he has published Don Quijote, *Symbol of a Culture in Crisis* and *The Voice of the Phoenix: Metaphors of Death and Rebirth in Classics of the Iberian Renaissance*. He also is a translator.

MYRIAM YVONNE JEHENSON is a professor emerita at the University of Hartford and the author of *The Golden World of the Pastoral* and *Latin-American Women Writers*.

PETER N. DUNN is a professor emeritus at Connecticut's Wesleyan University and the author of *The Spanish Picaresque Novel*, *Spanish Picaresque Fiction*, and other works.

BARBARA FUCHS is a professor at the University of Pennsylvania. She is the author of *Passing for Spain: Cervantes and the Fictions of Identity* and other works and has been coeditor of two special issues of *Modern Language Quarterly*.

Bibliography

Ardila, J.A.G., ed. *The Cervantean Heritage: Reception and Influence of Cervantes in Britain.* London: Legenda, 2009.

Bowers, Fredson, ed. *Vladimir Nabokov: Lectures on* Don Quixote. New York: Harcourt Brace Jovanovich, 1983.

Burningham, Bruce R. *Tilting Cervantes: Baroque Reflections on Postmodern Culture.* Nashville: Vanderbilt University Press, 2008.

Cascardi, Anthony J., ed. *The Cambridge Companion to Cervantes.* Cambridge, England: Cambridge University Press, 2002.

Childers, William. *Transnational Cervantes.* Toronto; Buffalo: University of Toronto Press, 2006.

Close, Anthony. *Cervantes and the Comic Mind of His Age.* Oxford; New York: Oxford University Press, 2000.

———. *A Companion to* Don Quixote. Woodbridge, UK; Rochester, N.Y.: Tamesis, 2008.

Cruz, Anne J., and Carroll B. Johnson, ed. *Cervantes and His Postmodern Constituencies.* New York: Garland, 1999.

Echevarría, Roberto González, ed. *Cervantes'* Don Quixote: *A Casebook.* Oxford; New York: Oxford University Press, 2005.

Eisenberg, Daniel. *A Study of* Don Quixote. Corrected ed. Newark, Del.: Juan de la Cuesta, 2001, 1987.

El Saffar, Ruth, ed. *Critical Essays on Cervantes.* Boston: G. K. Hall, 1986.

El Saffar, Ruth Anthony, and Diana de Armas Wilson, ed. *Quixotic Desire: Psychoanalytic Perspectives on Cervantes.* Ithaca, N.Y.: Cornell University Press, 1993.

169

Friedman, Edward H. *Cervantes in the Middle: Realism and Reality in the Spanish Novel from* Lazarillo de Tormes *to* Niebla. Newark, Del.: Juan de la Cuesta, 2006.

———. "Making Amends: An Approach to the Structure of *Don Quixote*, Part 2." *Vanderbilt e-Journal of Luso-Hispanic Studies* 2 (2005): (no pagination).

Gallegos, Jose L. "Don Quixote as Lover: A Neoplatonic Paradigm." *Indiana Journal of Hispanic Literatures* 5 (Fall 1994): 127–44.

Gaylord, Mary Malcolm. "Don Quixote's New World of Language." *Cervantes: Bulletin of the Cervantes Society of America* 27, no. 1 (Spring 2007): 71–94.

Glover, Douglas. *The Enamoured Knight.* Normal [Ill.]: Dalkey Archive Press, 2005.

Gorfkle, Laura J. *Discovering the Comic in* Don Quixote. Chapel Hill: Department of Romance Languages, University of North Carolina, 1993.

Graf, E. C. *Cervantes and Modernity: Four Essays on* Don Quijote. Lewisburg: Bucknell University Press, 2007.

Ife, B. W. "Cervantes and the Credibility Crisis in Spanish Golden-Age Fiction." *Renaissance and Modern Studies* 26 (1982): 52–74.

Johnson, Carroll B. *Cervantes and the Material World.* Urbana: University of Illinois Press, 2000.

———. *Madness and Lust: A Psychoanalytical Approach to* Don Quixote. Berkeley: University of California Press, 1983.

Johnson, Carroll B., ed. Don Quijote: *Across Four Centuries: 1605–2005.* Newark, Del.: Juan de la Cuesta, 2006.

Lauer, A. Robert, ed. *Central Institute of English and Foreign Languages Bulletin* 15–16, nos. 2–1 (December 2005–June 2006): 1–173.

Lauer, A. Robert, and Kurt Reichenberger, eds. *Cervantes y su mundo III.* Kassel, Germany: Reichenberger, 2005.

Mancing, Howard. *Cervantes'* Don Quixote: *A Reference Guide.* Westport, Conn.: Greenwood Press, 2006.

Martinez-Bonati, Felix. Don Quixote *and the Poetics of the Novel.* Ithaca, N.Y.; London: Cornell University Press, 1992.

Maurya, Vibha, and Ignacio Arellano, ed. *Cervantes and* Don Quixote: *Proceedings of the Delhi Conference on Miguel de Cervantes.* Hyderabad, India: EMESCO, 2008.

Mieder, Wolfgang. *"Tilting at Windmills": History and Meaning of a Proverbial Allusion to Cervantes'* Don Quixote. Burlington, Vt.: University of Vermont, 2006.

Murillo, L. A. *A Critical Introduction to* Don Quixote. New York: Peter Lang, 1990.

Parr, James A. Don Quixote, Don Juan, *and Related Subjects: Form and Tradition in Spanish Literature, 1330–1630.* Selinsgrove [Pa.]: Susquehanna University Press; Cranbury, N.J.: Associated University Presses, 2004.

————. Don Quixote: *A Touchstone for Literary Criticism*. Kassel: Edition Reichenberger, 2005.

————. *On Cervantes: Essays for L. A. Murillo*. Newark, Del.: Cuesta, 1991.

Paulson, Ronald. Don Quixote *in England: The Aesthetics of Laughter*. Baltimore: Johns Hopkins University Press, 1998.

Prado, Francisco La Rubia, ed. *Cervantes for the 21st Century*. Newark, Del.: Cuesta, 2000.

Presberg, Charles D. *Adventures in Paradox: Don Quixote and the Western Tradition*. University Park: Pennsylvania State University Press, 2001.

Reichenberger, Kurt. *Cervantes and the Hermeneutics of Satire*. Kassel: Edition Reichenberger, 2005.

Ricapito, Joseph V. *Consciousness and Truth in* Don Quijote *and Connected Essays*. Newark, Del.: Juan de la Cuesta, 2007.

Sherman, Alvin F., ed. *Framing the* Quixote, *1605–2005*. Provo, Utah: Department of Spanish and Portuguese, Brigham Young University, 2007.

Vélez-Sainz, Julio, and Nieves Romero-Díaz, ed. *Cervantes and/on/in the New World*. Newark, Del.: Juan de la Cuesta, 2007.

Weiger, John C. *The Substance of Cervantes*. Cambridge; New York: Cambridge University Press, 1985.

Williamson, Edwin. *The Half-way House of Fiction:* Don Quixote *and Arthurian Romance*. Oxford: Clarendon Press, 1984.

Wilson, Diana de Armas. *Cervantes, the Novel, and the New World*. Oxford; New York: Oxford University Press, 2000.

Yamada, Yumiko. *Ben Jonson and Cervantes: Tilting against Chivalric Romances*. Tokyo: Maruzen, 2000.

Acknowledgments

Carolyn A. Nadeau, "Reading the Prologue: Cervantes's Narrative Appropriation and Originality." From *Women of the Prologue: Imitation, Myth, and Magic in Don Quixote I.* Published by Bucknell University Press/Associated University Presses. Copyright © 2002 by Rosemont Publishing and Printing Corp.

Howard Mancing, "Cervantes as Narrator of *Don Quijote.*" From *Cervantes* 23, no. 1 (2003): 117–40. Copyright © 2003 by *Cervantes.*

Edward H. Friedman, "Books Errant: The Objects of Invention in *Don Quixote.*" From *Anuario de Estudios Cervantinos* 1 (2004): 41–55. Copyright © 2004 by Mirabel Editorial.

Mario Vargas Llosa, "A Novel for the Twenty-First Century," translated by Johanna Damgaard Liander. From *Harvard Review* 28 (2005): 125–36. Copyright © 2005 by Mario Vargas Llosa.

Roberto González Echevarría, "The Knight as Fugitive from Justice: The Quijote, Part I." From *Love and the Law in Cervantes.* Published by Yale University Press. Copyright © 2005 by Roberto González Echevarría.

Manuel Durán and Fay R. Rogg, "Constructing *Don Quixote.*" From *Fighting Windmills: Encounters with Don Quixote.* Published by Yale University Press. Copyright © 2006 by Yale University.

173

Bryant Creel, "Palace of the Apes: The Ducal Chateau and Cervantes's Repudiation of Satiric Malice." From *Don Quijote Across Four Centuries: Papers from the Seventeenth Southern California Cervantes Symposium, UCLA, 7–9 April 2005,* edited by Carroll B. Johnson. Copyright © 2006 by Juan de la Cuesta—Hispanic Monographs.

Myriam Yvonne Jehenson and Peter N. Dunn, "Discursive Hybridity: Don Quixote's and Sancho Panza's Utopias." From *The Utopian Nexus in* Don Quixote. Copyright © 2006 by Vanderbilt University Press.

Barbara Fuchs, "*Don Quijote* 1 and the Forging of National History." From *Modern Language Quarterly*, vol. 68, no. 3 (September 2007): 395–416. Copyright © 2007 by the University of Washington. All rights reserved. Used by permission of the publisher, Duke University Press.

Every effort has been made to contact the owners of copyrighted material and secure copyright permission. Articles appearing in this volume generally appear much as they did in their original publication with few or no editorial changes. In some cases, foreign language text has been removed from the original essay. Those interested in locating the original source will find the information cited above.

Index

175

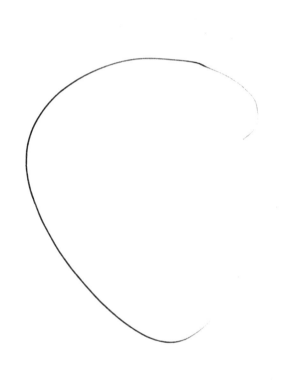